INCREDIBLE BASKETBALL
Lead-up Games and Drills

Kenneth M. Olynyk

**Faculty of Physical Education & Health
University of Toronto**

Sport Books Publisher

Graphics and design by Takao Tsuruoka and My1 Designs

National Library of Canada Cataloguing in Publication Data

Olynyk, Kenneth M.
    Incredible basketball lead-up games and drills

ISBN 0-920905-71-4

1. Basketball – Training. I. Title.

GV885.35.O49 2002   796.323   C2002-900847-6

Copyright © 2003, by Sport Books Publisher
All rights reserved. Except for use in review,
no portion of this book may be reproduced or
transmitted in any form or by any means without written
permission of the publisher.

Pictures reproduced with permission from the Faculty of
Physical Education and Health, University of Toronto.
Photo credits: Mark Brownson, Lewko Hryhorijiw, Bridget Bates

Distribution world-wide by
Sport Books Publisher
278 Robert Street
Toronto, ON M5S 2K8
Canada

http://www.sportbookspub.com
E-mail: sbp@sportbookspub.com
Fax: 416-966-9022

Printed in the United States

CONTENTS

EFFECTIVE COACHING METHODS 7
Dr. Peter Klavora, University of Toronto

MOTIVATION AND INSPIRATION 19
Dr. Peter Klavora, University of Toronto

LEAD-UP GAMES 33

DEVELOPING TECHNICAL SKILLS WITHOUT THE BALL 34
Starting and stopping 34
Turning 36
Evading and faking 37
Skipping and jumping 39

DEVELOPING TECHNICAL SKILLS WITH THE BALL 41
Getting used to the ball 41
Dribbling 42
Passing and catching 45
Shooting 49

DEVELOPING TECHNICAL AND TACTICAL SKILLS WITH AN OPPONENT 52
Dribbling with a defender 52
Passing with a defender 54

DEVELOPING ADVANCED PLAYING ABILITY 58
Half-court games 58
Full-court games 59

LEAD-UP GAMES & DRILLS

DRILLS *63*

OVERVIEW OF OFFENSIVE AND DEFENSIVE TACTICS *64*
Examples for competitive training and drill work *64*

TRAINING INDIVIDUAL OFFENSIVE AND DEFENSIVE SKILLS AND TACTICS WITHOUT THE BALL *68*
Tips for developing individual skills and tactics without the ball *68*

PASSING AND RECEIVING *76*
Tips for passing the ball *76*
Tips for receiving the ball *76*
Tips for defending against the pass *80*
Stationary passing and receiving—no position change *80*
Stationary passing and receiving—with position change *85*
Passing and receiving while moving *88*

DRIBBLING *98*
Tips for dribbling *98*
Tips for defending the dribbler *98*

PIVOTING *110*
Tips for pivoting *110*
Tips for defending the pivoting player *110*
Picking up the dribble and pivoting to pass *114*

SHOOTING *120*
Tips for shooting *123*
Tips for defending the shooter *123*
Lay-ups *124*
  • Lay-ups off the dribble *125*
  • Lay-ups off the pass *129*
Mid-range shots *136*
  • Free-throws (foul shots) *136*
  • Examples for competitive free-throw practice *136*
  • Jump shots *138*
  • Examples for competitive shooting practice *138*

FAKING *142*
Tips for faking *142*
Tips for defending against the fake *142*
Faking a pass *145*
Faking a shot *146*
Faking a pivot or dribble *147*

CONTENTS

COMBINATION DRILLS *148*
　　　Tips for combination drills *148*

ODD-PERSON ADVANTAGE SITUATIONS *156*
　　　Tips for executing odd-person advantage situations *156*
　　　Tips for defending against odd-person advantage situations *159*
　　　Two-on-one situations *159*
　　　Three-on-one situations *161*
　　　Three-on-two situations *163*
　　　Four-on-two situations *165*
　　　Four-on-three situations *165*

MOTION OFFENSE *166*
　　　Tips for player movement, screening, and shielding *166*
　　　Tips for defending against player movement, screening, and shielding *169*
　　　Basic forms of screening *169*
　　　Basic forms of shielding *171*
　　　Using basic screening and shielding techniques combined with player movement *172*

RUB SCREENS—WITH AND WITHOUT THE BALL *178*
　　　Tips for rubbing off a screen *178*
　　　Tips for defending players rubbing off a screen *180*
　　　Rubbing off a stationary player *180*
　　　Rub screens between moving players *183*

REBOUNDING *188*
　　　Tips for defensive rebounding *188*
　　　Tips for offensive rebounding *190*
　　　Rebound two-on-one *190*
　　　Rebound two-on-two *191*
　　　Rebound three-on-two *192*
　　　Rebound three-on-three *193*
　　　Rebound after free-throw *194*

CIRCUIT TRAINING *197*
　　　Circuit 1 *198*
　　　Circuit 2 *199*
　　　Circuit 3 *200*
　　　Circuit 4 *201*

PART I

TASK ANALYSIS 7

SKILL PRESENTATION TECHNIQUES 8

UNDERSTANDING THE PLAYER AS AN INFORMATION PROCESSOR 8

IMPORTANCE OF FEEDBACK IN EFFECTIVE COACHING 10

LEARNING STAGES 12

COACHING TACTICS 13

DEVELOPING COMPETITION SMARTNESS 14

PLANNING AN ALL-YEAR TRAINING PROGRAM 16

EFFECTIVE COACHING METHODS

Peter Klavora, University of Toronto

The basic idea of coaching basketball is the development of players' technical and tactical skills as well as his or her physical and psychological abilities. As a result, each of these components should be carefully developed during practice. These abilities and skills are initially tested in practice and training games, where conditions can be controlled and monitored, before moving on to more important competitive situations that serve as tests for future performance potential. The goal of practice should be developing consistent performance during competition, which is vital for success.

There is a growing body of research on a wide range of learning and coaching principles that make coaching basketball effective. Eight of these concepts, designed to enhance the methodology of coaching basketball are presented in this section. They deal with (1) the systematic analysis of the basketball task; (2) skill presentation techniques; (3) the understanding of the athlete's limitations in processing information; (4) the importance of feedback in effective coaching; (5) the appreciation of the learning stages; (6) coaching tactics; (7) developing competition smartness; and (8) the need to plan an all-year training program.

Task analysis

Any basketball skill can be broken down into a set of component movements which are quite distinct from each other in terms of the operations needed to produce an effective performance. The component movements of the task are envisaged as the ***subroutines*** involved in the total performance. Together, the subroutines form the overall task which is conceived as an ***executive plan***. This executive plan then is the overall goal, aim, or, objective the player is trying to master; at the same time it serves as an organizational process that controls the order in which a sequence of simpler tasks or movements is carried out.

Each subroutine can be further broken down into simpler movements, the ***sub-subroutines***. The process of division depends upon the complexity of the task at hand. It stops when all basic movements that comprise the task are identified.

It is advantageous, therefore, for the coach to break down each of the basketball tasks

LEAD-UP GAMES & DRILLS

into basic movements, ordered from the simplest to the most complex in a hierarchical fashion. Once these hierarchies are formed, the player can easily be introduced to new material at the level most appropriate given her or his past experience. The drill section of the book displays 22 charts that present skill hierarchies for all basketball tasks. Obviously, the less experienced a player, the lower in the hierarchy he or she should begin. Once the basic movements are mastered, the player can attempt movements at the next level in the task hierarchy structure. This process is continued until the most complex movements of the basketball task are learned.

When learned, the skills at the bottom of each task hierarchy become mainly automatic and "run off" without much attention by the player. Once they are mastered, these movements are relegated to the lower centres of the brain and do not overload the player's nervous system. Through practices using numerous lead-up games and drills, the execution of well-learned skills becomes automatic.

Skill presentation techniques

The best way to introduce a new skill is demonstration coupled with an explanation of the skill. If the coach does not possess the skill, it can be demonstrated by an athlete or an assistant coach. Other visual forms of visual information can be used, such as still pictures of proper actions, film clips or videos of successful performances, etc. The instruction should be kept brief and to the point, emphasizing only one or two key points at a time. Furthermore, the teaching formation must be such that all athletes are in front of the demonstrator and have a good view from the right angle. Several lead-up games and drills designed to develop the same skill must be selected very carefully as to assure the right progression in skill development and to prevent boredom. Furthermore, the selected drills should challenge the skill level of the athletes. If drills are too easy, the players may become bored quickly. Conversely, if the drills are too difficult, the athletes may become frustrated with lack of progress in skill development.

Understanding the player as an information processor

Coaches seldom realize that most coaching principles are based on knowledge of athletes' limitations and capacities in receiving and processing information. After a poor performance many coaches begin a long lecture about which bone does what and what muscles to use and at what particular time in the movement this or that muscle is to be activated. In essence, such coaches are observing and commenting only on the end result – the response of a whole series of interior processes that go on while the player is trying to execute the new skill at his or her very best. What are these processes?

Psychomotor processes (**Figure 1**) are part of the player's nervous system and are, in most cases, taken for granted. These mechanisms help the learner to sense, perceive,

COACHING METHODS

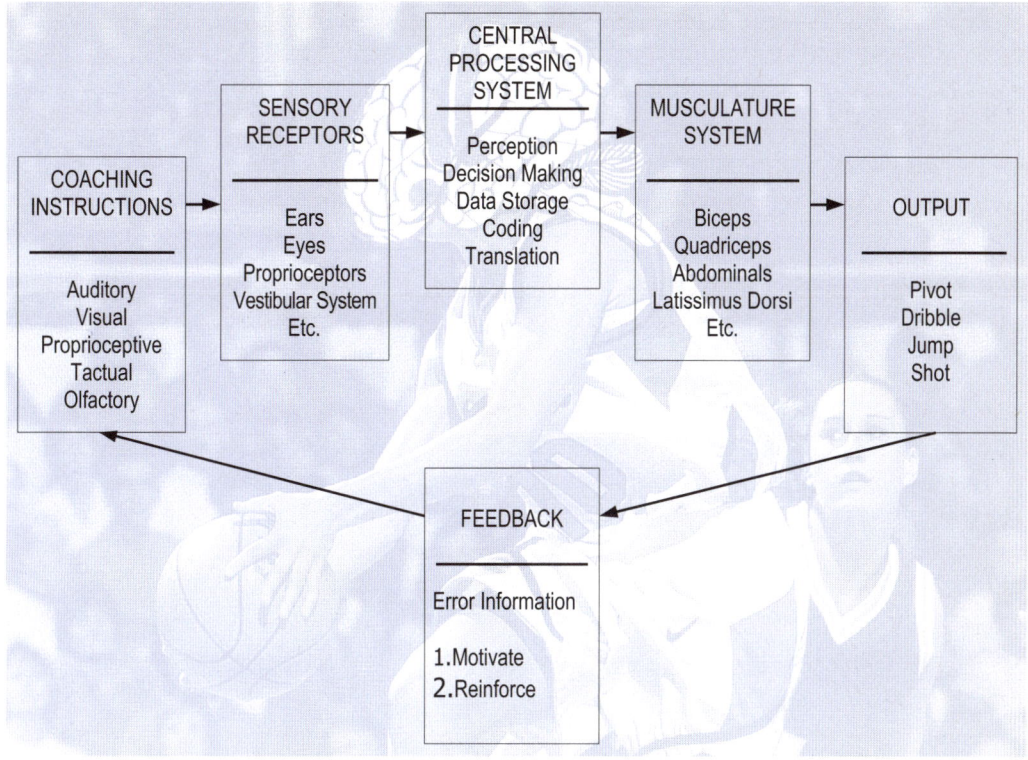

Figure 1 Psychomotor processes involved in executing a basketball skill.

attend to, store or memorize, decide, and organize an action in relationship to the demands placed on him by the coach and the environment. These mechanisms transmit information that is flowing between the athlete and the coach. However, these mechanisms are full of limitations that dictate our coaching approaches and teaching strategies. By keeping these limitations in mind, the coach becomes more effective which in turn helps players to progress faster. **Table 1** (see page 10) outlines some of the major limitations of an athlete's psychomotor system and main coaching strategies to overcome these limitations.

It is difficult to separate the player's sensory capacities from his perceptual processes. What input the athlete actually processes is highly dependent upon the quality of her sensory and perceptual mechanisms. In practice the athlete is constantly bombarded with stimuli coming in through various senses. These stimuli are provided externally by the coach and internally by proprioceptors (receptors in the muscles, tendons, ligaments, and vestibule sense). However, the player's single-channel system or selective attention that serves as a funnel gates out most of the available information presented to him. If the coach wants the player to perceive, i.e., hear or see, the right things, he would

Table 1 Characteristics of an athlete's psychomotor processes and coaching strategies.

MECHANISM	LIMITATION	COACHING STRATEGY
Sensory Mechanisms	• Poor visual skills, such as dynamic visual acuity • Athlete does not hear instructions	• Detect vision problems early • Limit noise in the gym; speak clearly and loudly
Perceptual Mechanisms	• One-track mind; selective attention; can attend to only one major point	• Provide only one critical component of a skill at a time
Short-term Memory	• Limited capacity • Significant rate of loss • Can be easily interfered with	• Provide only a limited amount of information; do not overload athlete • Minimize time between demonstration and rehearsal of skill • Avoid unrelated activities in gym, such as workers in the background, spectators yelling or commenting, other teams practicing, etc.
Long-term or Permanent Memory	• Must rehearse to encode and retain information	• Provide continuing rehearsal of skill until it is learned properly
Player's Psychological State	• Anxiety • Attention and fatigue • Boredom	• Provide non-threatening learning environment • Avoid practicing new skills when fatigued • Introduce new drills to coach same skill

have to select and present instructions carefully so that they have a chance to get through for interpretation and recognition. The single-channel system, selective attention, and short term memory are limitations of the player's perceptual mechanism that every coach must consider for optimal learning results in practice.

Importance of feedback in effective coaching

The coach's instructions, corrections, explanations, interpretations, comments, or notes, directed to the player during practice, evaluate her current performance. This evaluation is the feedback that systematically shapes the player's movements into the desired act, according to the coach's plan. According to motor-learning texts, "Practice alone does

COACHING METHODS

not make perfect, practice with appropriate feedback makes perfect... Feedback is probably the single most important factor during practice sessions." This and similar quotations indicate the significance of the presence of meaningful feedback in learning and performance.

The coach's feedback can be either ***descriptive*** or ***prescriptive*** in nature. A descriptive feedback statement indicates something about what the player did ("not so good on the follow through," "try better at next attempt," etc.); it presumes that the player knows what to do on the next attempt. Prescriptive feedback, on the other hand, provides the athlete with information he or she can use to make more effective corrections in their subsequent attempt ('focus on the wrist at the point of release') at the task. In general, prescriptive feedback is considered more effective than descriptive feedback.

There are four fundamental questions concerning the efficacy of coach's provision of feedback: (1) when is feedback most beneficial; (2) how much feedback is necessary; (3) how precise should feedback be; (4) what should the timing of feedback be; and (5) motivation properties of feedback.

Stages of learning and feedback The coach's feedback is especially vital early in the learning process. Later in his or her training, however, after he or she has gained experience and developed an internalized model of the correct basketball skill or task which he or she uses as a reference pattern, the coach's attention can be reduced and eventually completely withdrawn.

How much feedback is necessary The earlier discussion about the athlete as an information processor should answer the question of how much feedback is necessary for an effective instruction process. Particularly during coaching of novel skills or plays, an athlete's 'one-track mind' can process and attend to only a limited amount of information. The athlete can effectively concentrate on only one novel movement. Only later, when he or she becomes familiar with the novel task, can he or she shift her attention to other novel tasks and/or share the attention with other requirements of the movement or play. Although the athlete is limited in his capacities to process the coach's information, intense but selective coaching is nevertheless required in the early stages of the player's development if he or she is to progress at an optimal rate. In other words, no more and no less information about a performance should be provided than the athlete is capable of handling. The instruction must be adjusted to the amount of information the player can use.

How precise should feedback be Motor learning research has suggested that precise coaching generates far better results than any other type. The coach must formulate a precise standard of each task or play he wants to coach. Then, he or she must develop a trained eye in order to be able to provide precise information to the athlete abut his errors and how to correct them.

To decrease the dependency of athletes on coach's feedback as they become more skilled the coach may consider using ***bandwidth*** feedback. With this method, the coach only gives feedback when an athlete's movements fall outside some acceptable level of correctness, or bandwidth. This type of feedback has many advantages. The coach gives feedback less frequently and athletes' intrinsic feedback gains in importance which allows them to strengthen their permanent memory of the skill or play.

Timing of feedback To consider the timing of the coach's feedback to the athlete is to apply his short-term memory limitations to the coaching situation. Short-term memory bank is very susceptible to loss, and generally the greater the delay before giving the athlete information about her performance, the less effect the given information has. Thus, an intense, continuous instruction is more beneficial to the development of skills than the provision of coaching at the end of practice when the team is ready to leave the gym.

Motivation properties of feedback The coach's encouraging words 'good,' 'excellent,' 'that's it,' etc., not only provide the athlete with information about her performance, but also act as a reinforcement. When the player is given precise information about his technique, this feedback strengthens the correct response. In this regard the coach's instruction increases motivation, and, in general, information about one's performance affects the incentive to do well. It is encouraging for the player to hear that he or she is improving. The improvements make the athlete happy and motivate him to maintain her interest and his desire to keep practicing. Thus, the coach's feedback fulfills a valuable motivational role. (see **Figure 1,** page 9)

Learning stages

Technical and tactical training play a central role in developing a complete player. Technical elements of the game are normally developed in three stages of learning: acquisition, stability, and application.

Acquisition stage The goal of this learning stage is to introduce to players new technical elements and have them perform the skills under simplified conditions, initially while standing, and later with movement. When introducing a skill for the first time, it is important that the coach introduces it in a simplified setting. Initially, rough forms of the skill are developed in relatively undemanding conditions. The player's performance is highly variable and he or she is generally not aware of exactly what should be done differently the next time to improve. As a result, he or she needs specific information that will assist him or her in correcting what he or she has done wrong. With some practice, the player moves on to the second (stabilization) learning stage.

Stabilization stage The main objective of the stabilization stage is to refine their skills. The errors are fewer and less significant. The players are developing an ability to detect some of their own errors in performing the various tasks and various game elements. This provides the athletes with some specific guidelines about how to continue practice. Variability of performance from one attempt to another also begins to decrease.

COACHING METHODS

Gradually, the coach introduces variations according to game demands. Variations can be with regards to movement speed (ball or player), distance, movement direction, etc. Scoring should be attempted during high speed, from different distances, from different angles, and, if necessary, from both, left and right, directions. An important step is to practice game-specific combinations where several game elements are combined into a more demanding practice. Initially, one should choose combination elements that occur immediately before or after the skill just learned. Then, the easiest form should be chosen (depending on the game) and should be practiced in more demanding complex game forms. When practicing dribbling, e.g., catching the ball standing or while running can be added, and after dribbling, playing the ball to another player can be added.

In order to further strengthen technical abilities, one has to include opponents, whose impact is guided by the coach. Initially the skill should be practiced with inanimate opponents (objects) and then with passive opponents (players). The player has to learn to take an opponent into account. The passive opponent eventually turns into a semi-active opponent that agitates the player but still lets him finish the exercise. The player now has to broaden his technical abilities in order to be successful.

The demands get even higher, when the opponent becomes an active opponent that not only tries to disturb the flow of movement but also tries to hinder it. At this point tactical training becomes important and must be introduced into practice gradually.

Application stage After much practice and experience with various skills, the athlete moves into the application stage of learning. Here, skills have become almost automatic or habitual. The player does not have to attend to the entire production of the skill but has learned to perform most of the skill without thinking about it at all.

The application stage is the result of a tremendous amount of practice; it allows players to produce basketball skills and movements without concentrating on the entire movement. Therefore, they are able to attend to other aspects of the game, such as tactics. The goal of practice becomes learning how to apply the learned technical elements and the game's complex combinations in a game situation within a determined tactical framework. Thus, learning of tactical skills becomes a very important aspect of practice in the application learning stage.

Coaching tactics

The development of tactical abilities is a complicated process because it consists of a multi-layered system of sub-processes that normally develop in three steps:

Step 1 This step is mainly concerned with strengthening of individual and collective tactical methods and variations to solve a specific tactical problem. This includes training of individual movement forms and team combinations with the goal to use them at the right time at the right place, either alone or with other players.

LEAD-UP GAMES & DRILLS

An example of an individual attack tactic is to "get past a player with a ball." To solve this problem there are several basic forms with variations that can be practiced; initially without an opponent, then with a passive opponent and a half-active opponent. Basic forms include: (1) to get past a player while moving with change of pace; (2) to get past a player while moving with a cross-over dribble; (3) to get past a player from a standing position using an attack fake; (4) to get past a player from a standing position using a passing fake; and (5) to get past a player from a standing position with shooting fakes.

These basic play forms and their variations should be introduced one after the other and practiced diligently with the main goal to strengthen their correct execution.

Step 2 The second step involves perceptual and cognitive tasks where the players are learning to correctly assess a game situation and then correctly respond to the specific demand of the game. This requires learning to make quick and good judgments with a semi-active or active opponent.

The player has to learn to recognize a specific game situation or even create it, in order to use certain tactical elements. For this type of training, lead-up games that closely simulate competition situations can be effectively employed. Various forms of lead-up games are still easier to play compared to scrimmage practice, or competition games (fewer players, fewer opponents, smaller court area, etc.).

Step 3 The goal of this step is the correct application of the acquired basic forms and variations in a game. The tasks of this step are to develop the abilities to use tactics in the right situations, and also to develop the ability to create situations where a certain tactic can be used. The latter should be practiced under simpler conditions and in scrimmage practice, so that they can be applied appropriately in actual games. In some cases, the practice conditions should be harder than in actual competition.

Developing competition smartness

Training of competition smartness should occupy an important part of teams practice. It is mainly developed by playing competitive games under four progressively more demanding conditions: (1) simplified conditions; (2) scrimmage practice; (3) very demanding conditions; and (4) competition.

Practice games played under simplified conditions This introductory level of competition is characterized by playing simplified preparatory games using half court, lower baskets, smaller lighter balls, reduced number of players or uneven number of players, simplified rules, etc. This results in lower technical requirements. Initially, only simple technical skills are required. With regard to tactics, individual and simple group tactical actions are predominant (**Table 2**).

COACHING METHODS

Table 2 Practice games played under simplified conditions.

RULES	TECHNIQUE	TACTICS
• Fewer main rules • Shorter play time • Altered number of players: ⇒ Fewer players ⇒ One-sided player advantage • Scaled-down equipment: ⇒ Lower baskets ⇒ Smaller balls ⇒ Half-court	• Simple technical skills and abilities required	• Easy tactical applications in attack and defense: ⇒ Mainly individual tactical acts ⇒ Simple group tactical acts

Scrimmage practice Scrimmage practice involves practice games within the own team, with full number of players and regular game rules. From scrimmage to scrimmage, the coach progressively increases the demands by introducing more rules, increasing playing time, and demanding higher intensity of play. Each player should be provided with plenty of opportunities to apply the acquired skills in scrimmage practice. Furthermore, it is important to work on the gradual elimination of technical mistakes.

Another purpose of scrimmage games is to practice the individual and group tactical elements that were practiced in training. In scrimmage practice, the coach has the possibility to interrupt the game and point out mistakes and explain or demonstrate certain aspects or situations. Each player is assigned very specific goals which they are encouraged to apply during practice games.

The constant development and refinement of individual and group tactical elements, as well as the conscious application of these elements during scrimmage practice, lead to a constantly higher quality of play. The coach must insure that all players have an equal opportunity to play during this stage of development.

Practice games played under more demanding conditions In order to prepare players really well, we recommend practicing games under more demanding conditions. These games provide greater challenge than the standard of competition games. This can be done with regard to physical, tactical, technical, or psychological aspects, but often, the increase of one aspect makes the other aspects harder, too. **Table 3** (see page 16) shows a few possibilities. When planning games under more demanding conditions, the coach must take into account several factors, such as skill and fitness level of the athletes, the team's tactical abilities, etc. It is important that the players are able to effectively meet more demanding conditions.

LEAD-UP GAMES & DRILLS

Table 3 Practice games played under more demanding conditions.

PHYSICAL ASPECT	TECHNICAL ASPECT	TACTICAL ASPECT	PSYCHOLOGICAL ASPECT
• Longer play time • Fewer no. of players • Strenuous tactical demands • Carrying weighted vests, weighted wrist bands, etc. during play	• Decreasing basket rim size • Altering no. of players • Playing with weaker hand only	• One-sided team superiority • Playing against much stronger opponent • Playing game with four baskets • Making higher tactical demands, etc.	• Providing high noise background • Playing game after physical exhaustion • Giving one-sided instructions • Demanding additional training

Competition games played under normal conditions   Successful competition is the goal of all coaching efforts. The players have to demonstrate how successfully they can apply their acquired technical and tactical skills and whether their technical, tactical, physical and psychological preparation was thorough enough. It is important to find the right tactical concept with its specific variations and to apply it, based on the performance ability of one's own team and of the opponents, as well as their strategy. Competition games should be evaluated thoroughly and conclusions should be drawn for future training.

Planning an all-year training program

Overall planning of training aims at producing the highest possible individual performance. Since this can be achieved only after many years of preparation, intermediate goals must be set, guaranteeing a systematic build-up of performance. Planning thus comprises: Long-term development plans and multi-year plans for individual development stages, annual plans, and plans for specific periods and stages within an annual plan, such as preparation for a tournament, tapering for playoffs, etc.

The master plan   To achieve optimal performance in players and the team, an all-year training program must be adopted. Only a carefully planned annual plan over an entire year will assure an optimal development of the athletes' physical and psychological capabilities and skills. No matter what level it is for, an annual plan should contain the following: goals and tasks for each player; performance goals for the team; dates for testing of skills, fitness medical examination, and competitions; specific plans for skill, tactics and fitness training; and a clear division of the year into sub-phases.

COACHING METHODS

Table 4 An example of a master plan for basketball.

DATES	APR	MAY	JUN	JUL	AUG	SEP	OCT	NOV	DEC	JAN	FEB	MAR
PERIOD-IZATION	Transition	Preparation				Competition						
	Transition	General Preparation		Specific Preparation		Pre-Competition		Competition		Taper		Playoff

(NOTE: For more detailed information on periodization, refer to the book, *Periodization Theory and Methodology of Training*, by Tudor Bompa. Human Kinetics, 1999)

The master plan must assure a systematic development of training throughout the year until the peak of the competitive season, the playoffs. Detailed division of the plan into shorter periods, also known as ***periodization of training***, helps the coach maintain tight control over the continuous improvement of the athletes' performance. The various phases in the annual plan, the preparation, competitive and transitory phase, are determined on the basis of the most important competitions in the season. For most teams, these competitions include respective playoffs (**Table 4**).

The preparation period The main objectives during the preparation period is to create fitness, technical, and tactical prerequisites for further increase in team's performance during the subsequent competitive period. The preparation period includes a general physical preparation period and a basketball-specific period. Each period lasts approximately six to eight weeks.

The competitive period The competitive period is divided into pre-competition, main competition, tapering, and playoffs competition periods. The principal task of pre-competition period is to convert all basic capacities of the preparation period into competitive performance. The pre-competition period may include the training camp, and exhibition schedules. The main competition period includes the regularly scheduled league games. A short tapering period may be scheduled just before the playoff competition period, the concluding part of the season, begins.

The transition period The transition period commences immediately after the conclusion of the competitive period and may last up to a month. During this period, the players are taking a break from basketball-related training but should regularly cross train to maintain a good general fitness level.

PART II

THE COACH AS A MOTIVATOR *19*

MOTIVATION FOR PRACTICE *20*

USEFUL MOTIVATIONAL STRATEGIES *20*

FINAL THOUGHT *23*

INSPIRATIONAL SLOGANS *23*
    Attitude *24*
    Challenge *24*
    Concentration *24*
    Confidence *24*
    Courage *25*
    Desire *25*
    Discipline *25*
    Effort *25*
    Excellence *26*
    Goals *26*
    Leadership *26*
    Motivation *26*
    Persistence *27*
    Practice *27*
    Success *27*
    Teamwork *27*

MOTIVATION & INSPIRATION

Peter Klavora, University of Toronto

Motivation in athletes is the key to their effective learning of skills and persistent training at high levels of intensity. It is considered to be the intangible that makes the difference between successful and unsuccessful participation in competition.

One of the most important roles played by the coach is that of motivator. The coach's personality, attitudes and convictions, his goals and motivational strategies are of primary importance to the development of interest, motivation, and attitudes of his players toward training and competition. All of these, in turn, affect the degree of success the athlete will achieve. Therefore, the coach must make an effort to understand the motivational forces that stimulate an individual's athletic participation. The coach must realize that there are different sources of motivation that direct a youngster into the game of basketball and that later inspire her to work long and hard toward achieving success in competition. The coach must accept the fact that his athletes' reasons for participation differ greatly. Therefore, the coach must (1) make an effort to know and understand each player's specific needs, interests, and motives related to participation in basketball; (2) know the various assessment techniques which will help him identify his athletes' motives; and (3) learn and study the various motivational techniques and strategies designed to motivate players.

The coach as a motivator

The coach's ability to motivate his athletes is essential because, when all factors are fairly equal, teams who succeed are those who are *the most highly motivated during practices* and those who are also mentally well prepared for competition. When the coach is able to instill a burning desire to succeed in a team, that team will be the hardest-working unit. In other words, if properly motivated, the team will always train hard as long as necessary; this in turn leads to competitive success.

The affection and respect the coach succeeds in generating within the team have always been among the greatest motivators in keeping an athlete working hard in practice. This affection and respect of his athletes must be earned by demonstrating not only a solid technical knowledge, but also a number of personal qualities that make the coach effective in handling and working with the team. A well-liked coach (1) sets the right mood for practice—this mood is confident and relaxed; (2) is interested in his athletes' overall development and not merely in their athletic achievement; (3) is not an authoritarian nor is he excessively permissive. He sets reasonable rules for practice and is consistent in enforcing them; (4) is a hard worker, well organized, and tries very hard to make the training environment a pleasant place where athletes usually stay for several hours a day; (5) tries to be supportive and understanding because athletes often arrive at practice tired and weary after a long day of studying and/or work. The coach's smile and concern help the athlete to forget his problems more quickly and to settle into an effective practice.

There is no one way for the coach to earn the aforementioned affections since the personalities of coaches vary. Every effective coach provides leadership that is unique and suited to his personality. However, effective leadership also results from several standardized motivational techniques that can be learned.

Motivation for practice

Every player on the team must develop training discipline and an ability to push oneself to the maximum at every practice. These psychological qualities can be acquired only if the player becomes involved in basketball through a highly motivated program. Such a program makes each athlete approach practice with zest and eagerness and makes each athlete look forward to practice with anticipation. The daily practice becomes an entertaining and satisfying experience which challenges the team intellectually as well as physically. This positive attitude does not happen accidentally; it is the result of a carefully planned motivational program designed by the coach. The program must include several specific, carefully selected procedures that are highly motivational and that incite the team to ever greater training demands. Such a program develops pride in athletes about their acquired skills and physical fitness.

Useful motivational strategies

There are many motivational strategies that have been used effectively in many successful programs. It is not expected that a coach will be able to introduce into his program all of the techniques suggested here, but by incorporating a few ones into the ones he already practices the coach can expect a positive reaction and a heightened enthusiasm from his players.

Educating the athlete The contemporary practice on any level of participation taxes the athlete physically and mentally. The athlete who understands the purpose of each phase of his training will give the coach more cooperation and will be more motivated

MOTIVATION

during each practice session than the one who is completely uninformed. Therefore, the coach is wise to take time to explain to the team such concepts as (1) skill biomechanics; (2) the principles of various training methods and the effect on the athlete's physiological adaptation; (3) peaking phenomena; (4) the overload principles of training, etc.

The education of players can be done at regular team meetings. These meetings should be very carefully planned. Such matters as the progress of the team, training plans for the next phase, and the review of the videotapes should also be discussed. Athletes' concerns could also be aired at such meetings in order that the athletes be involved in the program intellectually as well as physically.

The education of athletes should be an ongoing process, before, during, and after practices, when the coach reviews the purpose of these practices and justifies his daily coaching methods. A brief comment or statement, hardly longer than a sentence, often does the job.

Variety in training Contemporary training is a demanding activity, requiring many hours of work from the athlete. The volume and intensity of training are continuously increasing, and the players repeat drills and technical elements numerous times. This, unfortunately, may lead to monotony and boredom, which negatively affects team's motivation. Therefore, the coach needs to be creative, with knowledge of a large variety of drills that allow developing skills and movements of similar technical pattern. The coach's capacity to create, to be inventive, and to work with imagination is an important advantage for successful variety in training. Only the coach's imagination limits the variety of activity, which can be introduced into daily training. However, it is important that the designed training program follows some general principles that guarantee the necessary short- and long-range goals.

Self-planned workouts One aspect of successful coaching is to develop self-reliance in athletes. To develop this quality and to further motivate practice sessions the coach may, on a given day every week, let a team member plan the entire or part of the workout for the team within certain guidelines. The 'self-planned workouts' procedure adds to the variety in training and reinforces the education of athletes. This certainly increases motivation for practice because athletes perceive that they are responsible for their own actions as they become more involved.

Rewards as motivators The coach can set up a reward system that provides symbols of recognition for a practice well done. The system can provide great incentive in practice for most players, since athletes generally demonstrate a considerable need for recognition. The rewards for special achievements can be simple. The coach may award special hats or shirts to the most improved player of the week; or, each week the coach may let the athlete who worked the hardest wear a specially colored shirt; or all players who can hit ten 3-pointers in a row receive a pound of jelly beans. Again, the only limitation in setting a successful reward system is a coach's imagination.

It is amazing how much motivation within the team this kind of costless reward system generates. It adds a great deal to the quality of practice as most players try very hard to earn at least one such award here and there. It is important, however, that the reward system be set up in such a way that even the less gifted players can experience some measure of success. It boosts their spirit enormously and lets them know that they too are important and necessary members of the team.

Performance evaluation Regular performance evaluation throughout the year keeps most athletes enthusiastic and motivated for daily practice at the desired intensity levels. The performance evaluation provides the athlete with the necessary feedback about his own progress from test to test and from year to year. Continuous progress is one of the strongest motivators to an athlete. Achieving short- and long-term goals gives him a tremendous sense of accomplishment which drives him even harder in practice.

Performance evaluation provides the coach with the necessary feedback about the effectiveness of his program as well. Continuous progress of most team members from test to test is an indication of a well-designed program and a highly motivated team. Additionally, the test scores provide a useful ranking of the athletes and can be used for selection of the team or starting players.

Setting team and individual goals The establishment of goals and consequent training programs to achieve them is another strong form of motivation that leads to greater zest for training. There exist two types of goals: ***team goals*** and ***individual goals***. Both are equally important. Initially, individual goals are more important since each individual really wants to see an improvement. He or she must see regular progress in order to want to continue; these goals, if well set, will allow the athlete to see the progress.

To be achieved, team goals require a contribution from all team members. Just as with individual goals, there are team goals for each practice, each week, each month, each testing, each tournament, and each season. They are usually discussed and determined at team meetings. Team discussion and team decision increase both goal awareness and commitment. They produce a form of psychological contracting which binds the team to serious practice. Once set through the coach's assistance, team goals increase team unity and continuously exert strong social pressure upon all members to continue according to expectations since each member is an integral and necessary part of the whole.

Psychologists have suggested several guidelines that can be helpful in using goal-setting as a motivational tool.

(1) Goals should be ***objective*** and ***specific*** (shoot 65% from the foul line, improve speed-drill time by 8 seconds, improve the vertical jump by 2 cm, etc.) rather than general ('do your best,' 'try and improve by as much as you can,' etc.);

(2) Goals should be ***meaningful*** (the player's vertical jump compares well - at the top - to the norms of his age group, etc.);

(3) Goals should be ***obtainable*** (realistic and yet demanding objectives - 50 % chance of achievement – are most effective goals for the player to strive for); and

MOTIVATION

(4) Goals should be *individualized* and should be based on past experience. The coach must know the athlete's abilities and limitations, as well as his aspiration levels. Only then can the coach formulate the athlete's realistic but challenging goals fairly accurately.

Final thought

It will be impossible for a coach to employ all of the motivational suggestions presented in this section. He or she may choose a few and build on them with ideas that may develop as he or she continues with his or her program. There are virtually no limits to the types of motivational ideas that can be developed and/or borrowed from other successful programs (not necessarily from basketball). However, every coach must also realize that no motivational procedure or strategy will have a lasting effect unless he or she knows how to teach correct basketball skills and strategies, how to apply contemporary training methods, and how to work with athletes.

Inspirational slogans

To increase his motivational effectiveness the coach may use inspirational words and phrases that will get his team focused and motivated. Slogans for the day, week, or a specific game can be a useful tool. A small selection of inspiring slogans taken from *The Great Book of Inspiring Quotations,* a Sport Books Publisher publication, has been compiled in the next section. The coach can select whatever suits his or her team best.

LEAD-UP GAMES & DRILLS

Attitude

Pride is a personal commitment. It is an attitude that separates excellence from mediocrity.
ANONYMOUS

A man is not hurt so much by what happens, as by his opinion of what happens.
MICHEL EYQUEM MONTAIGNE

We can do only what we think we can do. We can be only what we think we can be. We can have only what we think we can have. What we do, what we are, what we have, all depend upon what we think.
ROBERT COLLIER

Leadership is an attitude before it is an ability.
ANONYMOUS

The first and most important step toward success is the feeling that we can succeed.
NELSON BOSWELL

A mind free of negatives produces positives. Think victory, get victory.
ANONYMOUS

Challenge

Your biggest task is not to get ahead of others, but to surpass yourself.
ANONYMOUS

Becoming number one is easier than remaining number one.
BILL BRADLEY

The impossible is what nobody can do until someone does it.
ANONYMOUS

Accept that some days you're the pigeon, and some days you're the statue.
SCOTT ADAMS

Adversity makes some people break and makes others break records.
ANONYMOUS

By having adversity in life we can see in others and in ourselves who quits and those who won't quit; and in the end, adversity will make winners of those who won't quit.
ANONYMOUS

Every great achievement once seemed impossible.
ANONYMOUS

INSPIRATION

Concentration

The most important thing in communication is to hear what isn't being said.
PETER F. DRUCKER

Concentrate... put all your eggs in one basket, and watch that basket....
ANDREW CARNEGIE

The weakest living creature, by concentrating his powers on a single object, can accomplish something; whereas the strongest, by dispersing his over many, may fail to accomplish anything.
THOMAS CARLYLE

There is no job so simple that it cannot be done wrong.
ANONYMOUS

Concentrate all your thoughts upon the work at hand. The sun's rays do not burn until brought to a focus.
ALEXANDER GRAHAM BELL

The minute you start talking about what you are going to do if you lose, you have lost.
GEORGE SHULTZ

Confidence

When you have confidence, you can have a lot of fun; and when you have fun, you can do amazing things.
JOE NAMATH

The team that won't be beaten, can't be beaten.
FRANK BROYLES

I am only one, but I am one. I cannot do everything, but I can do something. What I can do, I should do and, with the help of God, I will do!
EVERETT HALE

Fear is your best friend or your worst enemy. It's like fire. If you can control it, it can cook for you; it can heat your house. If you can't control it, it will burn you every time.
CUS D'AMATO

Confidence comes from hours and days and weeks and years of constant work and dedication.
ROGER STAUBACH

One important key to success is self-confidence. An important key to self-confidence is preparation.
ARTHUR ASHE

25

Courage

A ship in a harbour is safe, but that is not what ships are built for.
ANONYMOUS

He who fears he shall suffer, already suffers what he fears.
MICHEL EYQUEM DE MONTAIGNE

Behold the turtle – he only makes progress when he sticks his neck out.
ANONYMOUS

Bravery is being the only one who knows you're afraid.
FRANKLIN P. JONES

Success is never final and failure is never fatal. It is courage that counts.
WINSTON CHURCHILL

It is not because things are difficult that we do not dare; it is because we do not dare that things are difficult.
LUCIUS ANNAEUS SENECA

Don't be afraid to go out on a limb—that is where the fruit is.
ANONYMOUS

Desire

Desire! That's the one secret of every man's career. Not education. Not being born with hidden talents. Desire.
BOBBY UNSER

A champion must have the desire for perfection, and the will to punish himself in the process.
ANONYMOUS

If everyone got what they wanted, there wouldn't be enough to go around.
ANONYMOUS

Man's desires are limited by his perceptions; none can desire what he has not perceiv'd.
WILLIAM BLAKE

The first principle of success is desire—knowing what you want. Desire is the planting of your seed.
ROBERT COLLIER

If you really want something, you can figure out how to make it happen.
CHER

INSPIRATION

Discipline

Only those who have the patience to do simple things perfectly will acquire the skill to do difficult things easily.
ANONYMOUS

The problem is not that people don't know what to do. The problem is they find reasons not to do it until there are no tomorrows.
ANONYMOUS

A man must learn to endure patiently that which he cannot avoid conveniently.
MICHEL EYQUEM DE MONTAIGNE

The reason some men do not succeed is because their wishbone is where their backbone ought to be.
ANONYMOUS

A lot of people love their jobs. It's the work they hate.
ANONYMOUS

There are no secrets to success. Success is doing the things you know you should do.
ANONYMOUS

Effort

Nothing good comes in life or athletics unless a lot of hard work has preceded the effort. Only temporary success is achieved by taking short cuts.
ROGER STAUBACH

I firmly believe that any man's finest hour, his greatest fulfillment to all he holds dear, is the moment when he has worked his heart out in a good cause and lies exhausted on the field of battle victorious.
VINCE LOMBARDI

What really counts is not the number of hours you put in, but how much you put in the hours.
ANONYMOUS

The harder you work, the harder it is to surrender.
VINCE LOMBARDI

It is said that good things come to those who wait. I believe that good things come to those who work.
WILT CHAMBERLAIN

I had rather wear out than rust out.
GEORGE WHITEFIELD

Excellence

It isn't hard to be good from time to time in sports. What's tough is being good every day.
WILLIE MAYS

I know it sounds selfish, wanting to do something no one else has done. But that's what you're out here for... to separate yourself from everyone else.
JACK NICKLAUS

I put the most pressure on myself because of my ambition to be the best basketball player ever. What happens around me can't put any more pressure on me than that.
JULIUS ERVING

I don't ask our athletes how many of them want to win. The question I ask is can you live with losing, can you live with failure, can you live with mediocrity?
LOU HOLTZ

Next year is not about winning another championship, or having one more ring, or developing bigger reputations. It's about leaving footprints.
PAT RILEY

Goals

All my life I wanted to be somebody. Now I see that I should have been more specific.
JANE WAGNER

Be aware that the only ceiling life has is the one you give it.
ANONYMOUS

We see obstacles when we take our eyes off our goals.
ANONYMOUS

Who shoots at the midday sun, though he be sure he shall never hit the mark, yet as sure he is he shall shoot higher than who aims but at a bush.
SIR PHILIP SIDNEY

Planning is bringing the future into the present so that you can do something about it now.
ALAN LAKEIN

The direction of the mind is more important than its progress.
JOSEPH JOUBERT

INSPIRATION

Leadership

The speed of the leader determines the rate of the pack.
ANONYMOUS

Real leaders are ordinary people with extraordinary determination.
ANONYMOUS

The very essence of leadership is that you have to have a vision.
THEODORE HESBURGH

A real leader faces the music, even when he doesn't like the tune.
ANONYMOUS

A leader has been defined as one who knows the way, goes the way, and shows the way.
ANONYMOUS

A good leader takes a little more than his share of blame; a little less than his share of credit.
ARNOLD H. GLASGOW

Leadership is action, not position.
DONALD H. MCGANNON

Motivation

The biggest mistake you can make is to believe that you are working for someone else.
ANONYMOUS

You are today where your thoughts have brought you. You will be tomorrow where your thoughts take you.
JAMES ALLEN

Remember it is better to have little talent and much purpose, than little purpose and much talent.
ANONYMOUS

In baseball and in business, there are three types of people. There are those who make it happen, those who watch it happen, and those who wondered what happened.
TOMMY LASORDA

Even if you are on the right track, you'll get run over if you just sit there.
WILL ROGERS

Life is like a ten-speed bike – most of us have gears we never use.
CHARLES SCHULZ

Persistence

Defeat doesn't finish a man – quit does. A man is not finished when he's defeated. He's finished when he quits.
RICHARD NIXON

It's not whether you get knocked down. It's whether you get up again.
VINCE LOMBARDI

A hero is one who knows how to hang on one minute longer.
NORWEGIAN PROVERB

It is better to burn out than to fade away.
NEIL YOUNG

You just can't beat the person who never gives up.
BABE RUTH

We may encounter many defeats, but we must not be defeated.
MAYA ANGELOU

Paralyze their resistance with your persistence.
ANONYMOUS

Practice

By nature, men are really alike; by practice, they get to be wide apart.
CONFUCIUS

You never get a second chance to make a good first impression.
ANONYMOUS

Everyone has the will to win, but few have the will to prepare to win.
BOBBY KNIGHT

Remember the five P's: proper preparation prevents poor performance.
ANONYMOUS

Failure to prepare certainly means preparing to fail.
JOHN WOODEN

I will get ready, and then perhaps my chance will come.
ABRAHAM LINCOLN

It takes years to become an overnight success.
EDDIE CANTOR

INSPIRATION

Success

You can win and still not succeed, still not achieve what you should. And you can lose without really failing at all.
BOBBY KNIGHT

He who does not hope to win has already lost.
JOSÉ JOAQUÍN OLMEDO

A winner respects those who are superior to him and tries to learn something from them; a loser resents those who are superior to him and tries to find chinks in their armour.
ANONYMOUS

Success is to be measured not so much by the position that one has reached as by the obstacles that one has overcome while trying to succeed.
MARK TWAIN

If you are average, you are as close to the bottom as you are to the top.
ANONYMOUS

Sometimes something worth doing is worth overdoing.
DAVID LETTERMAN

Teamwork

Coming together is a beginning; keeping together is progress; working together is success.
HENRY FORD

You may be on top of the heap, but remember, you are still part of it.
ANONYMOUS

It's amazing what a team can accomplish when no one cares who gets the credit.
JOHN WOODEN

One man can be a crucial ingredient on a team, but one man cannot make a team.
KAREEM ABDUL-JABBAR

The nice thing about teamwork is that you always have others on your side.
MARGARET CARTY

Together
Everyone
Achieves
More
ANONYMOUS

PART III

DEVELOPING TECHNICAL SKILLS WITHOUT THE BALL *34*

DEVELOPING TECHNICAL SKILLS WITH THE BALL *41*

DEVELOPING TECHNICAL AND TACTICAL SKILLS WITH AN OPPONENT *52*

DEVELOPING ADVANCED PLAYING ABILITY *58*

LEAD-UP GAMES

The collection of lead-up games in this section includes mainly game forms that have an immediate relationship to playing effective basketball. They are an important part of the general, as well as basketball-specific, practice because of their joyful and performance-stimulating character. They are the connecting link between necessary basic preparation and more basketball-specific training because they prepare, develop, and strengthen players' technical and tactical skills. As part of modern basketball training they should be used in a way that they are well balanced with other aspects of training.

Each lead-up game has a certain function to fulfill in physical, technical, or psychological respect. It should have a specific purpose and meet the objectives the coach has set for the practice. The following tips should be considered:

- Use lead-up games mainly as an introduction for new movements and techniques of the game. However, they can also serve as a relaxing part during the middle part of training and provide some counter balance to the more demanding basketball-specific drills and training elements. Lead-up games can be used as fun drills at the end of practice to end workout on a joyful note.

- Lead-up games should follow a progression, moving from the simple to more complex. Build up on previous experiences, and develop a progression of lead-up games for each skill taught.

- Know the game very well. Small organizational mistakes confuse the players and lower the value of practice. Well-planned lead-up games make practice enjoyable and increase players' motivation for further improvements.

- Explain each lead-up game clearly and demonstrate it before the players practice it. The explanation should be clear and concise making sure that every player has a clear understanding of the task.

- Equipment has to be ready to ensure a quick start of the game. This also applies to team markings, floor markings, etc.

- Make sure that the lead-up games are executed correctly. After a clear explanation and demonstration, it is the coach's responsibility to see that the lead-up game is done correctly. If the execution is sloppy or incorrect, the practice must be stopped and correct method emphasized one more time.

- As much as possible, introduce competition into lead-up games. This raises the intensity level of practice. Acknowledge the winner and praise good work.

- Check whether everything was done to give the selected lead-up game a joyful aspect.

LEAD-UP GAMES

Developing technical skills without the ball

Starting and stopping

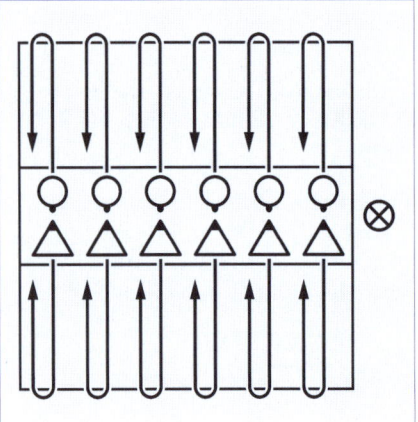

G1 The best group Two groups of equal number stand facing each other along the centre of the playing area. At the signal, each group turns and runs to the baseline behind them and back. The first group to return to its original position receives a point. Starting positions (e.g., prone, sitting, etc.) and mode of locomotion (e.g., skipping, hopping, etc.) can be varied. The team with the most points after several rounds is the winner.

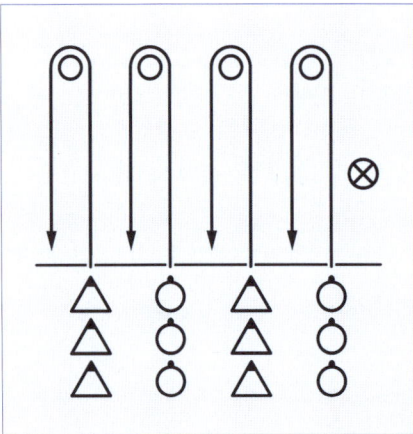

G2 Relay competition Several groups of equal number line up in rows behind a designated start line with adequate separation between the groups. Each group has a marker (e.g., flag, pole, etc.) positioned several metres ahead of it. At the signal, the first member of each group runs up to and around the marker, returns to the baseline, and tags the next player in line, and so on. The first group to return to its original position wins. If numbers are uneven to start, one player can go twice.

WITHOUT THE BALL

G3 **Start tag** One player is chosen to be IT and stands at one end of a playing area divided into three equal parts. The remaining players stand at the opposite end of the playing area. At the signal, all players try to successfully make it from one baseline to the other without being tagged by IT. Before tagging any players, IT must first run across a third of the playing area to pick up a pinnie or ball to be used to tag other players. All players tagged must also pick up pinnies or balls and help IT tag other players in subsequent rounds. The winner is the last player tagged.

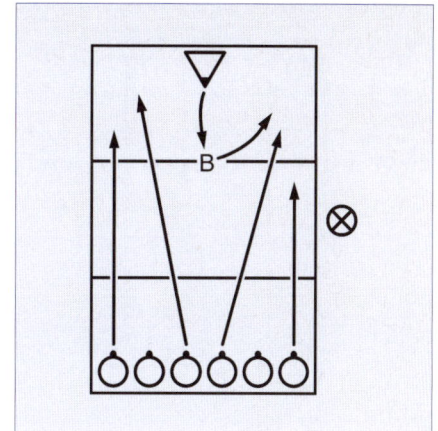

G4 **Black & white** Two teams of equal number stand facing each other some distance apart along the centre of the playing area. One team is called "black" and the other is called "white." At the signal of the coach ("black" or "white"), each member of that team must run to the baseline behind them as they are pursued by members of the opposing team. The goal of the other team is to tag as many players as possible before they reach the baseline safely. The team gets a point for each opposing player tagged. After repeating the game several times, the team tallying the most points is the winner.

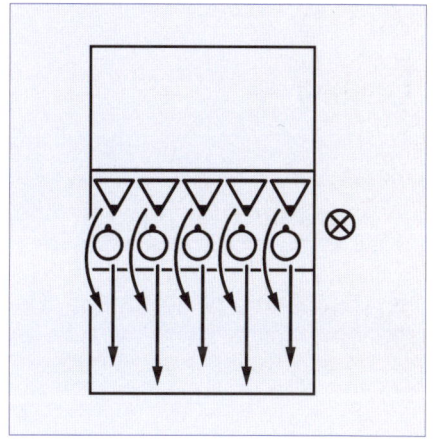

G5 **Position change** Two teams of equal number stand facing each other at opposite ends of a rectangular playing area. At the signal, both teams run to opposite sides. The first team to stand in a row along the opposite baseline wins.

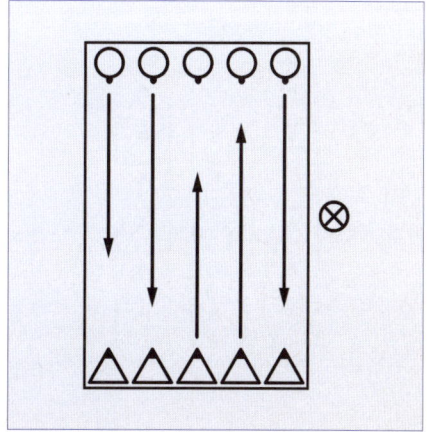

LEAD-UP GAMES

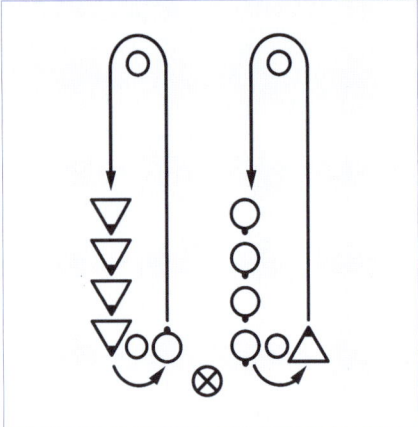

G6 Chase Two teams position themselves as shown. Each team assigns one player to be IT, who lines up next to the opposing team. At the signal, players begin circling around two pylons placed several metres apart. The player who is IT for each team must chase and try to tag the last player on the opposing team. Each team tries to prevent this as long as possible without losing their original order. The first team to successfully tag a player gains a point. New players are chosen to be IT for each round.

Turning

G7 Save your soul Players stand behind one baseline of a rectangular playing area. At the signal, all players run to the opposite baseline and back. The last player to return to the starting baseline after each round receives a point and starts one metre ahead of everyone else in the next round. The object is to finish the game with as few points as possible.

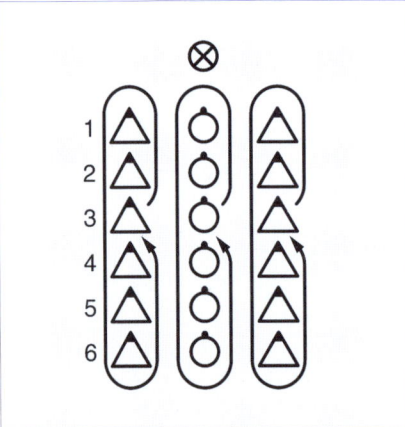

G8 Number run in a row Teams of equal number stand in rows next to each other. All players are given a number. When the coach calls out a number, the player from each team with that number must run around his or her team in a counterclockwise direction before returning to his or her original position. The first player to return to his or her original position receives a point for the team. Different numbers are called out in each round until all players have run at least once. The team accumulating the most points wins.

WITHOUT THE BALL

G9 Circle tag A small group (not more than 10 players) stands in a circle formation holding hands. A player chosen to be IT stands outside the circle and must try to tag a designated player from the circle. The circle tries to protect this player from being tagged by turning, but must do so without breaking the circle (i.e., releasing hands). When the player is successfully tagged, a different player becomes IT.

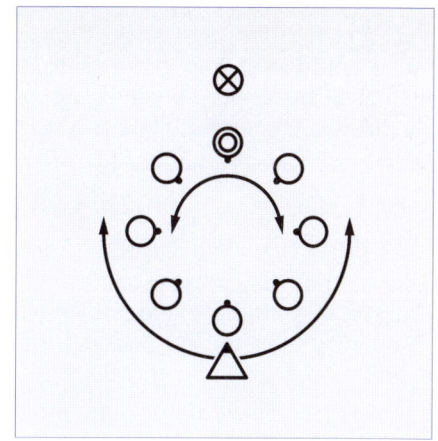

G10 Circling A group (not larger than 12 to 15 players) stands in a circle formation. One player (runner) stands in a small circle within the larger circle of players and two others (both IT) stand outside the circle. At the signal, the runner must try to circle around a player forming the circle without being tagged. Players who are IT cannot enter the circle of players at any time. Once the runner has successfully circled three different players or is tagged by IT, the players switch positions or are replaced by three new players.

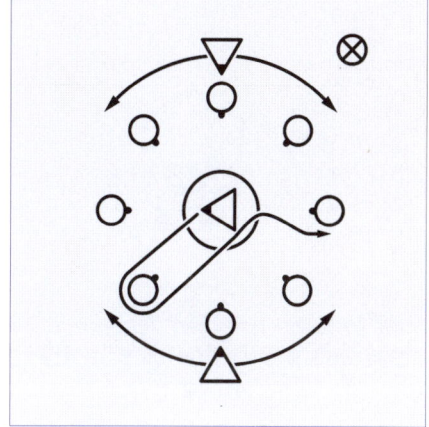

Evading and faking

G11 Simple tag One player is chosen to be IT and must try tagging another player in the group within a bounded playing area. A tagged player then becomes IT. Touchbacks are not permitted.

LEAD-UP GAMES

G12 **Protection tag** As described in "simple tag" (G11), except players can use specific positions agreed upon before the game (e.g., squat, piggyback with another player, hold hands with another player, stork stand, etc.) to avoid being tagged. Players are only "protected" for a limited period of time (up to five seconds) before IT can tag them again, but IT cannot guard protected players.

G13 **Time tag** One player is chosen to be IT. In a clearly defined playing area, IT must tag as many players as possible within a specified period of time (e.g., one minute). Tagged players must squat down where they are tagged and become obstacles for the remaining players. For added difficulty, the number of players who are IT to start the game can be gradually increased.

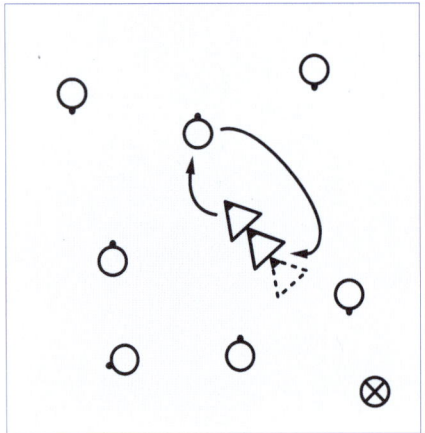

G14 **Chain tag** One or more players are IT to begin the game. As players are tagged, they must join hands with IT, becoming part of a longer chain. The chain must remain connected at all times, so only the first and last players forming the chain are able to tag remaining players. The game continues until all players have been tagged.

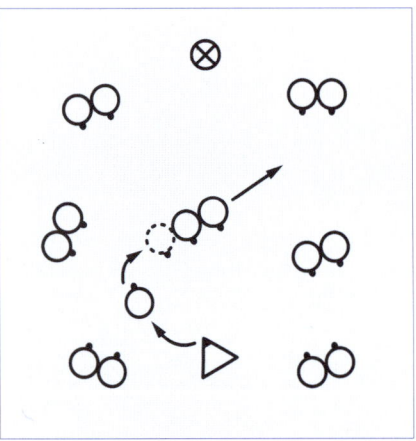

G15 **Tag the third** Players are paired (linked by the arms) and scattered throughout the playing area. Two players remain unpaired, one of whom begins the game IT. IT tries to tag the other unpaired player, who can save him- or herself by linking arms with one of the pairs. Only two players can be linked at one time, so when a third player links up with a pair, the outermost player must release and form a new pair while avoiding being tagged, and so on. If IT successfully tags another player before he or she is able to link up with another pair, that player becomes IT. Touchbacks are not permitted.

WITHOUT THE BALL

G16 Two catch one Players are divided into groups of three. Two players are IT and must hold hands as they try tagging the third player within a bounded playing area. The player who successfully tags the third player, without letting go of his or her partner's hand, switches roles with the tagged player.

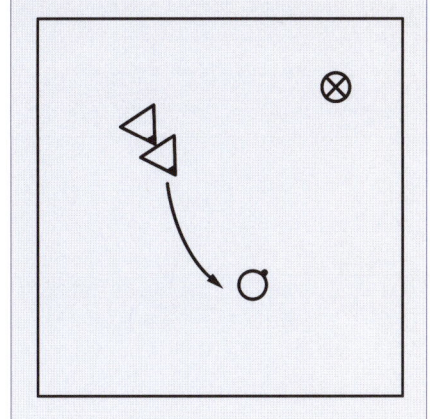

G17 Collecting pinnies Everyone is IT in this game. All players tuck a pinnie into the back of their pants or shorts and must try grabbing as many other players' pinnies as possible, while protecting their own. The player who successfully collects the most pinnies after a specified period of time is the winner.

Skipping and jumping

G18 Jumping over Two groups each form a circle lying on their stomachs (prone position) with their heads towards the centre. At the signal, the first player in each group gets up and jumps over the other players in a counterclockwise direction until returning to his or her original position. As soon as the first player has jumped over the person next to him or her, this player also gets up and begins jumping over the others in the same direction, and so on, until each player has jumped over every other player. The first team to have each member return to his or her original position is the winner. Be cautious.

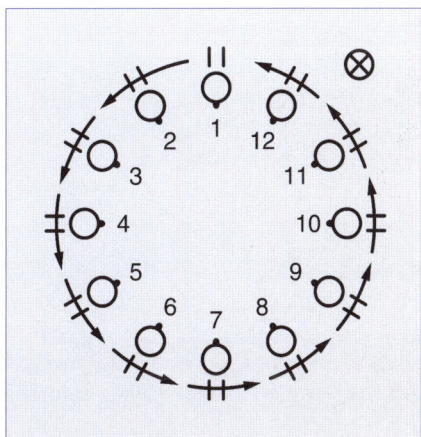

39

LEAD-UP GAMES

G19 Jumping circle The coach or instructor stands in the centre of a circle formed by the players. The coach swings a rope with a sandbag (or similar object) attached to the end of it just above the ground in a clockwise direction. Players in the circle must jump over the rope as it passes them. If a player touches the rope at any time, he or she is out of the game. The coach can vary the speed and height of the swing or instruct players to move in the opposite direction of the swing to add difficulty. The last remaining player is the winner.

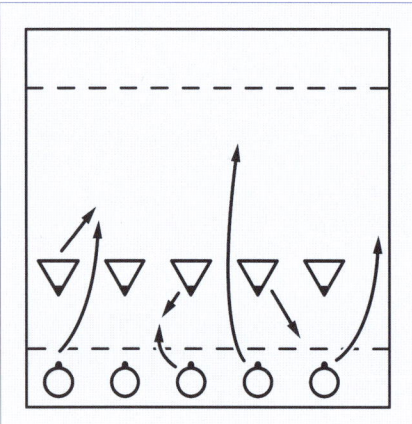

G20 Jump tag Two groups stand facing each other a few metres apart at one end of the playing area. One group is IT to start the game. At the signal, the players must begin jumping or hopping towards a goal line at the opposite end of the playing area. Players who are IT must try tagging as many of them as possible before they safely reach the goal. Groups switch roles after each round. Points are totalled after a few rounds to determine the winner.

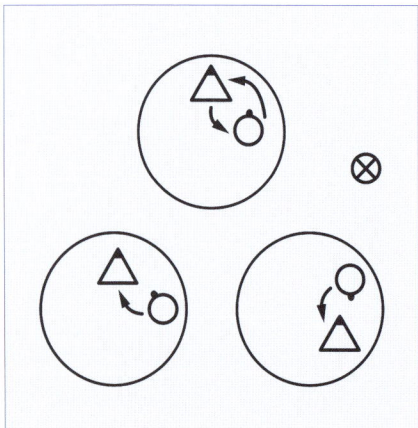

G21 Rooster fight Two players face each other in a fighting position (arms crossed in front, standing on one leg). At the signal, players try knocking each other off balance without unfolding their arms until one player is forced to put both feet on the ground. *Variations:* (a) multiple players can play at the same time, with teams fighting for a specified period of time. The winning team would be the one with the most players still on one leg with arms crossed after the allotted time; (b) a circular fighting ring may also be used to make the game more difficult. Any player stepping out of the ring would be eliminated.

WITH THE BALL

Developing technical skills with the ball

Getting used to the ball

G22 Goal ball Players are divided into two equal teams. Players on one team are each given a ball and stand around a basketball hoop. At the signal, the players try to make as many baskets as possible within a given time (20-60 seconds). The teams then switch, and the drill is repeated for the other team. The team that makes the most baskets in the allotted time is the winner.

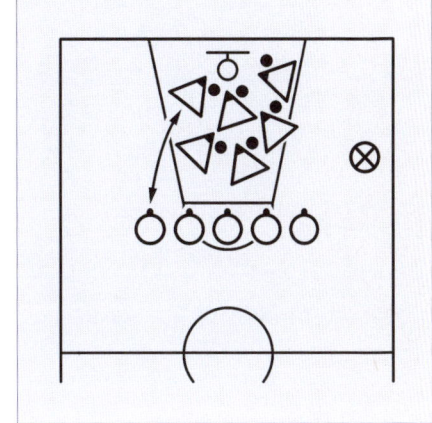

G23 Ball toss Players are each given a ball and divided into two equal teams. Each team stands on opposite sides of a playing area divided into two equal halves. Members of each team distribute themselves along both baselines. At the signal, players on both teams try tossing their balls into a basket located in the centre of each half of the playing area. The ball must remain in the basket to count as a point. When all players have attempted a shot, players retrieve their own balls. The team making the most baskets after several rounds is the winner.

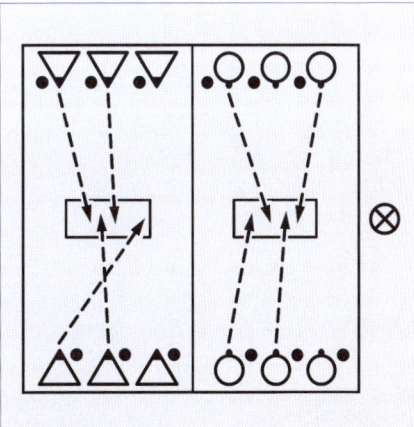

LEAD-UP GAMES

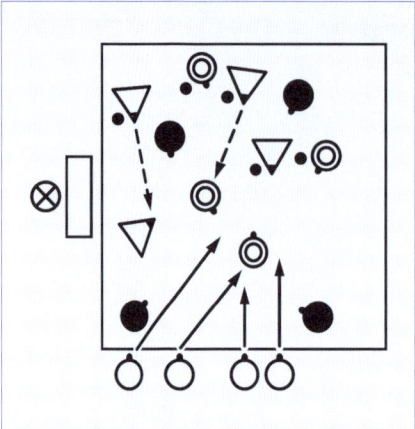

G24 Catch ball Three teams of equal number spread out in a playing area and pass several balls among themselves. A fourth team of equal number starts along the baseline wearing pinnies to distinguish themselves from the other players. At the signal, the fourth team enters the playing area and tries to intercept as many passes as possible. Intercepted balls are removed from the playing area. When all the balls have been intercepted, the time is stopped and recorded. The game continues until every team has played as the intercepting team. The team successfully retrieving all the balls in the shortest time is the winner.

Dribbling

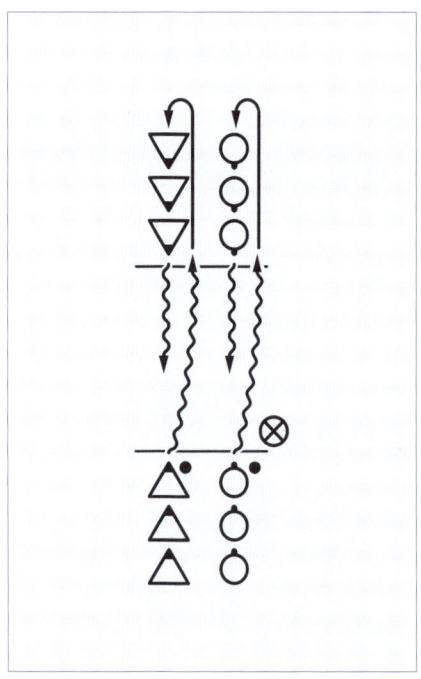

G25 Pendulum dribbling Two teams of equal number are each divided in half, with each half lined up facing the other from a given distance. The first player from each team is given a ball and, at the signal, dribbles over to the first player in line across from them, passes off the ball to this player, and then joins the back of the line. The player receiving the pass repeats the drill, and so on, until every member of the team has switched sides. The first team to completely switch sides and have every player seated in a row is the winner.

WITH THE BALL

G26 Turn dribbling Players line up in a row one behind the other. The first player in line is given a ball and dribbles up to and around one or more markers before dribbling back, passing the ball off to the next player in line, and joining the back of the line. This game can be played with several teams as a relay, where the first team to have the first player return to the front of the line is the winner.

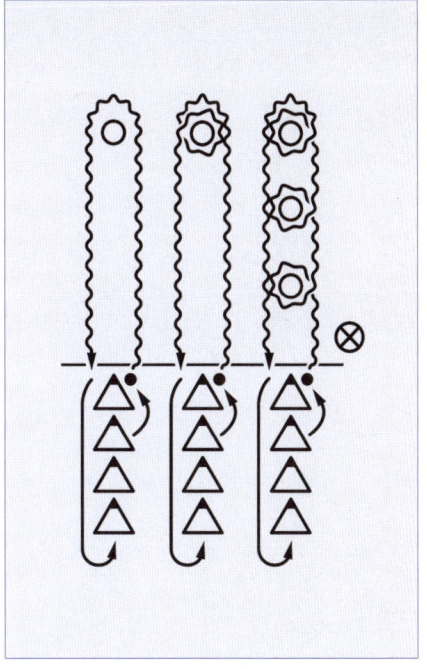

G27 Circle dribbling Players form two or more groups of equal number and stand along a large circle with some separation between groups. The first player in each group is given a ball and dribbles around the circle in a counter-clockwise direction. When he or she has completed the full circle, the ball is passed off to the next player in line and he or she joins the back of the line. This continues until the first player reaches the front of the line again. The first team to have all players return to their original positions is the winner.

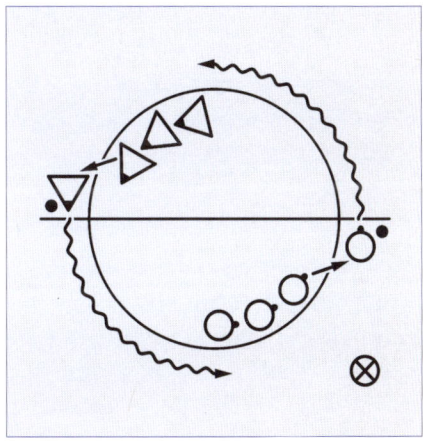

G28 Dribble tag Players spread out within a clearly defined playing area. One or more players are chosen to be IT and must try tagging the other players while dribbling. Any player who is tagged also becomes IT and is given a ball. As a variation, all players can begin the game with a ball, and players who are IT must wear pinnies to distinguish themselves from the other players. The winner is the last player tagged.

LEAD-UP GAMES

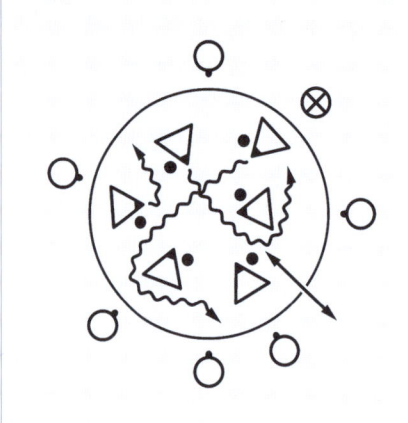

G29 Autodrome Players are divided into two groups. Each member of one group is given a ball and dribbles within a confined circular playing area for one minute. Players must continue moving and dribbling within the circle at a brisk pace determined by the coach, trying not to bump into other players, step out of bounds, or lose control of the ball. The next group then repeats the drill. Players from each team lasting the full minute without a fault then play one more round to determine a winner. In the final round, players actively try to knock the balls away from each other while dribbling. The last remaining player wins.

G30 Circular track dribbling Members of one team are each given a ball and dribble along a circular path (one to three metres wide) in a counterclockwise direction. Players' balls and feet must remain within the path at all times, and all players must remain in single file. Another team of equal number stands around the circle watching for mistakes. When the first group has completed five full trips around the circle, the time is recorded. Additional time is added for mistakes (i.e., one mistake = five seconds). Teams then switch roles. The team completing the rounds in the fastest time wins.

G31 Chase dribbling Players are divided into equal teams and form a large circle, standing in alternating order, facing the centre. Each player from each team is given a number (e.g., from 1 to 4 for teams of four players). When the coach calls out a number, all players with that number must dribble around the outside of the circle in a counterclockwise direction and try to tag the person in front of them. The winner of each round is the first player to successfully tag the player ahead of him or her while maintaining control of the ball.

WITH THE BALL

G32 Baseline saves Players are each given a ball and stand along one baseline. One player is chosen to be IT and stands on the opposite baseline at the other end of the playing area. At the signal, players must try dribbling to the opposite baseline without being tagged. Before being able to tag any players, IT must first run to pick up a ball a few metres ahead of him or her. A player who is tagged also becomes IT and helps tag the remaining players in subsequent rounds.

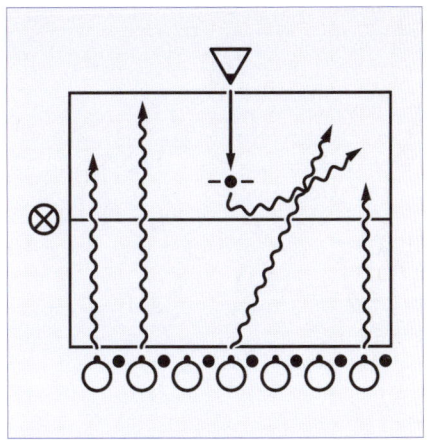

G33 Team dribbling tag Two teams of equal number stand on opposite sides of the playing area. Each player is given a ball. One player from each team is chosen to be IT and stands at the centre line. At the signal, these two players dribble into the opposing team's half of the playing area and try to tag as many players as possible. Tagged players sit or stand where they are tagged and become obstacles for remaining players. The first player to tag every player on the opposing team in each round is the winner. When each member of both teams has been IT once, the final scores are tallied to determine a winner.

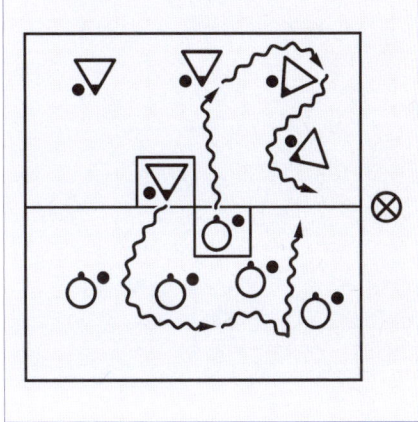

Passing and catching

G34 Combination ball Players are divided into two equal teams. At the signal, players on one team begin moving and passing several balls among each other within a defined playing area for a specified period of time. The coach or instructor keeps track of how many balls are dropped. Teams then switch. The team with the fewest number of dropped passes is the winner. *Variations:* (a) players are given a number and must pass to teammates in sequential order; (b) each team plays with only one ball and players pass among each other either in a random or predetermined order.

LEAD-UP GAMES

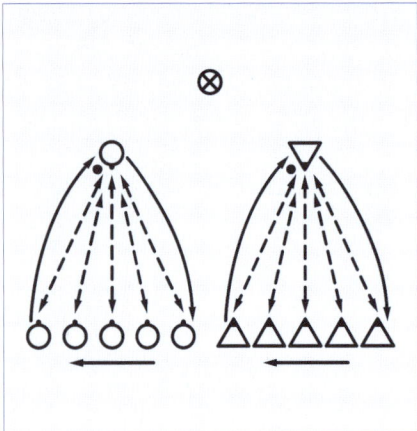

G35 **Exchange ball** Two or more groups position themselves in a triangular formation as shown in the diagram. One player is given a ball and begins the game as the passer from the top of the triangle. The passer passes to teammates one at a time from left to right, receiving a return pass after each pass, until every player has received a pass. Once the last player in line has made the final pass, he or she takes over as the passer, and the passer joins the end of the row. The game continues until each player has been passer once. The first team to have all players back in their original positions is the winner.

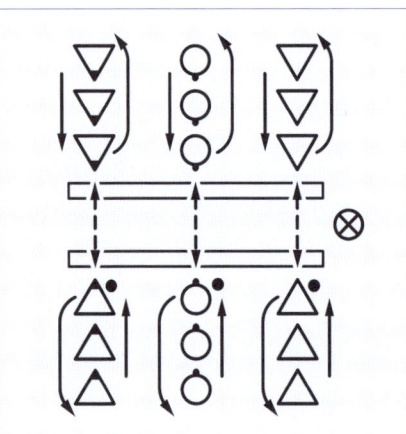

G36 **Ball throwing** Players are divided into two or more equal teams. Teams are then divided in half, each half lining up (single file) facing the other from a given distance behind two lines or benches. The first player from each team is given a ball and passes to the first player across from them and then moves to the end of the line, and so on. The winner is the first team to successfully complete a specified number of passes.

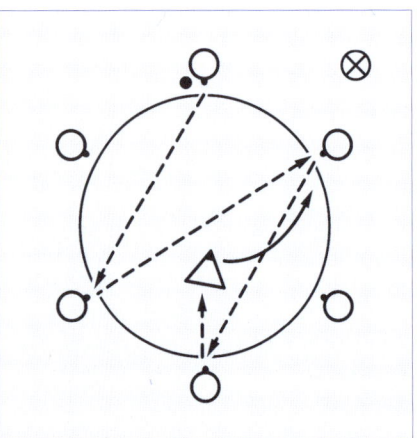

G37 **Tiger ball** Players form a large circle around one other player ("tiger"). The players forming the circle pass one or more balls among each other, and the goal of the tiger is to try to intercept a pass. The ball cannot be passed between players standing right next to each other in the circle. If the tiger successfully intercepts a pass, a new player becomes the tiger for the next round and the tiger joins the circle.

WITH THE BALL

G38 Double circle ball Two circles are marked on the floor as shown in the diagram. All but three players stand outside the outer circle, with one player inside the inner circle, and two other players in the area between the two circles. A ball is passed back and forth between the player inside the inner circle and the players outside the outer circle. The two players between the circles must try to intercept the ball. If the ball is caught or knocked away by one of these two players, he or she switches positions with the player who threw the pass.

G39 Four sections Players are divided into two equal teams. A rectangular playing area is divided into four equal sections, with half of each team occupying alternate sections. The team starting with the ball must try to pass to a player on their team two sections over. The ball can be passed within a section once before attempting another pass. A successful pass between sections earns a point for the team. If a pass is dropped, bounces more than once, or is intercepted by the opposing team, possession of the ball changes hands. The team with the most points after a specified amount of time wins.

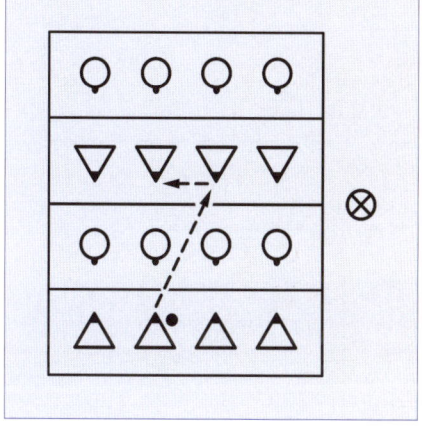

G40 Hunter ball Two equal teams spread out in a large playing area. One team of players are hunters (and wear a pinnie) and the others are rabbits. When the coach throws the ball into play, a hunter picks up the ball and tries to hit a rabbit (below the waist). The ball can be passed among hunters before shooting at a rabbit. The same rabbit cannot be hit twice in a row. Hunters receive a point each time a rabbit is hit; rabbits receive a point if they catch a ball thrown at them or if a pass is dropped by the hunters. The team with the most points after a specified period of time is the winner. Teams then switch roles.

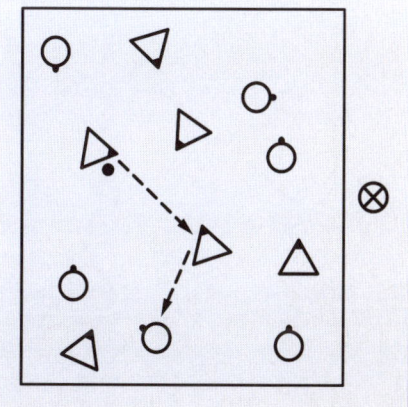

LEAD-UP GAMES

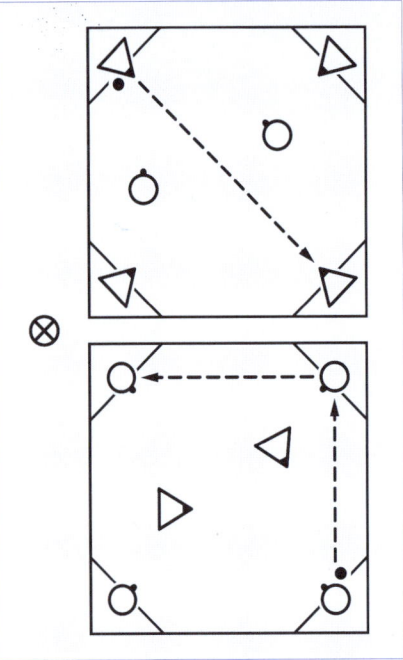

G41 Square ball Players are divided into two teams of six and arrange themselves in two square playing areas as shown in the diagram. The corners of each square are marked with a small box or triangle—one player stands in each marked corner. One corner player from each team is given a ball and must try passing the ball to other corner players in the square, always keeping at least one foot in the marked area. The ball cannot be passed back to a player who just threw the ball. Two players from the opposing team stand in the middle of each square and try to intercept the passes. Each successful pass earns a point for the passing team. If the middle players manage to intercept the ball or deflect a pass out of play, the passing team loses a point. After a specified period of time has elapsed, the games are stopped and the points for both teams are tallied to determine a winner.

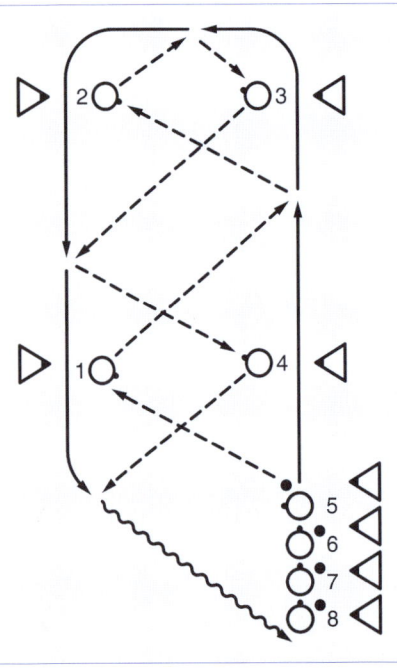

G42 Pass, run, catch Players are divided into equal teams of six or more. Only one team plays at a time. Each player is given a number and positioned as shown in the diagram. Players 1 through 4 stand in a rectangular formation near the top of the playing area, while the remaining players are given a ball and stand (single file) in the bottom right corner of the playing area. Player 5 begins the game by passing the ball to player 1 and begins running around the rectangle of players in a counterclockwise direction. As player 5 continues running, he or she must pass the ball to each player in the rectangle, receiving a return pass after each pass, before dribbling back to the original starting line-up. After each player starting with a ball has run the circuit twice, the time is stopped and recorded. Teams then switch. The team completing the circuit in the fastest time is the winner.

WITH THE BALL

G43 Ball at the wall Players are divided into two or more equal groups. Each group stands in a row (one behind the other) some distance away from a large, smooth wall. At the signal, the first player on each team throws a ball against the wall and catches it, before passing the ball on to the next player in line, and so on. If the ball is dropped, the player must attempt another throw, until the ball is caught. Each player must successfully catch the ball off the wall three times. The first group to have the first player back at the front of the line after three catches is the winner.

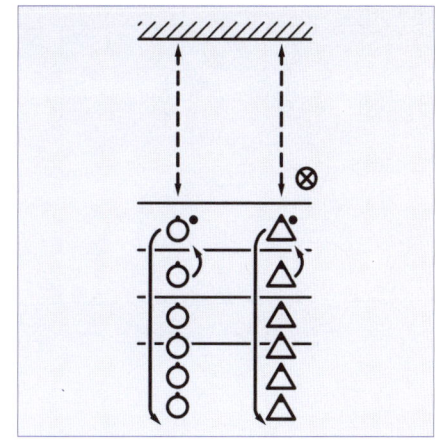

Shooting

G44 Who scores first? Two teams of equal number stand on opposite baselines of a basketball court. Each player is given a number. Two balls are placed at centre court. When the coach or instructor calls out a number, the player from each team with that number must run to the centre, pick up a ball, dribble back towards the basket, and try to score as fast as possible. The player who scores first earns a point for the team. After everyone has gone twice, the team accumulating the most points wins.

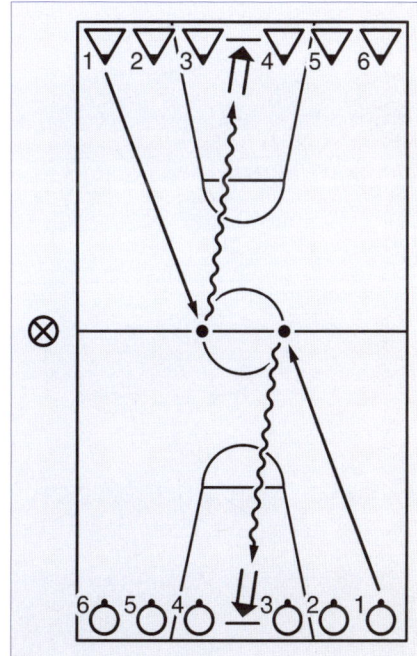

LEAD-UP GAMES

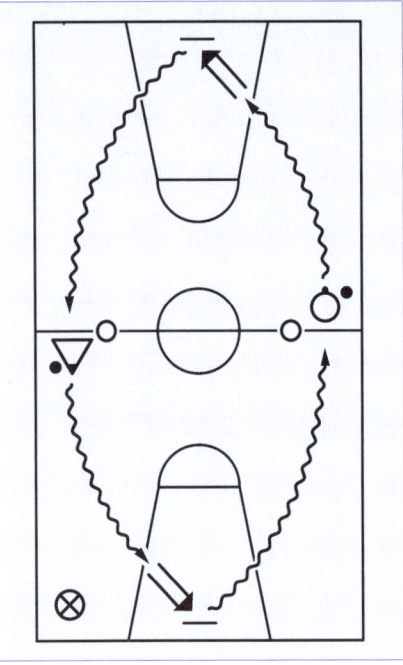

G45 Catch up Players are divided into two groups. One player from each group is given a ball and stands at half court. The two players stand on opposite sidelines facing opposite ends of the court. At the signal, each player dribbles towards his or her own basket, shoots a lay-up, and continues dribbling (now in the opposite direction) towards the other basket, and so on. A player can only continue towards the other basket after a shot has been made. When one player has caught up to or passed the other player, the round is over. The winner in each round can sit out, while the loser goes again in the next round. However, no player will compete in more than two consecutive rounds. The game ends when every player has completed at least one round.

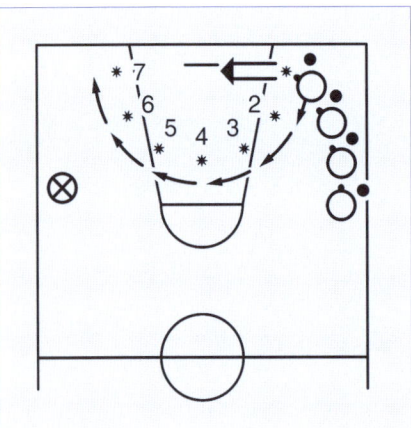

G46 Around the world Seven positions are marked along a half circle around the basket. Players begin at position one and try working their way around to position seven. Each player is permitted two shot attempts at each position. When successful, the player moves on to the next position. When unsuccessful, the player must wait until his or her turn comes up again. The first player to successfully make a shot at each position (or in the fewest number of shots) is the winner.

G47 Risk Similar to (G46) above, seven positions are marked along a half circle around the basket. Each player begins at position one and when a shot is made, players move on to the next position. When a shot is missed, players may choose to hold their position until their next turn, or risk it and try the shot again. If a player takes a risk and makes the shot, he or she moves on to the next position. If the shot is missed, the player returns to position one. The first player to make a shot at each position, or the player reaching the highest position after a specified amount of time, is the winner.

WITH THE BALL

G48 Rapid fire Five players stand with a ball somewhere along a half circle drawn around the basket. At the signal, each player shoots at the basket, rebounds the ball, dribbles back to a position on the half circle, shoots again, and so on. The first player to make a certain number of baskets, or the player who makes the most shots after a certain period of time, is the winner.

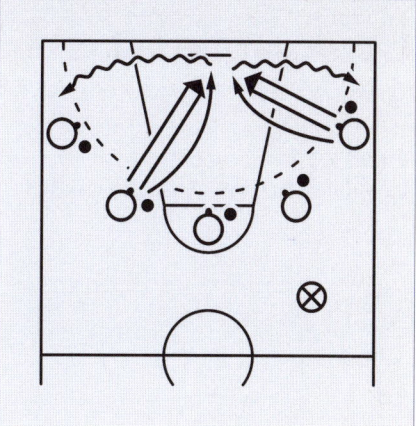

LEAD-UP GAMES

Developing technical and tactical skills with an opponent

Dribbling with a defender

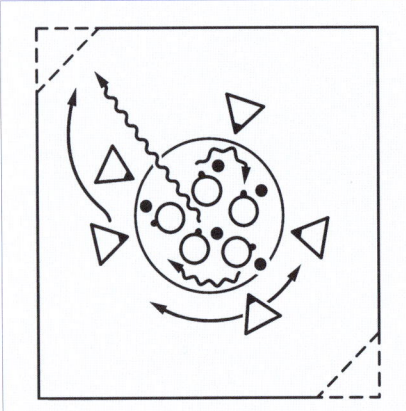

G49 Partner tag Players are divided into dribblers and non-dribblers. Dribblers are each given a ball and stand inside a circle in the centre of the playing area. Non-dribblers are defenders and stand outside the circle. Defenders cannot enter the circle at any time. The goal of the dribblers is to dribble to one of two safe zones in opposite corners, while the non-dribblers try to tag them (with two hands). If a player is tagged before reaching a safe zone, he or she must return to the centre circle. After two minutes, the groups switch roles. The group with the most players reaching the safe zone in the allotted time wins.

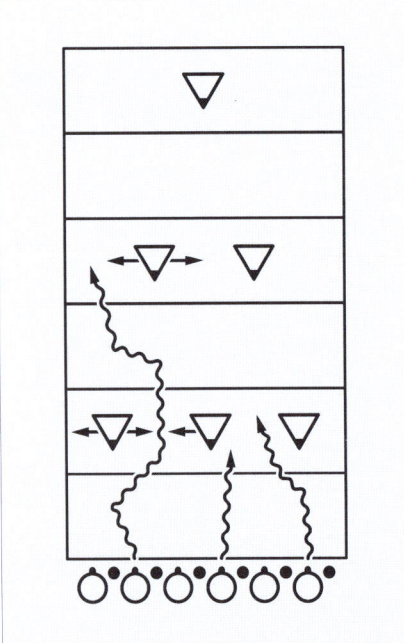

G50 Dribbling through zones A rectangular playing area with six equal sections is marked as shown. Players are divided into two equal teams. The members of one team are each given a ball and stand along one baseline. The members of the opposing team stand in alternate sections of the playing area as defenders. At the signal, players along the baseline must try to dribble to the opposite baseline without losing their balls to a defender. Dribbling players face one less defender in each successive section. Players successfully making it across the playing area (still in possession of their ball) earn a point for the team. Players losing their ball must wait until the next round before rejoining the game. When teams have completed four rounds, roles are switched. The team accumulating the most points is the winner.

WITH AN OPPONENT

G51 Row dribbling A rectangular playing area is divided into as many equal sections as there are players (up to eight) as shown in the diagram. One attacking player stands on the baseline with a ball. The remaining players each guard one section of the playing area. The attacking player must try dribbling past each line of defense before reaching the opposite baseline. Defenders must remain on the line bordering their section at all times. When the attacker has passed the line, the defender can no longer interfere with the progress of the attacking player. When the attacker reaches the opposite baseline, he or she becomes the last line defender, and the first line defender in the last round becomes the attacking player in the following round, and so on. The player making the fewest mistakes after several rounds is the winner.

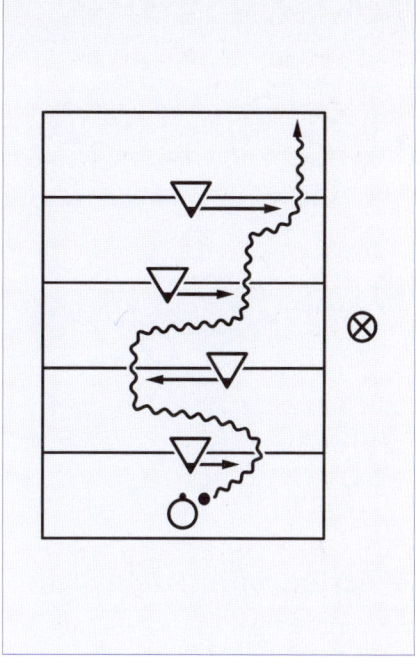

G52 Fight over balls Players are divided into two equal teams and stand along opposite baselines of a basketball court. Players on each team are given a number and stand in sequential order according to their assigned numbers. Several balls, equal to the number of players on each team, are placed along the centre line of the court. When the coach calls out a number, the players from each team with that number must run towards the ball directly ahead of them at centre court. The first player to retrieve the ball must dribble back towards his or her own baseline as quickly as possible. The opposing player must try to prevent him or her from successfully reaching the baseline with the ball. A point is awarded for each ball returned to the baseline. The team accumulating the most points is the winner. *Variations*: (a) the player returning to the baseline must attempt and make a shot at the basket to earn a point for the team; (b) the coach calls out more than one number at a time.

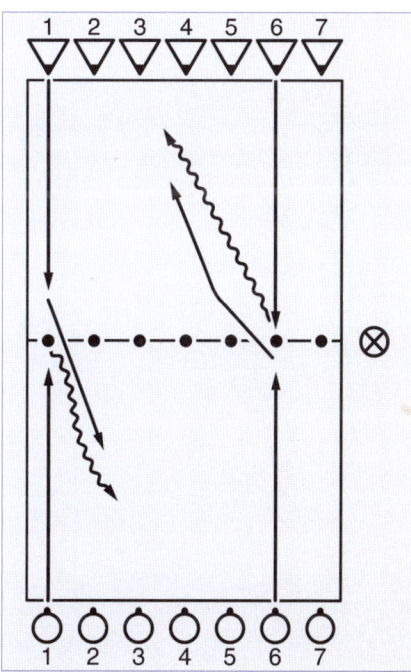

LEAD-UP GAMES

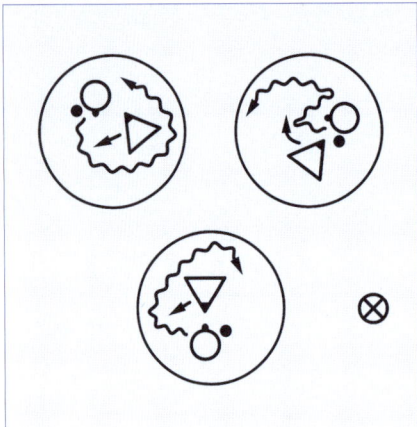

G53 Dribble duel Players are divided into pairs and stand within a small circular playing area. One player begins with the ball and must dribble within the boundaries of the playing area trying to maintain control and possession of the ball. The opposing player must try to steal the ball or knock it away from the ball carrier. The defending player receives a point each time the ball is stolen or knocked away. After two to four minutes the players switch roles. The player accumulating the most points is the winner.

Passing with a defender

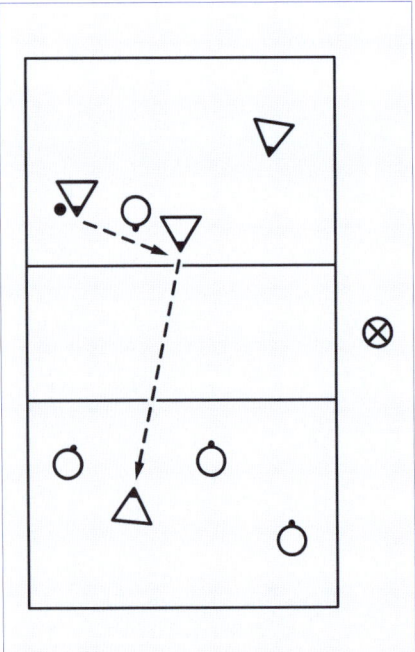

G54 Catch the ball Two teams of equal number, wearing different coloured pinnies, stand facing each other on opposite sides of a rectangular playing area. The playing area is divided by a neutral zone that cannot be entered by any player during the game. Each team sends one player into the opponent's section of the playing area. One team begins with the ball and must try to pass to their teammate in the opponent's section of the playing area without entering the neutral zone or going out of bounds. A successful pass earns a point for the team. If the opposing team intercepts the ball, two new players are selected to play in the opponent's section. If a rule is broken (a player steps into the neutral zone, the ball goes out of bounds), the last player to touch the ball before the infraction occurred gains possession of the ball. The team with the most points after a certain period of time is the winner.

WITH AN OPPONENT

G55a Party ball Two teams of equal number wear different coloured pinnies and stand in a large playing area. One team starts with the ball and must pass among themselves, earning a point for each successful pass. The opposing team must try to intercept the ball to earn points. The winner is the first team to reach 20 points or the first team to successfully pass the ball to five different teammates in succession.

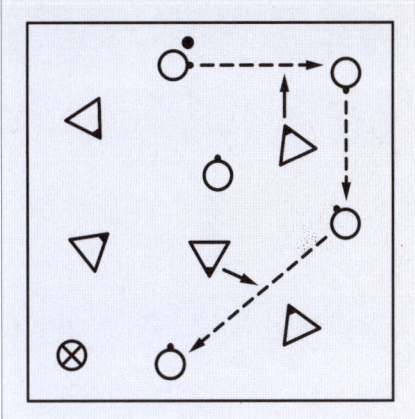

G55b Passing order As described above (G55a), except players are numbered and must pass the ball in sequential order (player 1 to player 2, to player 3, etc.), without losing possession of the ball to the opposing team. The team earns a point when a series of passes is successfully completed. The ball changes hands after each attempted passing sequence. The first team to reach a specified number of points, or the team with the most points after a specified time, is the winner.

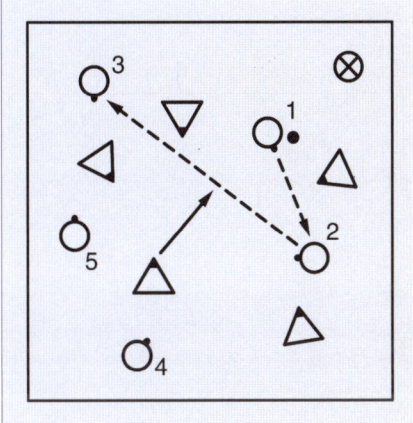

G55c End zone pass As described above (G55a), except the ball must be passed to a teammate beyond the opponent's baseline to earn a point. The first team to reach a certain number of points is the winner.

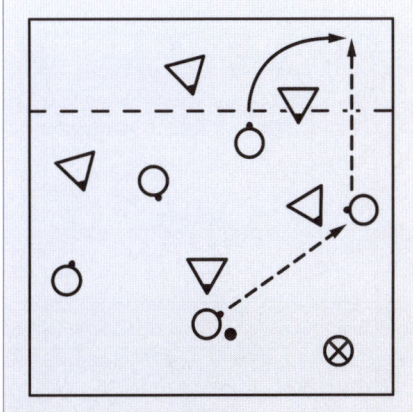

LEAD-UP GAMES

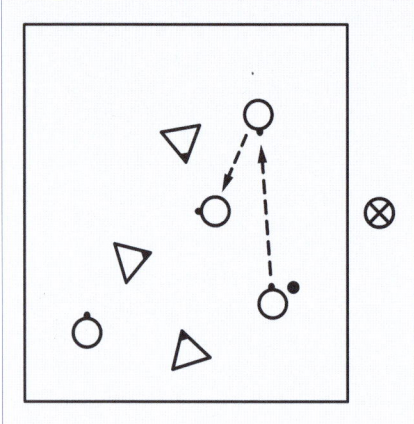

G56 Outnumbered Players are divided into two teams, one team outnumbering the other by one or more players. At the signal, the coach or instructor throws the ball into the playing area. The first team gaining possession of the ball must try to pass to each other, keeping possession of the ball as long as possible. A player cannot hold on to the ball more than five seconds before passing off to a teammate. The team earns a point for each minute the ball is kept away from the opposing team. Teams are rearranged every five minutes until everyone has been part of the outnumbered team at least once.

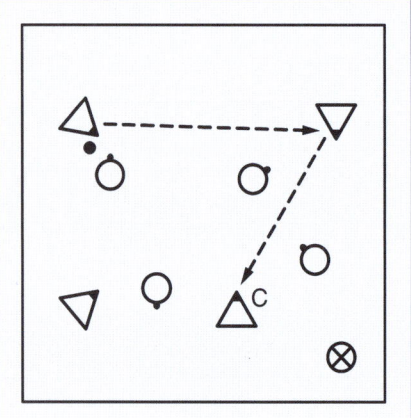

G57 Captain ball Two teams of equal number stand in a large playing area. Each team selects one player to be their captain. The team beginning the game with the ball must try to pass to their designated captain. Every time the captain successfully receives a pass, the team earns a point. The captain cannot receive a pass from the same player twice in a row. After a certain amount of time has elapsed, new captains are chosen for each team. The winner for each round is the team accumulating the most points.

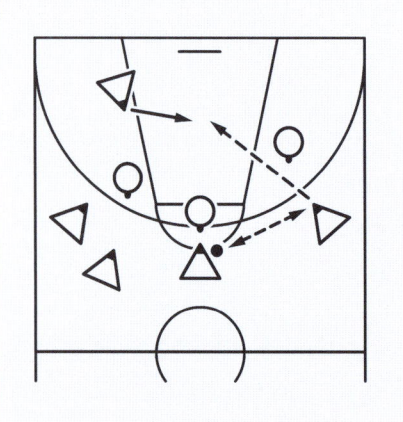

G58 Pass over Players are divided into five offensive and three defensive players. Offensive players stand outside the half circle, allowing only one player at a time to enter the area for three seconds. Defensive players must remain within the half circle at all times. When the offensive team is able to pass the ball to a teammate beyond the half circle, they earn one point. If they are able to score a basket upon receiving the pass, the team is awarded two additional points. After a specified time, players switch roles until all players have played both offense and defense. The team with the most points is the winner.

WITH AN OPPONENT

G59 Tower ball Two teams of equal number arrange themselves at opposite ends of a large playing area as shown in the diagram. At the signal, the team starting with the ball must pass among themselves, and eventually to the tower guard (a teammate standing on a box) in the opponent's end zone, to earn a point. The tower guard must catch the ball or the point does not count. The opposing team gets the ball after a point is scored. The first team to reach a certain number of points is the winner.

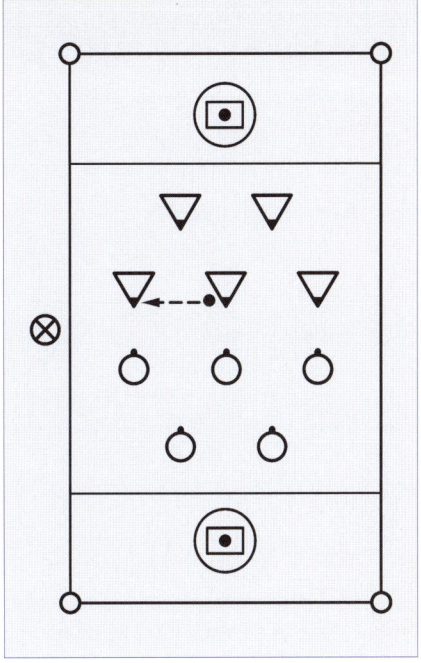

G60 One-on-one with substitute Players set up at one end of a basketball court as shown. The offensive player is given a ball and stands on one wing. He or she must try to score against one defender. Only one shot can be attempted. After each shot, the offensive player joins the end of the line and the ball is rebounded by the defensive player and passed to the next player in line. When the first offensive player returns to the front of the line, a new defender is chosen for the next round. After each player has had an opportunity to play as the defender, the winner is the player with the most made baskets.

Variation: The game can be played with both an offensive and defensive line, with players on offense and defense moving to opposite lines after each shot. This way, players never play the same role twice in a row.

LEAD-UP GAMES

Developing advanced playing ability

Half-court games

G61 One-on-one Players are divided into groups of three. Two players play a game of one-on-one at one basket and a third player sits off as a reserve. When a player successfully makes a shot, he or she is replaced by the reserve player, and so on. The player with the highest score after a certain amount of time is the winner.

G62 Two-on-two Players are divided into three pairs. Two pairs play two-on-two at one basket and the third pair sits off as reserves. When a pair successfully makes a shot, they are replaced by the reserve pair, and so on. The team with the highest accumulated score after a certain period of time is the winner.

G63 Three-on-three Players are divided into three groups of three. Two trios play three-on-three at one basket and the third trio sits off as reserves. When a trio successfully makes a shot, they are replaced by the reserve trio, and so on. The team with the highest score after a certain period of time is the winner.

G64 Two-on-four One offensive pair plays against two defensive pairs, without any reserves. Pairs rotate positions after each attempted shot. The pair with the most points after a certain amount of time is the winner.

ADVANCED PLAYING ABILITY

G65 Half-court game Players are divided into two equal teams and set up at one end of a basketball court as shown. One team starts with the ball at the top of the key. The ball must be passed at least once before a shot can be attempted at the basket. If a shot is missed and the opposing team secures the rebound, the ball must be taken back to the top of the key before being played at the basket again. If the same team that shot the ball gets the rebound, another shot can be attempted immediately. The team that scores retains possession of the ball. The first team to make ten baskets is the winner.

Full-court games

G66 Three-team pendulum Players are divided into three teams. One team begins the game on offense, one team on defense, and the other team sits off near half court. Starting at one end of a basketball court, the offense tries to score on the defense. When the offense scores or the defense gains possession of the ball, the defense goes on offense (towards the basket at the other end of the court), the offense sits off, and the team that was sitting off becomes the new defense. This pattern continues for a specified period of time. The team that scores the most baskets in the allotted time is the winner.

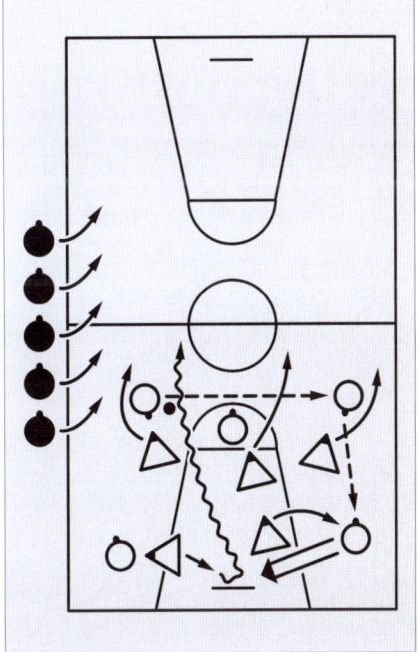

LEAD-UP GAMES

G67a,b,c Game with reduced player number

The game is played on a regular basketball court with all the rules, only with fewer players—one-on-one (G67a), two-on-two (G67b), three-on-three (G67c), or four-on-four (G67d).

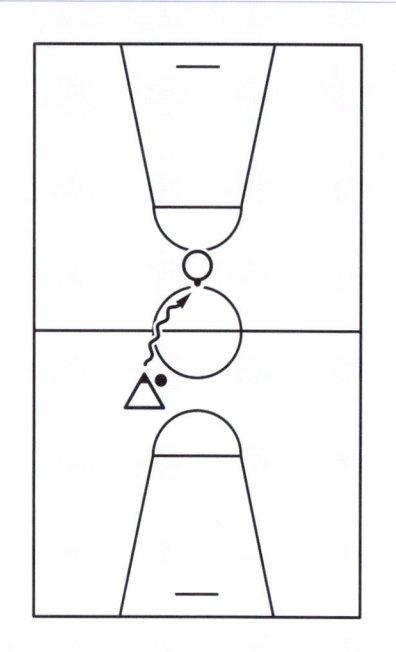
G67a

G67b

G67c

ADAVANCED PLAYING ABILITY

G67d

PART IV

OVERVIEW OF OFFENSIVE AND DEFENSIVE TACTICS *64*

TRAINING INDIVIDUAL OFFENSIVE AND DEFENSIVE SKILLS
AND TACTICS WITHOUT THE BALL *68*

PASSING AND RECEIVING *76*

DRIBBLING *98*

PIVOTING *110*

SHOOTING *120*

FAKING *142*

COMBINATION DRILLS *148*

ODD-PERSON ADVANTAGE SITUATIONS *156*

MOTION OFFENSE *166*

RUB SCREENS—WITH AND WITHOUT THE BALL *178*

REBOUNDING *188*

DRILLS

'How you practice is how you play!' is well known saying in coaching. Effective, well-run drills at game-like intensity levels are the essence of training and a key ingredient in today's coaching. How the athletes relate to the coach is in many ways directly related to how the drills and practices are implemented.

This section presents over 200 game-specific drills divided into 12 main sections, which aim to develop players' technical, tactical, and competition skills and abilities. The following guidelines should be considered when implementing drills into the training program:

- Drills should be applicable to the skills used in the game.

- Drills should challenge the skill level of the players.

- Drills should be varied. The coach should choose from a number of different drills that accomplish the same purpose. Include a fun drill in most practices.

- Generally, drills should be carried out at a tempo that simulates the action of the game. Practices conducted at high intensity are more enjoyable for the athletes and provide a valuable carry-over into the game situation.

- Drills that introduce complex skills must be practiced initially at a slower tempo. When the skill is perfected the tempo is correspondingly increased until it reaches game intensity levels.

- Drills must be executed correctly. If the execution is not correct or a lack of effort is apparent the coach must stop the activity and emphasize the correct method and demand required training effort.

- Most drills allow competition which increases athletes' interest in practice and elevates the intensity of workout. Weaker players must be supported which strengthens their self-esteem and increases their enthusiasm.

- Drills should flow from one to another with a minimum of time lost between drills. A well-planned drill progression flow makes an effective practice.

- Each drill should be evaluated after each practice. Were there noticeable improvements in the practiced skill levels of players?

DRILLS

Overview of offensive and defensive tactics

Charts 1 to 3 provide an overview of skills/techniques and offensive and defensive tactics for basketball. A more detailed version is discussed in the individual chapters

Examples for competitive training and drill work

The following exercises can be used as practice for competition and can be performed as individual or group competitions:

- Who or which group is fastest in completing a specific task (number of passes, tactical tasks, running a certain distance, etc.)

- Who or which group achieves the highest repetition score for a specific task (number of passes, number of goals, etc.)?

- Who or which group achieves the highest score within a given number of repetitions (20 shots—how many baskets?; five attempts at a certain skill or tactic—how many are successful?)

- Who or which group makes the fewest errors for a given task (catching balls, floor contacts, double dribbling, losing the ball, fouls, intercepted passes, etc.)

- Who or which group has the highest serial score of repetitions for a specific skill (how many successful free throws in a row? How many straight lay-ups?)

- Who or which group demonstrates better decision-making or problem-solving skills (qualitative evaluation, movement, tactical tasks)?

OFFENSIVE & DEFENSIVE TACTICS

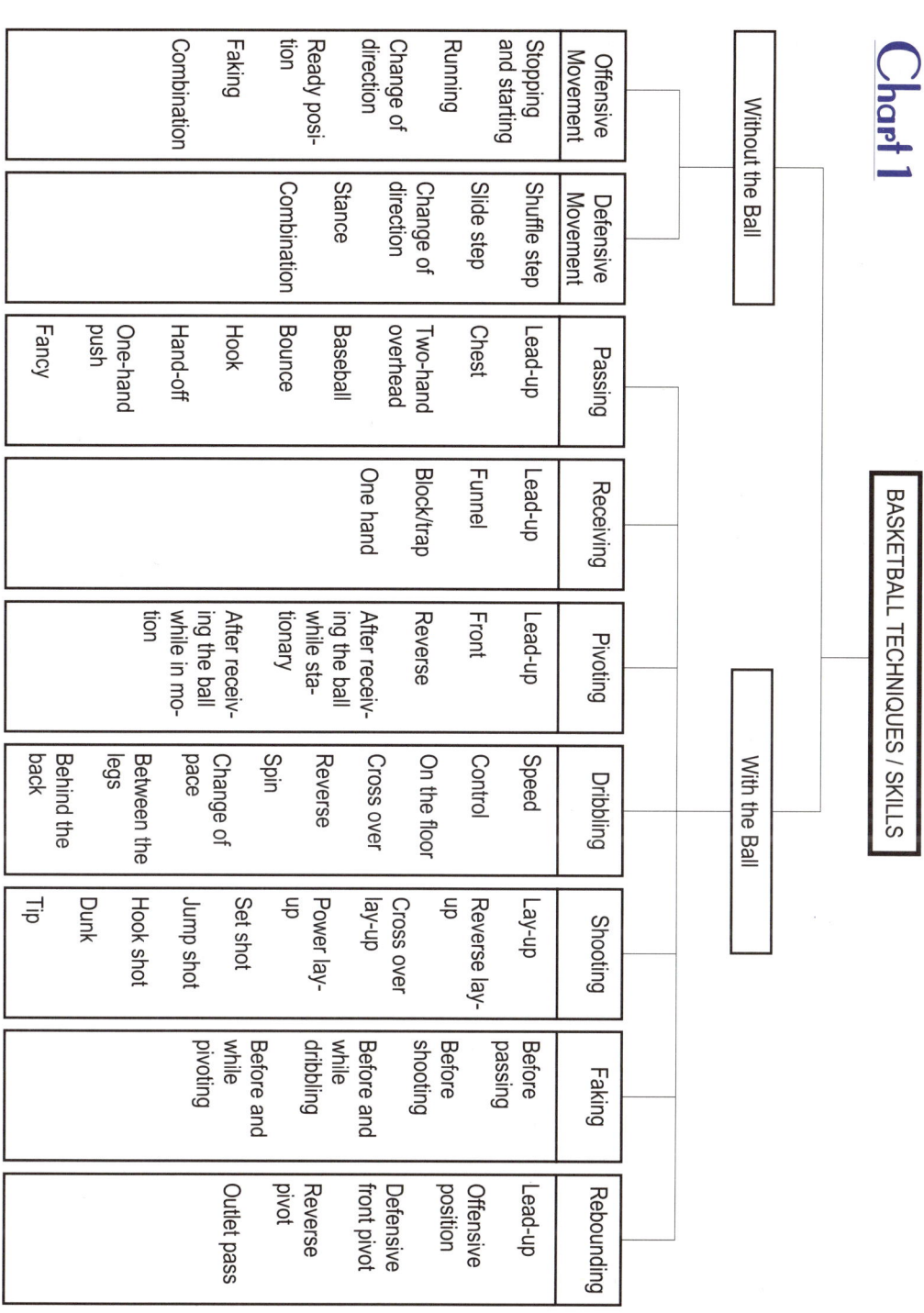

DRILLS

Chart 2

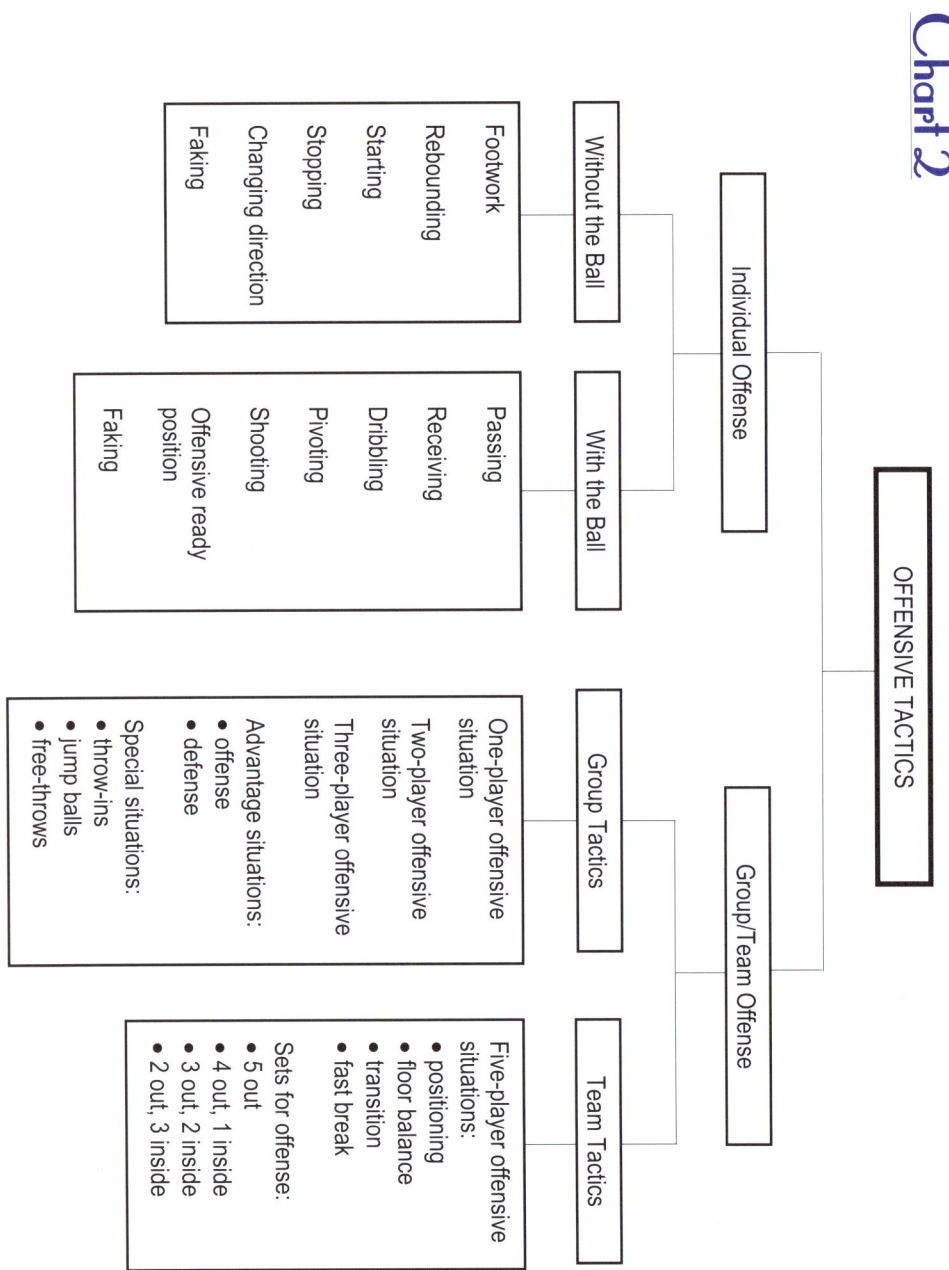

OFFENSIVE TACTICS

- Individual Offense
  - Without the Ball
    - Footwork
    - Rebounding
    - Starting
    - Stopping
    - Changing direction
    - Faking
  - With the Ball
    - Passing
    - Receiving
    - Dribbling
    - Pivoting
    - Shooting
    - Offensive ready position
    - Faking
- Group/Team Offense
  - Group Tactics
    - One-player offensive situation
    - Two-player offensive situation
    - Three-player offensive situation
    - Advantage situations:
      - offense
      - defense
    - Special situations:
      - throw-ins
      - jump balls
      - free-throws
  - Team Tactics
    - Five-player offensive situations:
      - positioning
      - floor balance
      - transition
      - fast break
    - Sets for offense:
      - 5 out
      - 4 out, 1 inside
      - 3 out, 2 inside
      - 2 out, 3 inside

OFFENSIVE & DEFENSIVE TACTICS

Chart 3

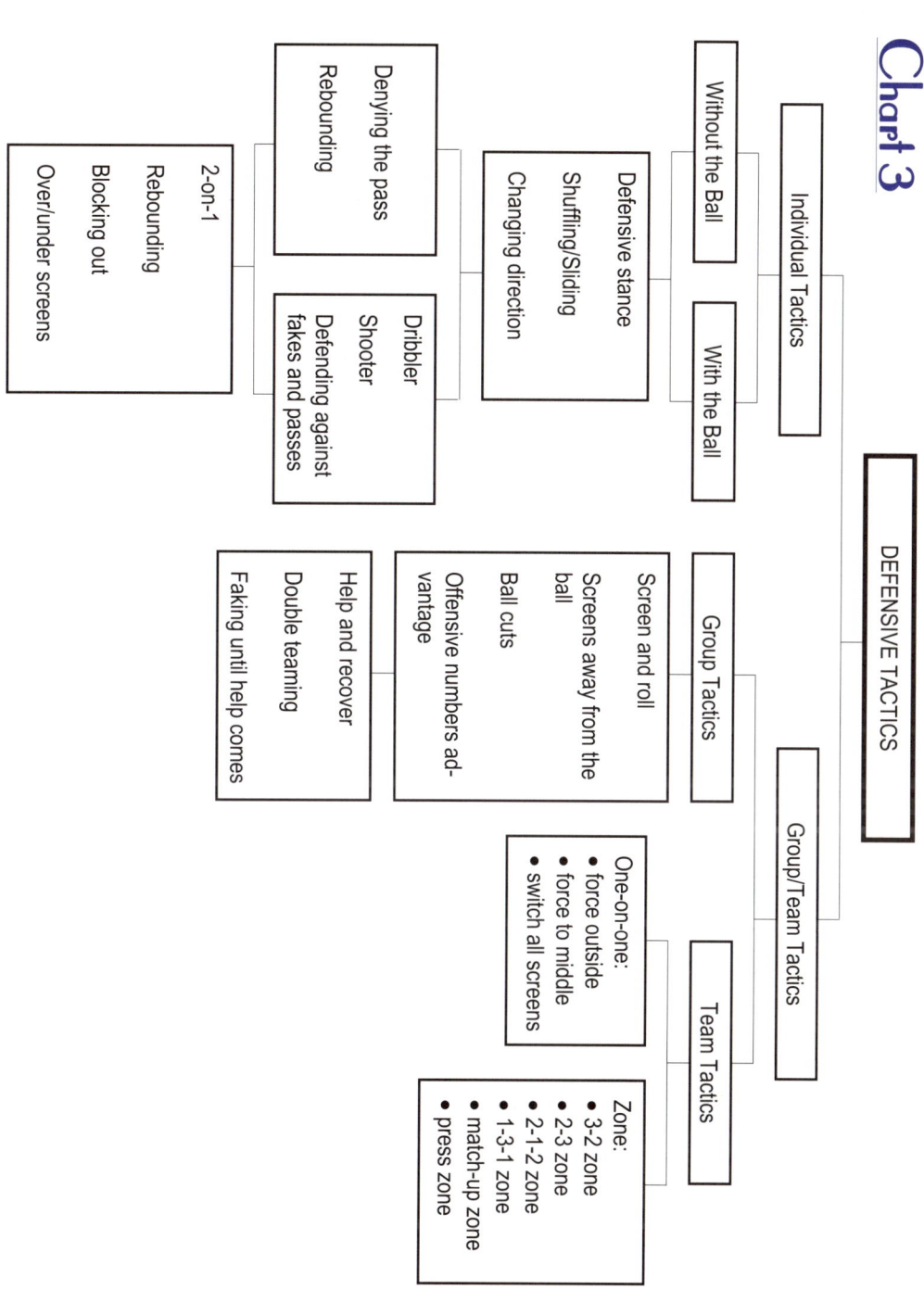

DEFENSIVE TACTICS

- Individual Tactics
  - Without the Ball
    - Denying the pass
    - Rebounding
    - Defensive stance
    - Shuffling/Sliding
    - Changing direction
  - With the Ball
    - Dribbler
    - Shooter
    - Defending against fakes and passes

- Group/Team Tactics
  - Group Tactics
    - 2-on-1
    - Rebounding
    - Blocking out
    - Over/under screens
    - Screen and roll
    - Screens away from the ball
    - Ball cuts
    - Offensive numbers advantage
    - Help and recover
    - Double teaming
    - Faking until help comes
  - Team Tactics
    - One-on-one:
      - force outside
      - force to middle
      - switch all screens
    - Zone:
      - 3-2 zone
      - 2-3 zone
      - 2-1-2 zone
      - 1-3-1 zone
      - match-up zone
      - press zone

67

DRILLS

Training individual offensive and defensive skills and tactics without the ball

We define individual skills and tactics without the ball as all the technical and tactical actions a player must perform during a game without the ball both on offense (**Chart 4**) and defense (**Chart 5**). Studies have shown that the average basketball player spends about 90% of the game without the ball. The importance of playing without the ball is often underestimated in basketball, so our attention is directed towards that part of the game here. Important prerequisites for enhancing performance while playing without the ball include speed, strength, endurance, reaction time, quickness, and agility. These physical skills and attributes need to be developed through general and specific athletic training, but are also developed trough individual offensive and defensive skill and tactical practice sessions related to game-specific situations.

Tips for developing individual skills and tactics without the ball

- Practice technique and individual offensive and defensive skills without the ball as intensely as you practice similar skills with the ball.

- Varying the use of fakes, changes of direction, changes of pace or speed, fake cutting to the ball or basket, and starting/stopping can get you past a defender. Continuously watching the defender will allow you to take advantage of his or her mistakes and is vital when playing without the ball on offense.

- Always maintain a low centre of gravity as a defender and always pay close attention to the offensive player's movements and options. The defensive player can react quickly to the quick movements of the offensive player by anticipating their movements and through good execution of shuffle steps forwards, sideways, backwards, as well as having active hands on defense to bother passes (both by the passer and the receiver) and contest shots.

TACTICS WITHOUT THE BALL

Chart 4

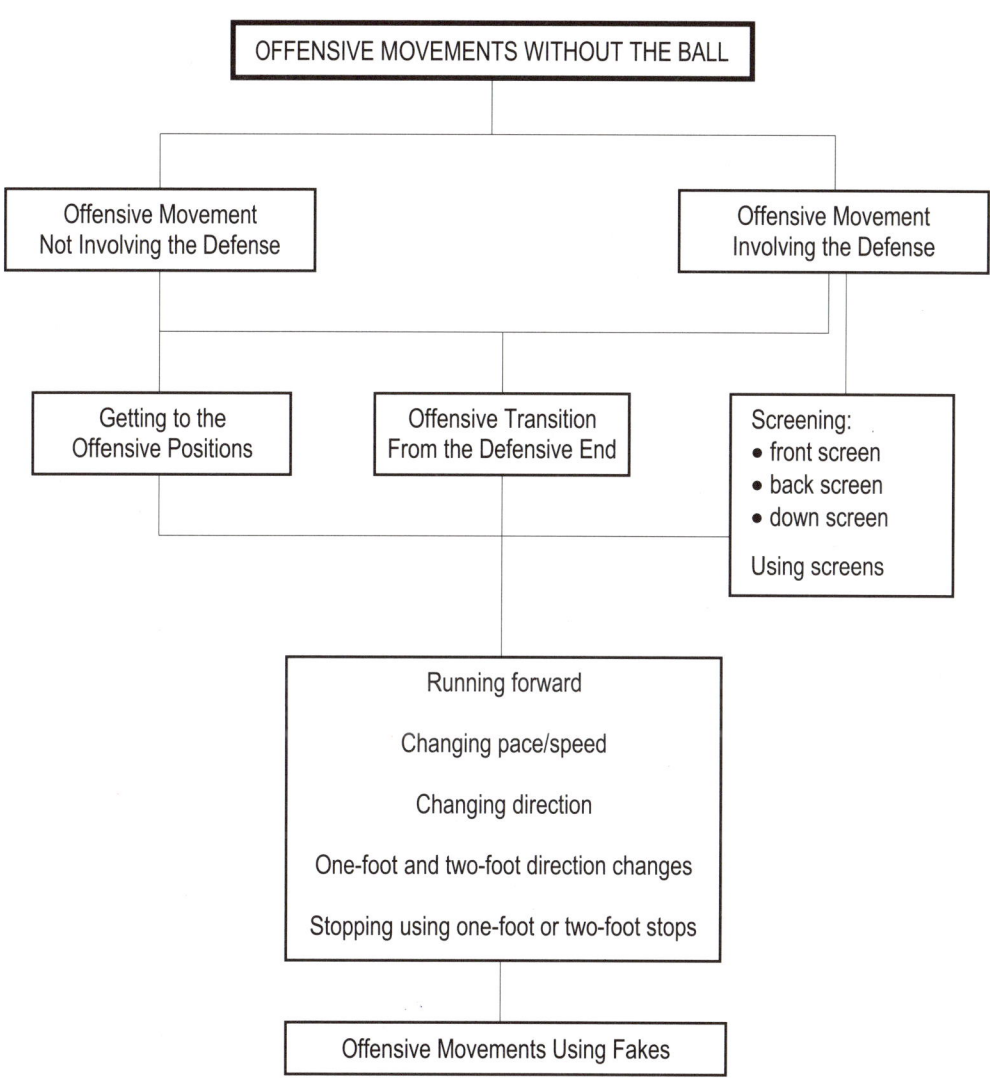

DRILLS

Chart 5

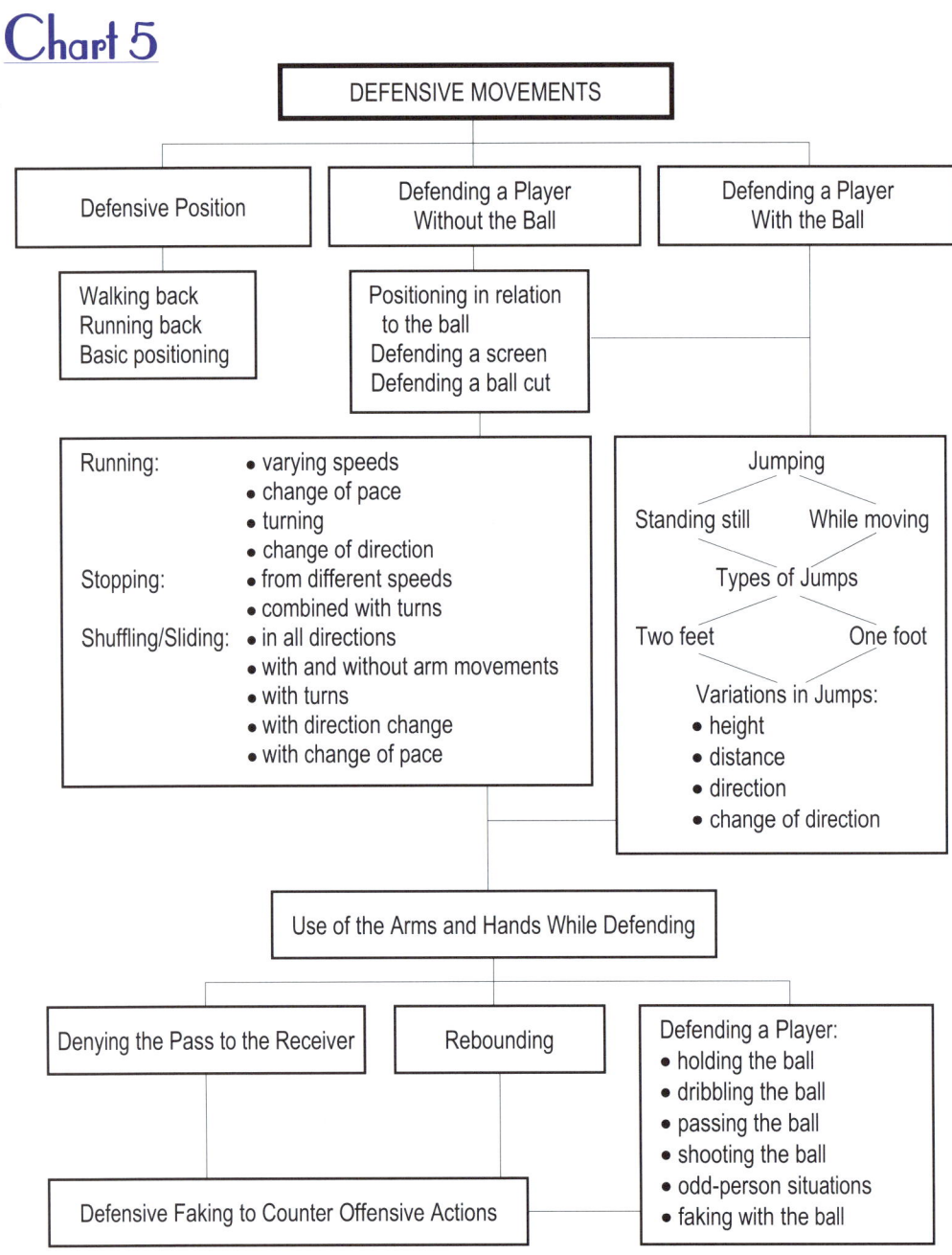

TACTICS WITHOUT THE BALL

D1 <u>Directional changes</u> The following drills are designed to develop and train basketball-specific movements involving directional changes (D1a to D1e). In each case, players are working on their movements without the basketball.

Variations:

- Players complete several continuous rounds along the depicted path (D1a to D1c).

- Determine a winner through individual (D1d) or group (D1a to D1c and D1e) competitions.

- Determine a winner by recording the time it takes to complete a specified number of series (D1a to D1d).

- The winner in D1e is the team able to catch up to and pass the other team.

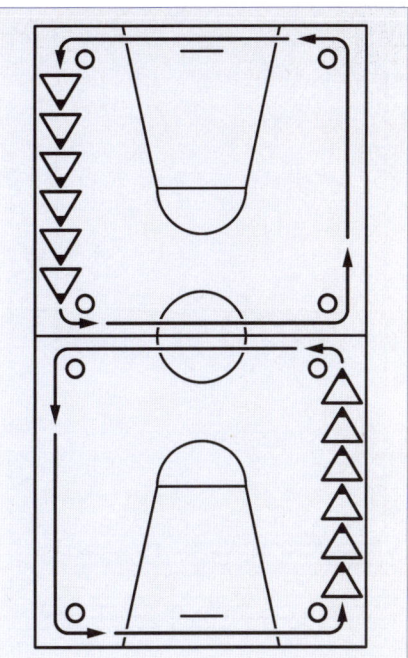

D1a

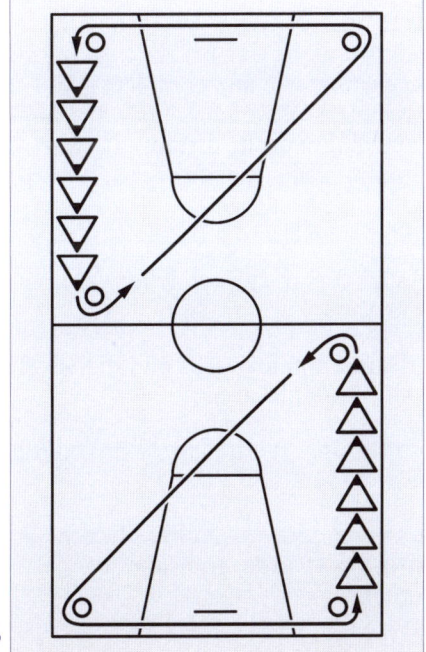

D1b

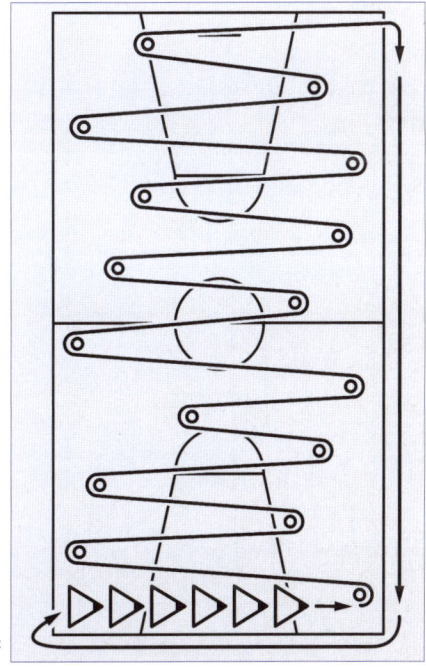

D1c

DRILLS

D1d

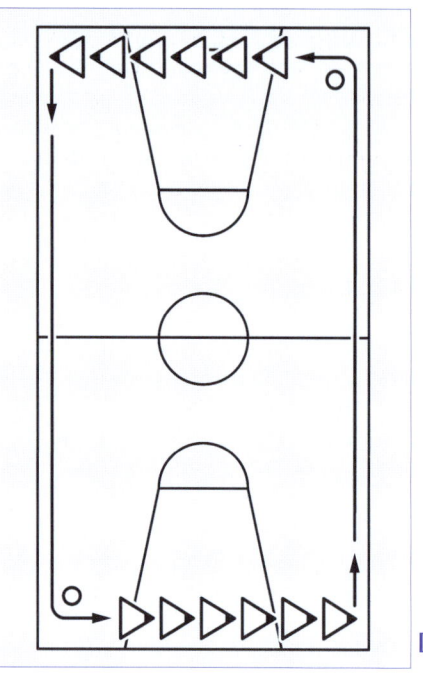
D1e

D2 Starting, stopping, and turning Players stand in a row along one baseline. At the signal, each player must run and complete a half-turn at each designated turning point, always facing forwards. The length of the distance between each turning point can be varied.

Variations:

- Players must run alternately forwards and backwards.

- Players must run forwards and then backwards using shuffle/slide steps.

- At each turning point, players must perform one or more jumps.

- Players must perform shuffle/slide steps forwards, backwards, and sideways (left and right).

TACTICS WITHOUT THE BALL

D3 Defensive stance and positioning Players must weave their way down the court from baseline to baseline performing the following movements: run forwards—stop—shuffle/slide steps sideways to the left—stop—run forwards—stop—shuffle/slide steps sideways to the right—etc. At each stop one or more jumps can be performed (from a squat or standing position).

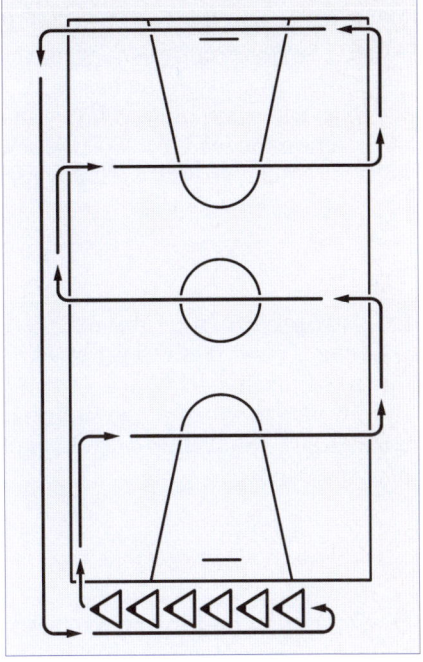

D4 Defensive slides and shuffles Players line up along the free-throw line extended at each end of the court as shown, and must shuffle back and forth between the free-throw line and baseline maintaining a low centre of gravity.

Variations:

- Players hold their knees or ankles with their hands to emphasize the low position.
- Players must roll a medicine ball along with the hands while shuffling.
- Shuffle and slide steps are combined with arm movements.
- At each turning point, players must touch the ground with both hands.
- At each turning point, players must perform maximal jumps using the arms and legs.

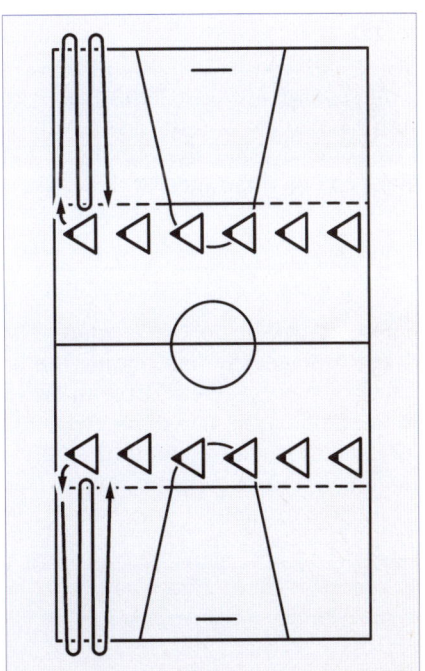

DRILLS

D5 Follow the leader shuffle Players line up along one baseline facing into the court. The coach or one other player ("leader") stands at the free-throw line facing the remaining players on the baseline. The leader then randomly shuffles/slide steps forwards, backwards, or sideways and all players must imitate each movement and change of direction the leader makes. A new player becomes the leader after a specified period of time has elapsed until all players have been leader once.

D6 Jump training This drill is designed to develop and train (one- and two-legged) jumping ability required for blocking shots and rebounding. *Variations*: (a) jumping to touch the mesh, backboard, or rim (with one or both hands) a certain number of times; (b) jumping to touch a "pendulum ball" (height can be adjusted accordingly) or a basketball held up at a certain height (player standing on a box holding up the ball to the appropriate height).

D7 Defending a player without the ball Players are divided into pairs and begin at on end of the basketball court. One player is on offense and the other is on defense defending the basket at the opposite end of the court. Offensive players (without the ball) try to lose their defenders using various head and body fakes as they move from one end of the court to the other. The defensive player must try to stay between the offensive player and the basket and try to direct him or her towards either sideline. *Variation*: a ball is passed to the offensive player half way down the court and the defensive player must try to prevent the pass from being completed or make the offensive player pick up his or her dribble after receiving the pass. If the offensive player gets past the defender, a shot can be attempted at the basket.

D8 Getting open for a pass This drill is designed to practice getting open (as an offensive player) and defending the pass (as a defensive player). The drill can be carried out in a two-on-one or two-on-two situation (without a basket). Within a bounded area (e.g., half court), one player tries to get open with fake cuts to receive a pass from another player with the ball (the player with the ball can also be defended in a two-on-two scenario). The defensive player tries to prevent the offensive player he or she is guarding from getting open or successfully passing or receiving the ball.

TACTICS WITHOUT THE BALL

DRILLS

Passing and receiving

Passing and receiving the ball are important components in basketball (see **Charts 6, 7, and 8**). Receiving a pass (pass reception) is a technical element resulting after a pass and is therefore not often practiced separately. However, there are times when one may be emphasized over the other. The drills to follow offer ample variety and variations for practicing these skills. Try using medicine balls instead of basketballs to increase speed strength (power) in the arms, or add defenders to the drills to help improve individual tactical abilities for both defensive and offensive players.

Tips for passing the ball

- The type of pass the player utilizes will depend on the situation. The surest pass is usually the two-hand chest pass. The fastest pass is the one-hand push pass or touch pass (redirecting the flight of the ball).

- Passing the ball from an attack position (triple threat – shoot, pass, or dribble) is the most economic and accurate way of passing. Therefore, passing should be practiced with both the right and left hand and utilizing both the right and left foot as the pivot foot. Variability and balance are the keys to being a good passer.

- Do not make a pass obvious to the defender (do not telegraph the pass). Avoid any exaggerated movements, keeping pass fakes short, quick, and controlled.

- Pass the ball when the receiver is expecting the ball (make eye contact).

Tips for receiving the ball

- The best method for receiving a pass is watching the flight of the ball into your hands and securing the ball with both hands. Passing the ball once it has been received can be done with either one or two hands.

- Practice one-handed ball catching with both the left and right hand. Always secure the ball with the off hand, especially if the defender is nearby, or if the ball is not being passed from the position it was caught or with the same hand used to catch the pass.

- Attempt to always take into account the direction, height, speed, and spin (bounce pass) of incoming passes.

PASSING AND RECEIVING

Chart 6

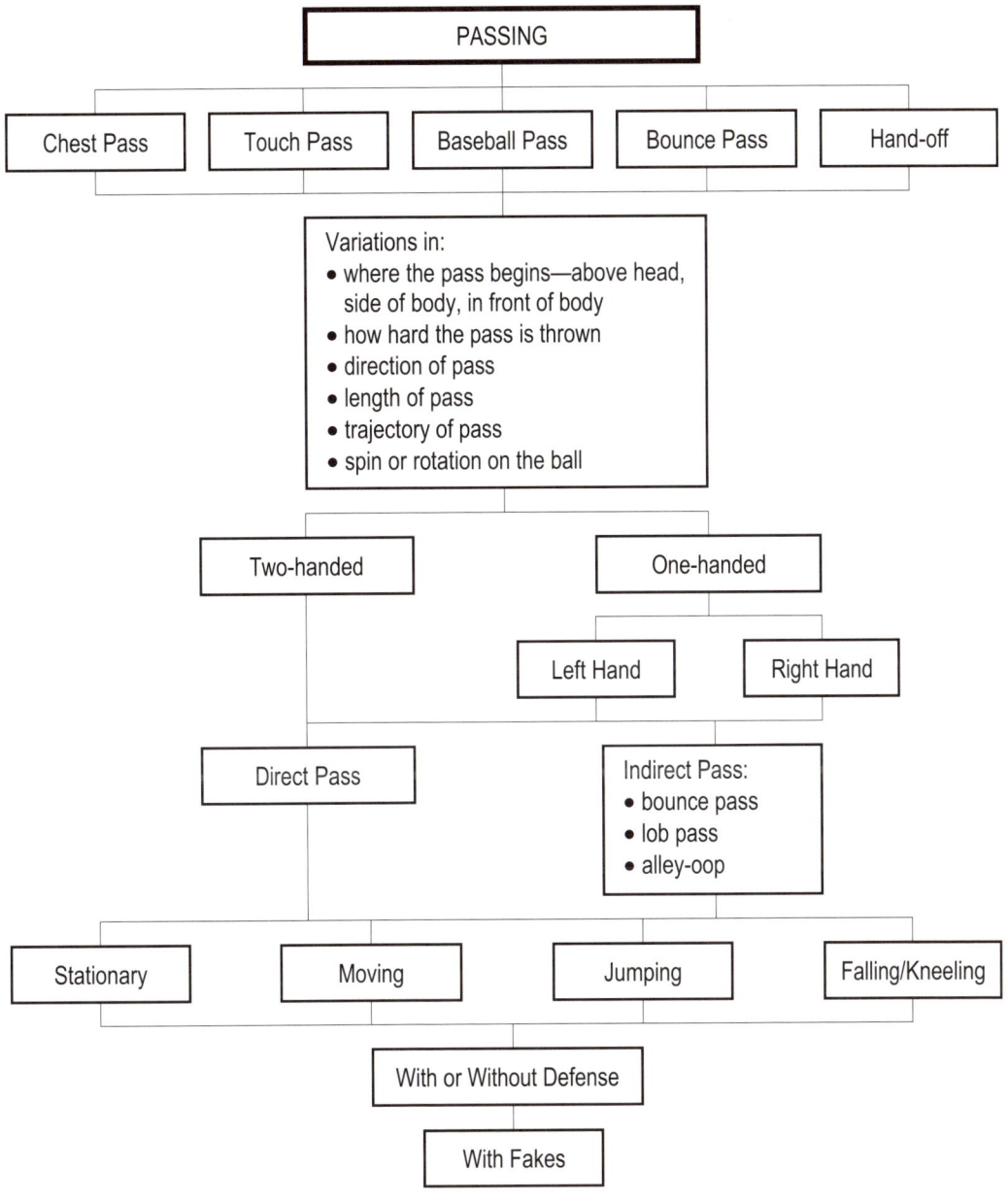

DRILLS

Chart 7

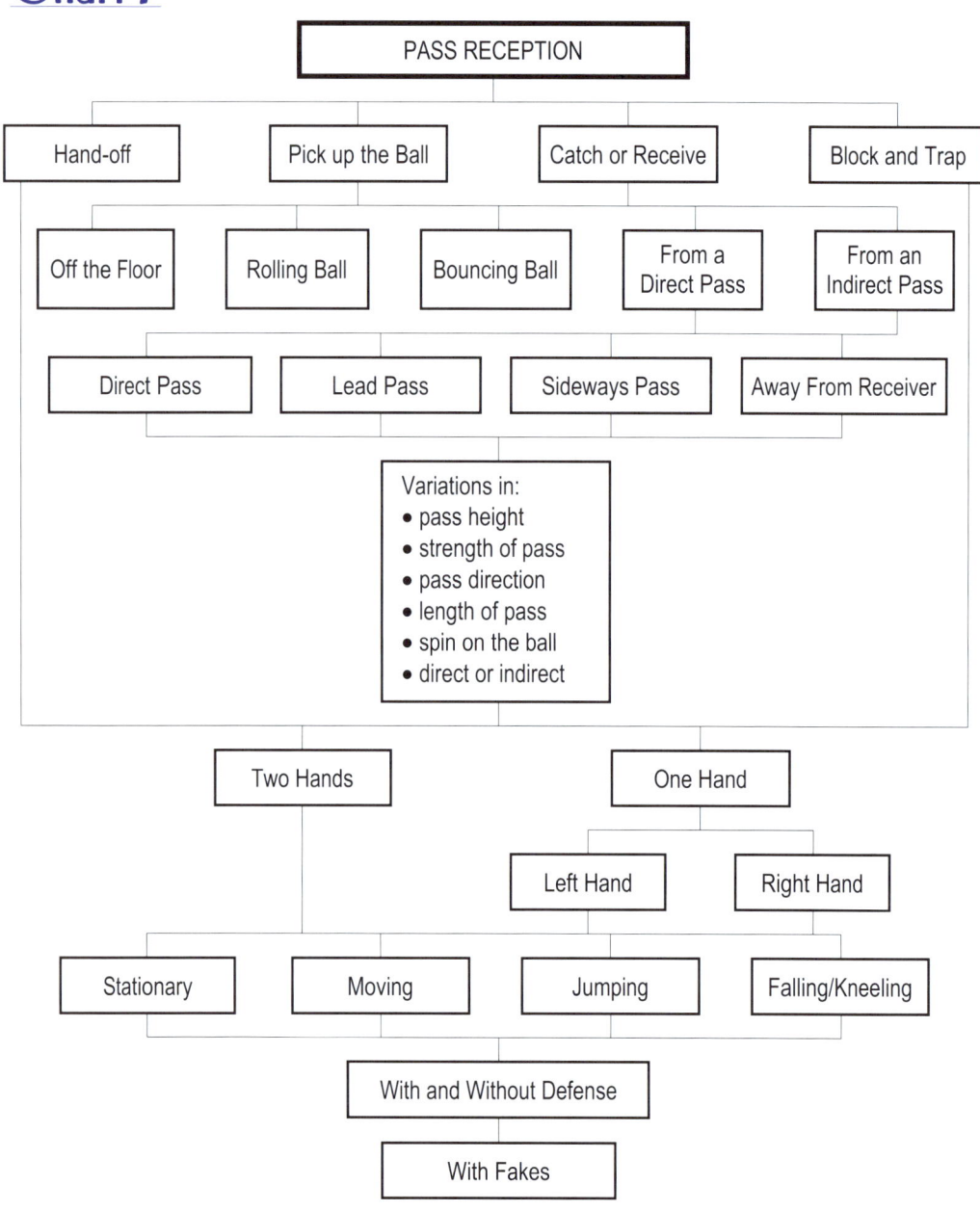

PASSING AND RECEIVING

Chart 8

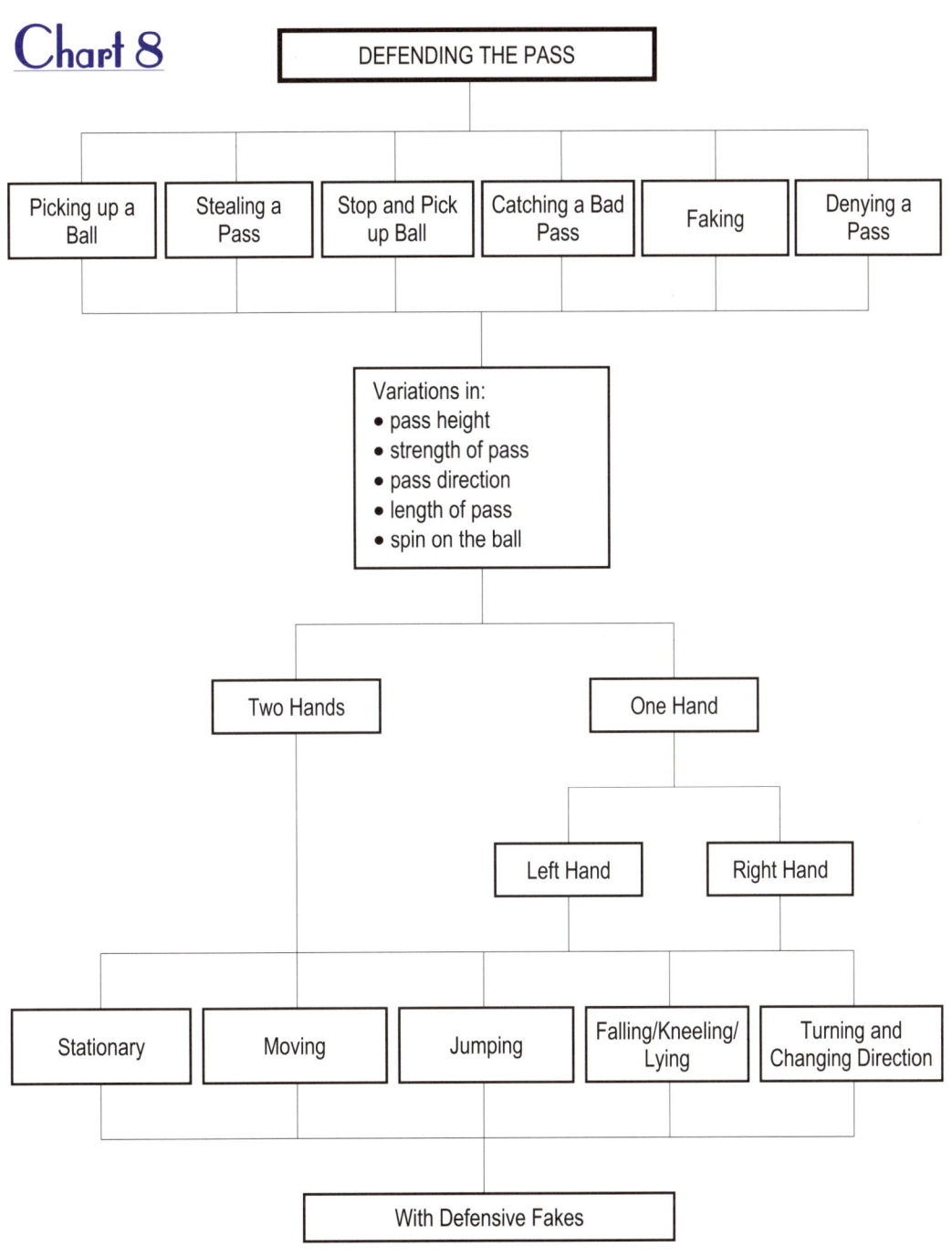

DRILLS

Tips for defending against the pass

- Closely observe passing lanes and try to anticipate passes by offensive players.

- Make passes difficult by harassing the ball handler or trying to prevent the intended receiver from getting the ball. An attempted pass that is tipped or deflected can often stray from the intended target and may be recovered by a defensive team player.

- Correct positioning is vital to successfully defending a pass. Players must identify the passing lanes (a direct line from the passer to the receiver) and always have an eye on the ball and the player being defended.

- Good hand positioning (mirroring the ball) and faking can lead the offensive player into making careless passes or distract the concentration of players receiving the ball.

Stationary passing and receiving—no position change

D9 **Back and forth** Players are divided into pairs and stand in two rows facing each other. Each pair is given a ball and passes back and forth according to the call of the coach (chest pass, bounce pass, lob pass, etc.) The distances between the players may be adjusted depending on the age and strength of participants, as well as the type of passes being performed. *Variations*: (a) both players in each pair are given a ball and begin passing at the same time, using different heights and types of passes (i.e., bounce pass and chest pass) to avoid a collision of balls; (b) one or more defenders are added to try to intercept passes. Various types of passes and pass fakes can be practiced to avoid having the ball intercepted. When the defender touches or intercepts the ball, he or she exchanges positions with the player who threw the ball.

D10 **Pass back** One player is given a ball and stands facing the remaining row of players from a given distance. The designated passer passes the ball to each player in line down the row, receiving a return pass after each pass, until each player in line has received and passed the ball twice. The passer is then replaced by a new player for the next round of passing. *Variation*: two rows of players face each other and the ball starts at one end of one row. The first player with the ball begins by passing to the first player in the other row, who passes to the second player in the first row, who passes to the second player in the other row, and so on down the line. When the ball reaches the end of the row, the ball is reversed and continues in the opposite direction until every player has passed the ball at least twice.

PASSING AND RECEIVING

D11 Around the circle Players form a large circle and pass one or more balls around the circle in one direction. When more than one ball is used, each ball starts at a different position in the circle and players can try to make one ball catch up to the other, always maintaining good pass and pass reception technique. *Variations*: (a) passes go in one direction from one player to the next, every second player, every third player, etc. This drill can also be carried out with two balls and two teams standing alternately in a circle. The goal for each team would be to get the ball around the circle in the shortest possible time without any dropped passes; (b) change of direction after a whistle or signal from the coach; (c) passes in either direction or across the circle—one or more defenders can be added in the middle of the circle to practice various passes and pass fakes.

D12 Player(s) in the middle Players form a circle with two passers in the middle (D12a). The middle players pass back and forth with players forming the circle. *Variations*: (a) every second player around the circle is given a ball (D12b). Middle players receive a pass from players with the ball and pass back to the next player in the circle in one direction; (b) number of balls can be varied to make the drill more challenging; (c) defenders stand around an inner circle and try to intercept passes to the middle player (D12c). Players on the outer circle can pass to each other before passing to the middle player.

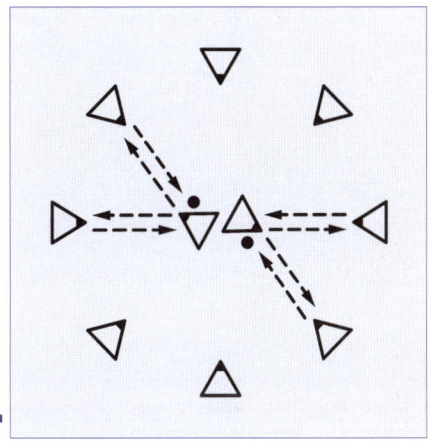

D12a

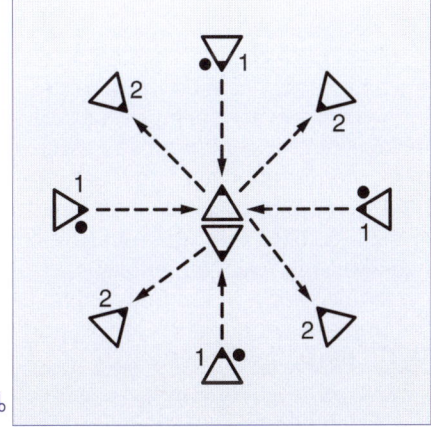

D12b

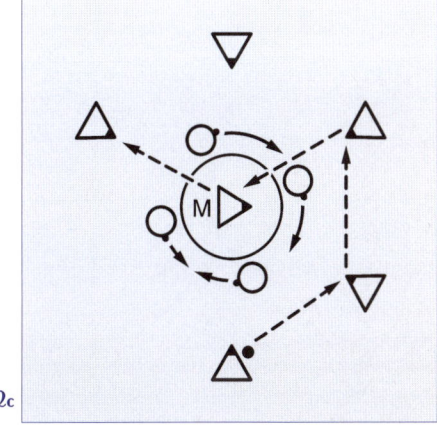

D12c

DRILLS

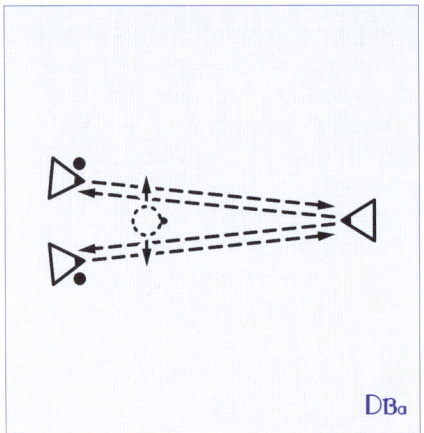

D13a

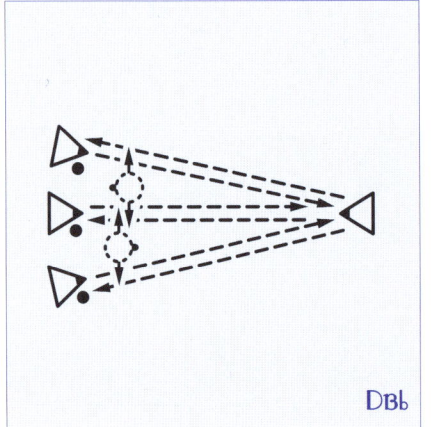

D13b

D13 Triangle passing Players arrange themselves in a triangular formation as shown (D13a). Two players forming the base of the triangle are each given a ball and pass to the third player one at a time. The point player in the triangle returns each pass to the same player who passed the ball to him or her. The speed of passes and distances among players in the triangle can be varied.

Variations:

- Passes are always made in a clockwise (or counterclockwise) direction among players.

- The point player must use a different type of pass when returning the pass (e.g., receive a bounce pass, throw a chest pass, etc.).

- Number of players can be increased to three or more within the triangle (D13b).

- Defenders can be added to try to intercept or bother the pass (D13a,b).

- The point player can return the pass to any other player in the triangle. Keep your hands up!

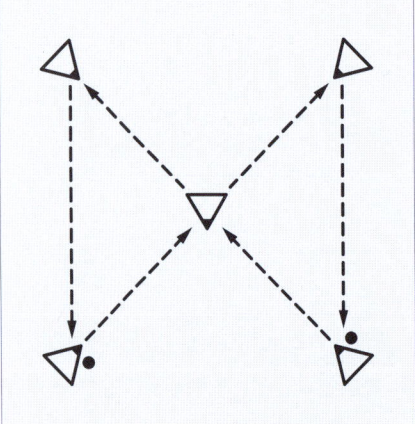

D14 Square triangles Five players form a square with one player in the middle as the pivot passer. Two players are each given a ball and alternately pass to the middle player. After receiving a pass, the middle player passes to the player opposite the player who passed the ball, turns to receive the next pass from the opposite corner, and so on, passing in a triangular pattern. *Variations*: (a) the position of the middle player can be adjusted to make some passes longer and others shorter; (b) the types of passes may be varied, or pivot passers must make a specific type of pass (bounce, chest, lob, etc.) to each corner.

PASSING AND RECEIVING

D15 Two balls around the square Four players arrange themselves in a square (diamond) formation as shown. Starting with two balls, player 1 passes to player 2 (one ball at a time), who then passes one ball to Player 3 and one ball to player 4. After receiving a pass from player 2, player 3 and player 4 return the ball to player 1. The sequence is therefore 1 – 2 – 3 – 1 for one ball and 1 – 2 – 4 – 1 for the other ball. This drill helps prepare players for passing the ball to a teammate who is ready to receive it and also works on passing the ball from the position it is received.

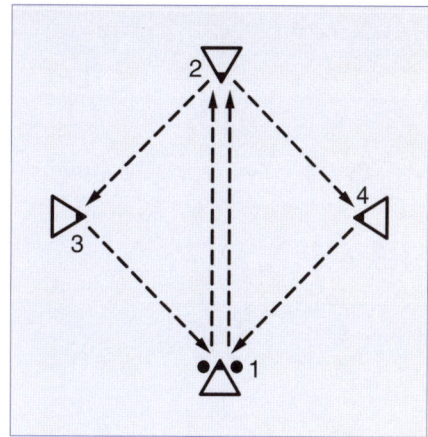

D16 Spider Six or more players arrange themselves in a large square formation with one passer in the middle as shown. Player 1 is given two balls and stands between two players along one border of the square. Player 1 begins by passing (one ball at a time) to player 2 in the middle. Player 2 then has the option of passing to any other player in the square, except player 1. Players receiving a pass from player 2 then return the pass to player 1 at the starting position. The drill continues in this manner for a specified period of time or until a passing error is made. Positions in the square should be changed periodically.

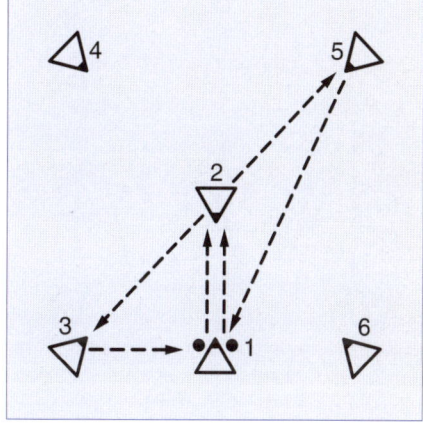

D17 Three-way passing Players form a square. Two players on the same side of the square (player 1 and player 4) are each given a ball to start. Each ball is passed among only three players. The ball beginning with Player 1 is passed 1 – 2 – 3 – 1 while the ball beginning with Player 4 is passed 4 – 2 – 3 – 4. Do not begin passing the balls at the same time! Positions in the square can be changed after a given period of time or after a certain number of passes have been successfully completed.

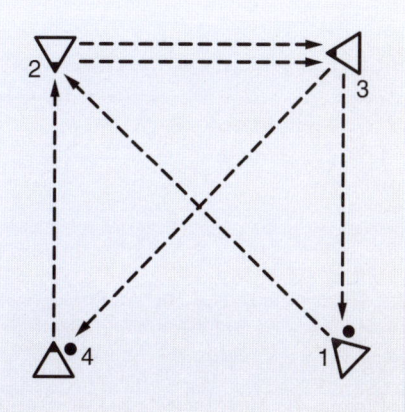

DRILLS

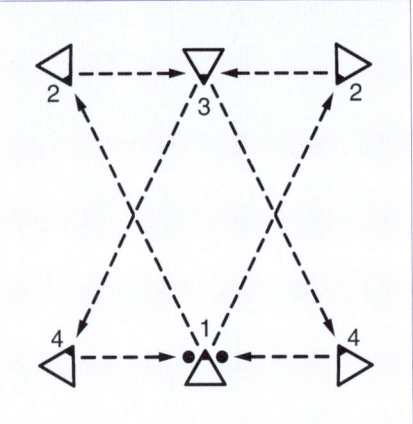

D18 Square rectangles Six players form a large square as shown. Player 1 and player 3 form an imaginary border dividing the square into two smaller rectangles. Player 1 begins with two balls and passes (one at a time) to player 2 in opposing corners of the square. The ball is passed in a 1 – 2 – 3 – 4 – 1 sequence within each smaller passing rectangle. Each ball is therefore only passed among four players within the larger square, with player 1 and player 3 the only common players to both rectangles. The drill continues following this pattern until a certain number of passes have been completed or a passing error is made.

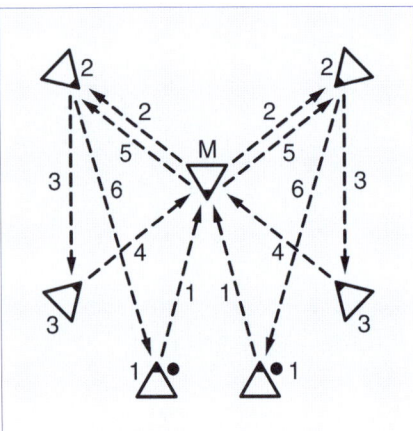

D19 Around and back Seven players arrange themselves in two half circles connected by one middle player (M) as shown. The ball is passed in a 1 – M – 2 – 3 – M – 2 – 1 sequence among four players, with M as the common player to each passing group. The drill continues following this pattern until a certain series of passes have been completed or a passing error is made. Players should change positions periodically. *Variation*: the type of pass (bounce pass, chest pass, one-handed push pass, etc.) thrown from each position may be varied.

PASSING AND RECEIVING

Stationary passing and receiving—with position change

D20 Pass and follow Two rows of players stand facing each other with one player standing to each side of the rows. The first player in each row (1 and 3) passes to the player to the right (2 or 4), before following his or her pass to replace that player. The players receiving the pass then pass the ball to the first player in the row to the right and follow the pass to join the end of the row. This pattern continues until each player has passed from each position at least twice. *Variation*: all players stand in a circle and randomly pass to any other player in the circle, following their pass to replace the player they passed to.

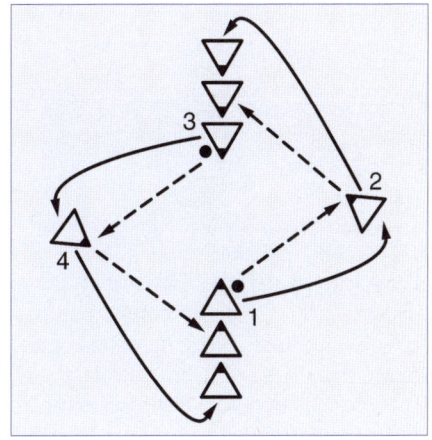

D21 Pass across and move Players stand in four equal rows in a cross formation. The first player in two adjacent rows starts with a ball and passes to the first player in the row directly opposite him or her. After throwing a pass, players run (in the same direction) to join the end of the row they passed to. Players receiving the ball throw a pass to the next player in the line directly opposite them and join the end of the row they passed to, and so on in a circular pattern. *Variations*: (a) vary the direction and type of pass being used; (b) the passer can move through the middle to the opposite row instead of going around.

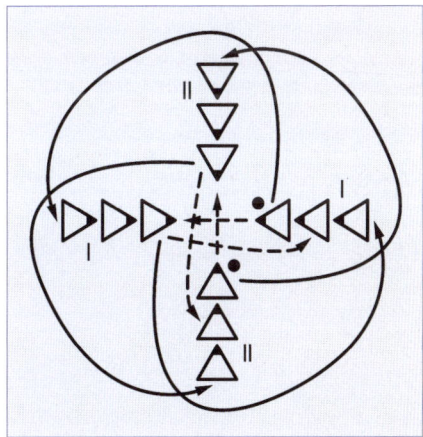

DRILLS

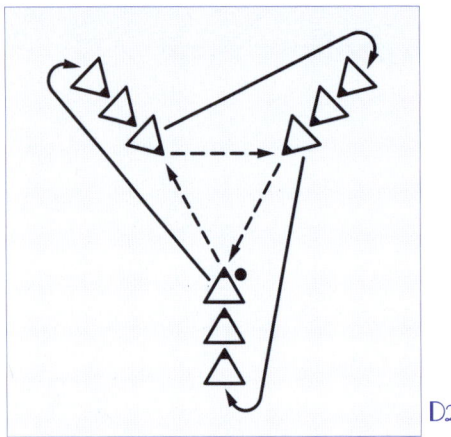
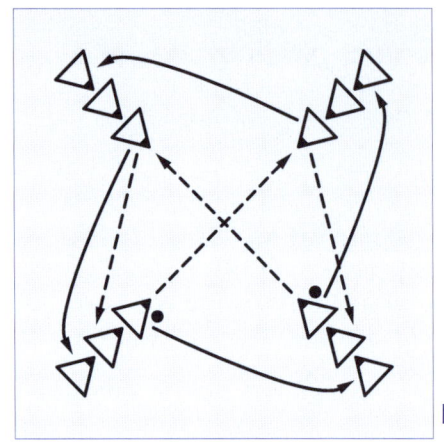

D22 Pass and go Players stand in three equal rows in a triangular formation as shown (D22a). The first player in one row starts with a ball. The ball is passed from one row to the next in the same direction. After throwing a pass, players must run in the same direction of their pass to join the end of the next row. *Variation*: players stand in four equal rows in a square formation (D22b). The first player in two adjacent rows starts with a ball and passes to the first player in the row directly opposite him or her and moves to join the end of the row to his or her right. The player receiving the pass then passes to the next player in the row to his or her right and moves to join the end of the row to his or her right, and so on.

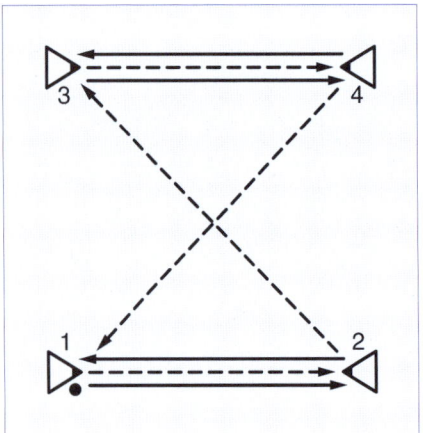

D23 Pass and switch Players stand in a square formation and player 1 is given a ball. The ball is passed 1 – 2 – 3 – 4 – 1 as shown. After passing the ball, players switch positions with the player next to them in the square (player 1 with player 2 and player 3 with player 4). The pattern is repeated for a specified period of time or until a passing error is made. *Variation*: player position changes can also be performed diagonally or vertically.

PASSING AND RECEIVING

D24 Four-row square Players are divided into four groups and line up in rows facing each other in a square formation as shown. One other player (M) stands in the middle of the square as a pivot passer. The closest players to the middle in facing rows (player 1 and player 3) start with a ball. Player 1 begins by passing to M, who passes to the first player in the next row on the same side, who then returns a pass to the starting position to complete the triangle. The same pattern is followed on the other side starting with player 3. Once a pass is made (by every player except M), players move to join the end of the facing row.

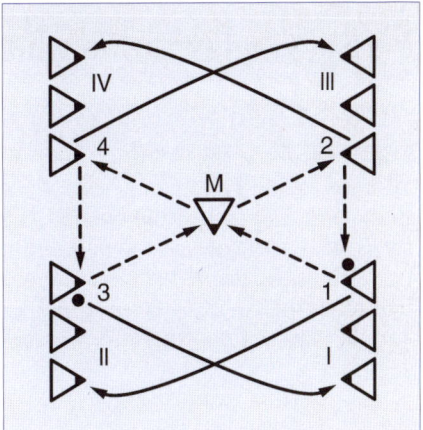

D25 Around the square Players form a large square with an equal number of players on each side. Two players directly opposite each other in the square are each given a ball to start. At the signal, the ball is passed by both players around the perimeter of the square in the same direction. After completing a pass, players switch positions with the player directly opposite them. Keep the pattern going as long as possible.

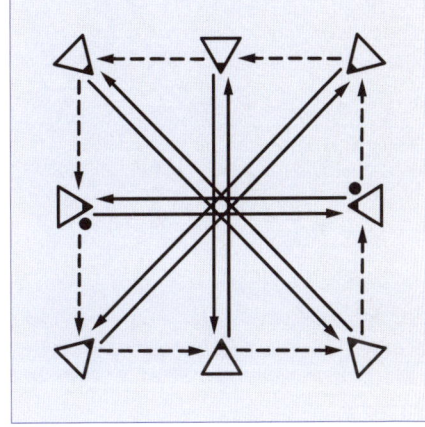

D26 Pass in order Each player is given a number (from one to as many players as are participating) and spreads out over the court. The ball must be passed from one player to the next in numerical order within a given time limit. Players call out their numbers when they are next in the passing order.

Variations:

- The coach calls out the next number in the passing order (random order).
- Two balls are used—one for the even numbers and one for odd numbers.
- The ball is passed among players in descending numerical order.

DRILLS

Passing and receiving while moving

For the drills in this section, the traveling rule is in effect, which means the two steps allowed by the rules can be practiced, either from a stationary standing position or while in motion. The allowable two steps need to be practiced by the players in order to effectively pass and receive the ball while moving, without losing balance or violating the traveling rule. Right-handed players should try working on passing and receiving the ball from their left leg (this is mechanically like a lay-up shot) and left-handed players should work on passing and receiving the ball from their right leg.

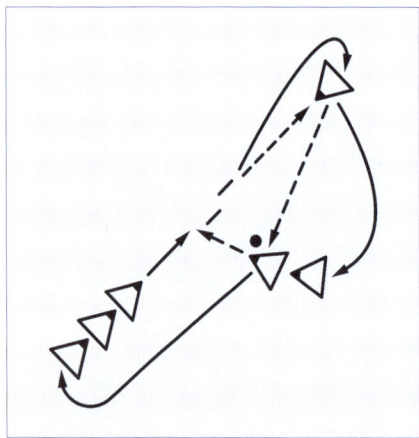

D27 Two-step rhythm The coach (or another player) holds out the ball for a moving player, who jumps off his or her left leg (right leg for left-handed players) to get the ball, and performs the allowable two steps (right—left for right-handed players), before passing the ball to the next player in line. The ball is returned to the starting position and the next player in line repeats the drill. *Variations*: (a) the ball can be thrown in the air instead of holding it; (b) the distance between players can be increased; (c) a defender can be added to make the pass more difficult.

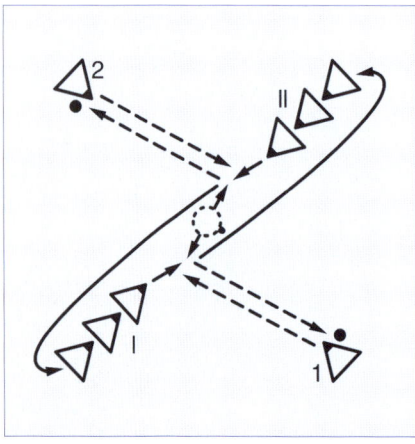

D28 Switch rows Players form two rows and face each other from a given distance. Two other players are given a ball and stand at right angles to the two rows. The first players in each row begin running towards each other, receiving a pass from the player on their right and returning the pass on their way to switching rows (row I passes with player 1 and row II passes with player 2). The players should practice catching and passing utilizing the two-step rhythm to avoid traveling. Player positions should be changed periodically. *Variation*: have a defender stand between the two rows trying to intercept passes.

PASSING AND RECEIVING

D29 **Pass left, go right** Players are divided into four rows and stand facing each other in an X formation. The first players in two opposite rows are given a ball to start. At the signal, each player passes the ball to the first player in the row to their left who runs to meet the pass. The pass is then returned to the next player in the same row the pass came from. After passing the ball, players run to join the end of the row to their right. This pattern continues for a specified period of time or as long as the rhythm can be maintained.

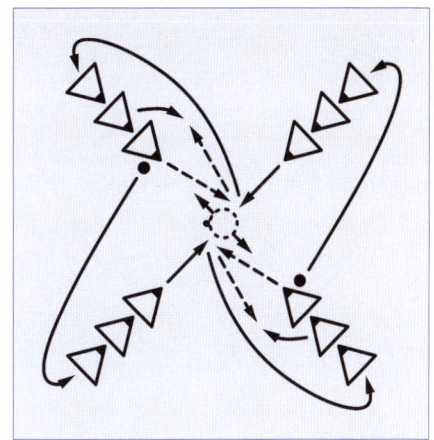

D30 **Pass right and follow** Similar to the drill above, players are divided into four rows and stand facing each other in an X formation. The first players in two opposite rows are given a ball to start. This time, players pass the ball to the first player in the row to their right and run to join the end of the row they passed to, always passing and moving in the same direction. *Variations*: (a) pass and move to the row to the left; (b) add a defender in the middle who must try to intercept passes.

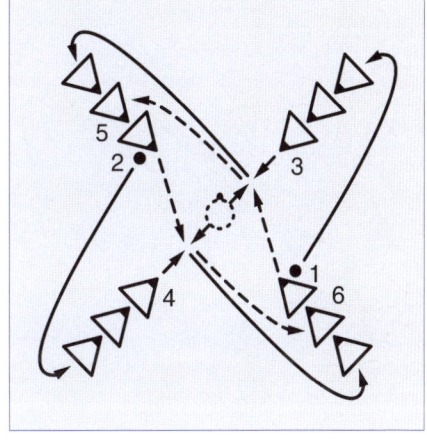

D31 **Passing player exchange** One player starts with a ball (passer) facing a row of players from a given distance. The ball is passed to the first player in the row who moves forward to meet the pass, returns the pass, and then runs behind the passer to form a new row. When there is only one player left in the original row, that player becomes the passer and the movement of players goes in the other direction. *Variation*: if a defender is used, the passer is exchanged more frequently.

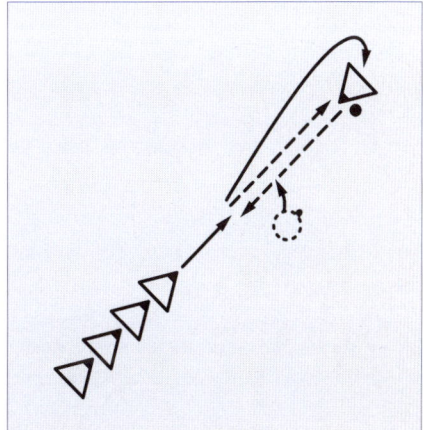

DRILLS

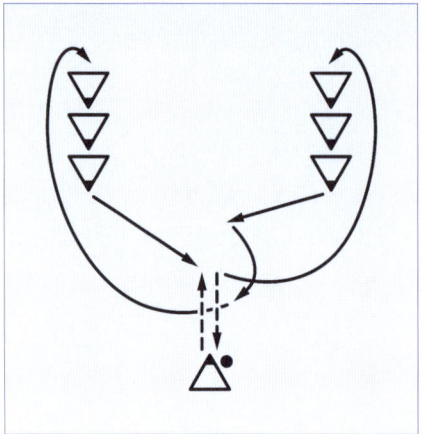

D32 Run, pass, and run Players stand in two rows facing one other player (passer) who has a ball. At the signal, the first player in each row begins running towards the passer, who has the choice of which player to pass to. The player receiving the pass returns the pass to the passer and circles around to join the end of the opposite row. The player not receiving the pass pivots and also circles around to join the opposite row. This pattern continues until every player is back to his or her original position, and a new player becomes the passer for the next round.

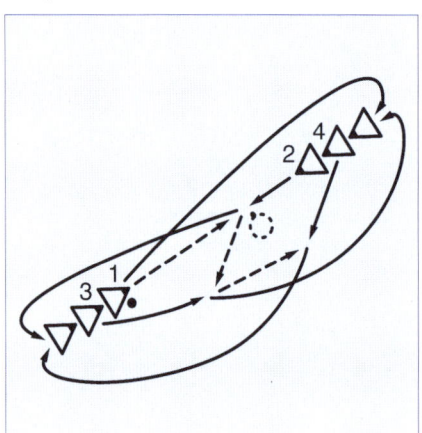

D33 Encounter Players form two lines and pass the ball back and forth between the two lines while moving. Players follow their passes and join the end of the opposite line they started from. The fewer the players involved, the higher the intensity of the drill. *Variations*: (a) the two lines do not face each other directly—one is shifted to one side (makes the passes longer); (b) two balls are used instead of one; (c) four rows are formed with players standing in a cross formation. Each player should go through every line; (d) a defender can try intercepting passes.

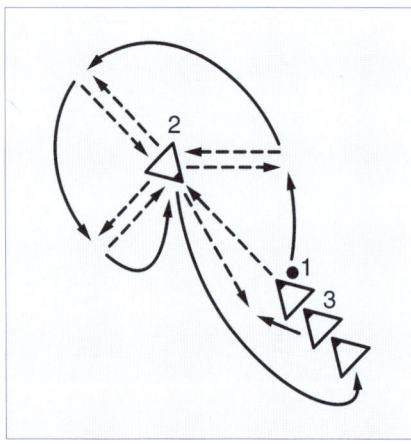

D34 Back and forth and around Players line up in a row facing one other player (passer) from a given distance. The first player in line (player 1) begins by passing the ball back and forth with the passer (player 2) as he or she runs a circle around the passer. When player 1 has completely circled player 2, the ball is passed to the next player in line (player 3), player 2 follows his or her pass to join the end of the row, and player 1 replaces player 2 as the passer. The drill continues following this pattern until each player has been passer at least once. The types of passes may be varied.

PASSING AND RECEIVING

D35 **Give and go return pass** Players are divided into two equal groups. One group forms two stationary rows (passers) facing each other from a given distance. The remaining players in the other group are each given a ball and stand in two additional rows facing each at each end of the two passing rows. While moving as fast as possible from one end of the passing line to the other, players pass and receive a return pass from each player in the passing line, join the end of the opposite row, and repeat the same pattern coming back down the other side. Players should switch periodically until every player has played every position. *Variations*: (a) players must make a specific type of pass (bounce, chest, etc.) to each player along the passing row; (b) players run up and down the same side of the row and join the end of the same row they started from, making it a relay against the opposite row.

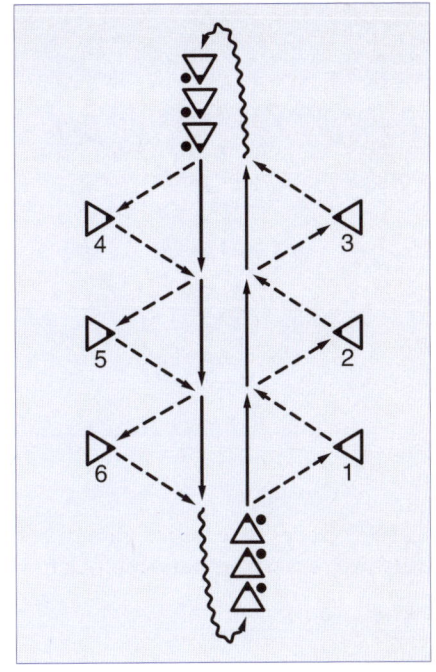

D36 **Tic-tac-toe** Players are divided into two equal groups and line up in rows facing each other from a given distance. The first player in each line is given a ball to start. At the signal, each ball is passed back and forth with two (passing) players for each row as the player moves towards the opposite row. After receiving the second return pass, the player passes the ball to the next player in the opposite row and joins the end of the row. The drill continues following this pattern until all players have returned to their original positions and new passers are chosen for the next round.

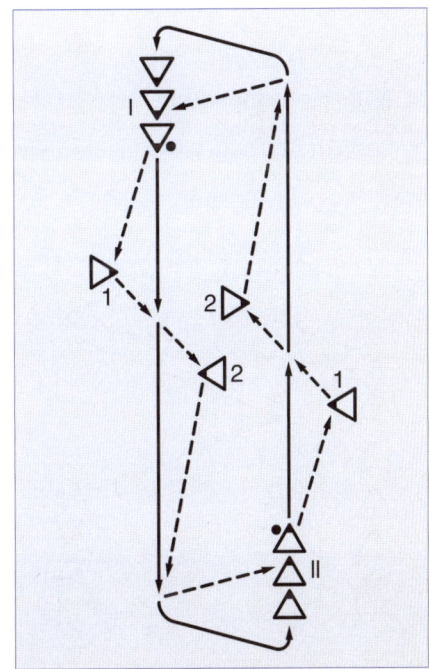

DRILLS

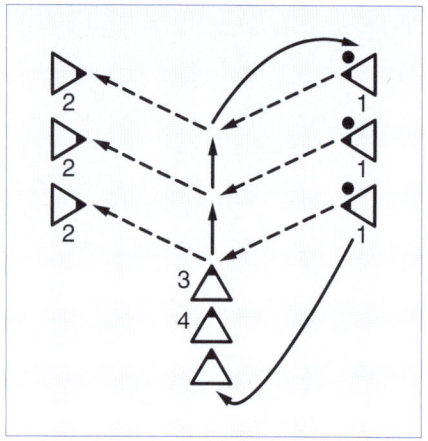

D37 Up the middle Players are divided into two rows (1's and 2's) and face each other from a given distance. Remaining players line up facing the two rows at one end. Player 1's each have a ball to start. The first player (1) begins by passing the ball to the first player in line (3), who passes to the first player (2) in the opposite row, moves forward to receive another pass from the next player (1), passes the ball to the next player (2) in the opposite row, and so on, until all the balls have been switched to the opposite row. Player 3 then joins the end of the original passing row, and the drill is repeated in the opposite direction.

D38 Weave The ball is passed between two (D38a) or three (D38b) players as they run forward. Distances between players and speed can be varied.

Variations:

- Pass two balls at the same time.
- Two groups practice in opposite directions at the same time. Keep your head up!
- As above, except passes can be intercepted by opposing groups.
- Add one or more defenders to try to intercept passes.
- Pass and go behind—players switch sides after each pass (D38b).

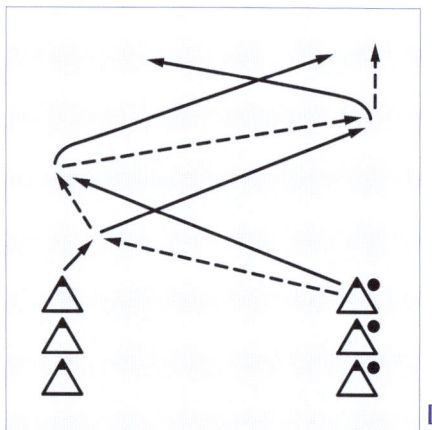

D38a

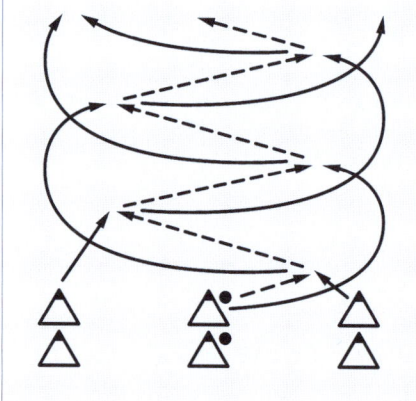

D38b

92

PASSING AND RECEIVING

D39 Running in a square Five players arrange themselves in a square formation (D39a). Apart from the first pass, all passes are made in motion. Player 1 passes the ball to player 5, who passes back to player 1 as he or she moves to the next corner of the square, and replaces player 1. Player 1 then passes to player 2, receives a return pass from player 2, and replaces player 2 as he or she now moves towards the next corner of the square occupied by player 3, and so on. The drill becomes continuous following this pattern around the square. *Variations*: (a) utilizing different passes, the ball begins with the second person in line, who throws a lob pass to the first person who is moving towards the next line. This player in turn passes to the second person in the next line, and so on, in a continuous pattern around the square (D39b); (b) the ball begins with the first person in line who passes it to the first person (moving) in the next line and moves to the end of the next line (D39c). When the pass is received the player passes the ball back to the second person in line, and a lob pass is thrown to the receiver over the shoulder. The drill becomes continuous following this pattern.

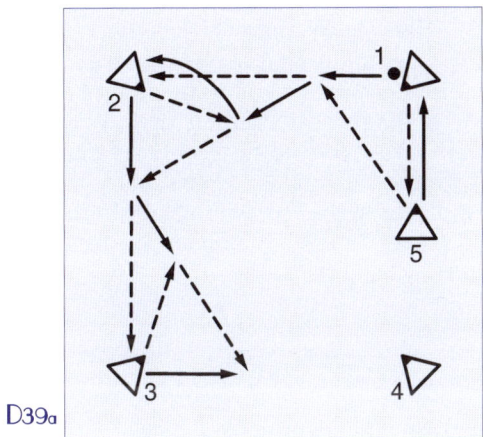
D39a

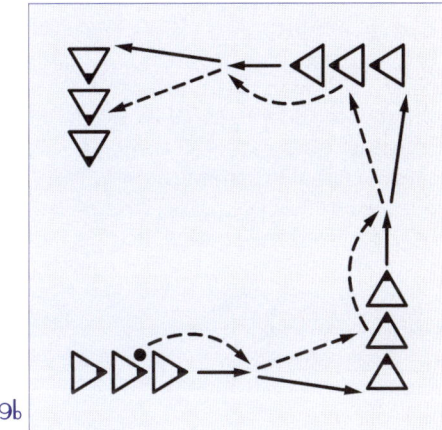
D39b

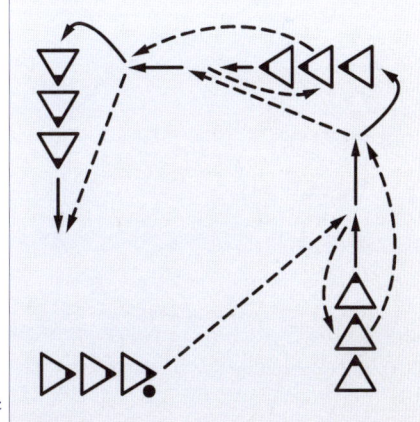
D39c

DRILLS

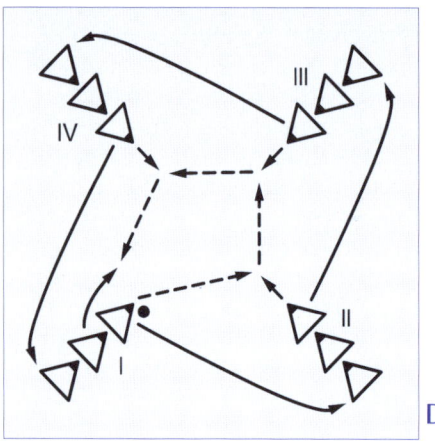 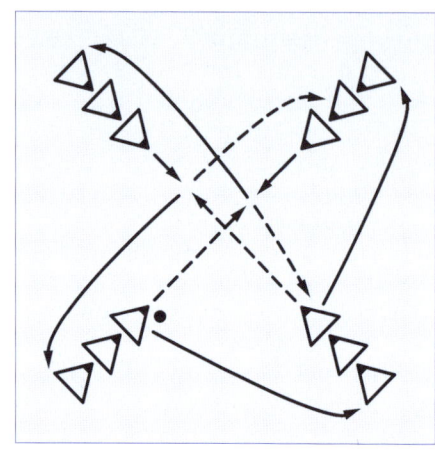

D40 Meet the pass and move Players are divided into four equal rows and line up in a square formation (D40a). Beginning with the first player in row I, the ball is passed to the first player in row II who meets the pass, passes to the first player in row III, who passes to the first player in row IV, and so on. After passing the ball to the first player in the row to their right, players run to join the end of the row also to their right. Players continue moving in the same pattern, I – II – III – IV – I, etc. until players are back in their original positions. *Variation*: the player with the ball begins by passing to the first player across the square, who passes to the first player to the left, who passes to the first player across the square, who passes to the next player on the left, and so on. Players always move to the end of the row to their right after each pass (D40b).

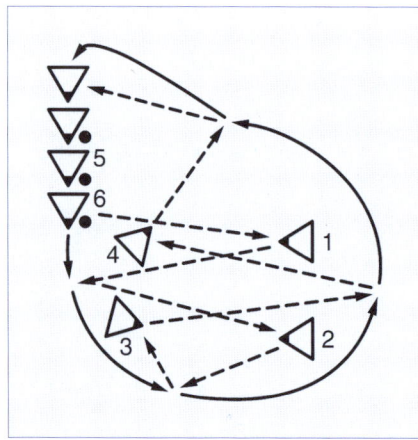

D41 Circling the square Four players (1, 2, 3, 4) form a square while the remaining players form another line to the side of the square. The first player in line (player 6) passes the ball to players 1, 2, 3, and 4 in order as he or she circles around the square, receiving a return pass from each player in turn. After receiving the final pass from player 4, player 6 passes the ball to the last player in line and joins the end of the line. Positions should be switched when players have returned to their original positions. The drill may be varied by using different types of passes or increasing the speed.

PASSING AND RECEIVING

D42 **Pass it around** Players spread out on the court and pass one or more balls among each other. Passes can occur in a random or predetermined order. The weave drill described above (D38a,b) can also be done with four or five players.

D43 **Circle pass** Two players are given a ball and stand inside a circle of players who move along a circular track. The balls are passed to the players around the circle either in a random or specific order as they move.

D44 **Passing, receiving, turning** Players are divided into four groups and stand in a square formation. The first player in one group (player 1) is given a ball. He or she begins by passing to player 2 and moves into position to receive a return pass. Player 1 then passes back and forth with player 3 and player 4 in the same manner, before passing to the next player in the starting line (player 5) and joining the end of the row headed by player 4. All other players move one row to their left after throwing the return pass to player 1. The drill continues until all players have passed around the square.

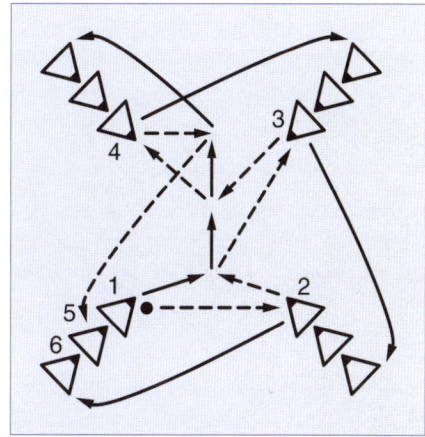

D45 **Pass and go left** Players are divided into three groups and line up in a triangular formation as shown. Beginning with player 1, the ball is passed in order, 1 – 2 – 3 – 4 – 5, and so on, with players meeting each pass and moving to join the end of the row to their left after throwing a pass.

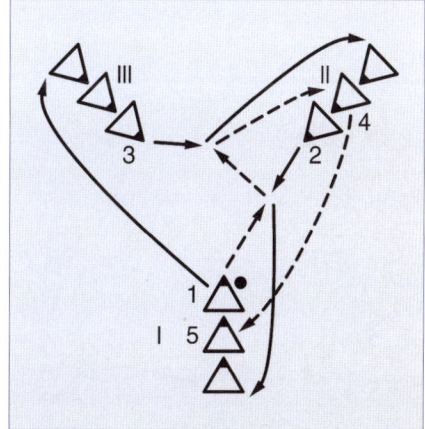

DRILLS

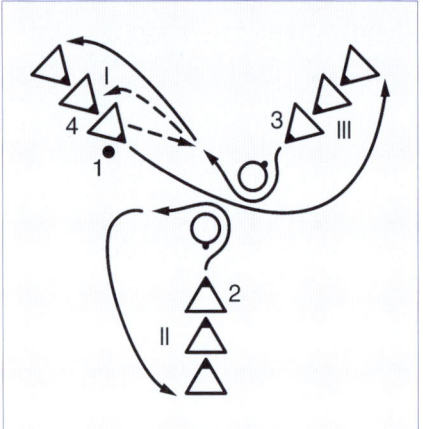

D46 Get open for the pass Players form 3 lines in a triangular pattern as shown. Player 1 begins with the ball and a defender stands between row I and rows II and III. The ball is passed from player 1 (row I) to player 2 (row II) or player 3 (row III) depending on the position of the defenders. The player receiving the pass returns the ball to the next player in row I and the drill continues. Players passing the ball always follow their passes to join the end of the row they passed to. The player not receiving the pass turns and joins the end of the same row.

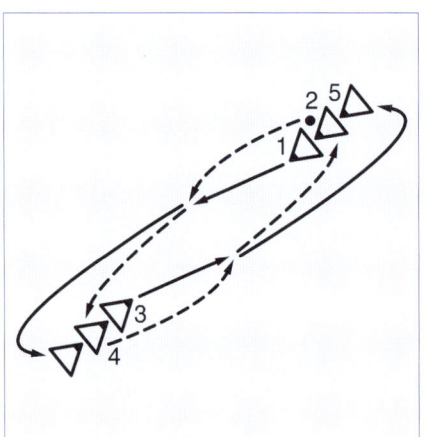

D47 Lead pass Players form two rows facing each other from a given distance. The second player in one row (player 2) is given a ball and passes ahead (lead pass) to the first player in the row (player 1). After the pass is caught, the receiver passes to the second player in the opposite row (player 4) and follows the pass to the end of that row. The drill is then repeated beginning with the opposite row, with player 4 throwing a lead pass for player 3, and so on.

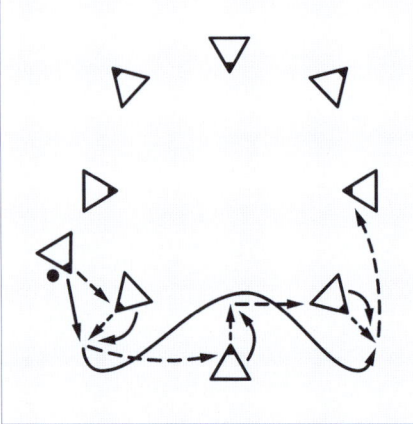

D48 Slalom Players form a large circle and one other player slaloms around them, passing back and forth with each player around the circle. *Variations*: (a) players on the circle can move in the opposite or same direction as the slaloming player; (b) players on the circle can become defenders after returning the pass to the slaloming player.

PASSING AND RECEIVING

D49 Circle line Players form a large circle and randomly pass one or more balls to each other while running in a circular pattern.

Variations:

- Players must run to the position they passed to.
- One or more players play within the circle as defenders.
- Players around the circle must try passing the ball to a designated player in the middle, keeping the ball away from a defender.

D50 Opposite directions Players form two circles (one inside the other) and move in opposite directions. One or more balls are passed in a random or specific order. *Variation*: defenders can be added between the two circles to make it more difficult for passes to make it through.

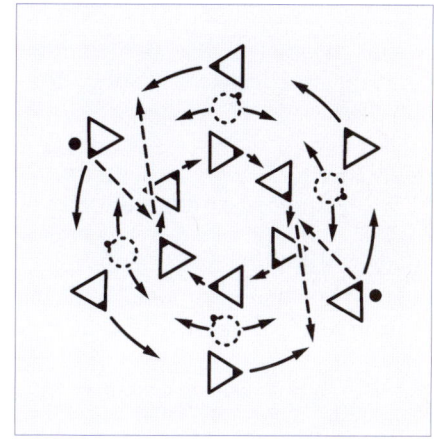

D51 Pass the ball Players run randomly around the court, passing one or ore balls to each other making sure not to travel with the ball.

Variations:

- Every player is given a number and passes are completed in order.
- Several small groups play on the same court at the same time with a separate ball.
- As above, except groups can intercept other groups' passes as well.
- Defenders are added to try to intercept passes. There can be as many defenders as there are passers.

DRILLS

Dribbling

Dribbling allows players to move around on the court in every direction with the ball. As long as a player is dribbling the ball, there cannot be a traveling violation (taking steps while carrying or holding the ball). The exercises to follow can be varied to make them suitable to each type of skill training for dribbling. Together with mastering the skills of dribbling, the skills of defending the dribbler should also be trained (see **Charts 9 and 10**).

Tips for dribbling

- Only dribble when a pass is not possible or useful at the time. A good rule is to only dribble to advance the ball up the court, improve a passing angle, take the ball to the basket, or to relieve pressure on the ball.

- Practice with both the right and left hand, trying not to look at the ball while dribbling. This enhances peripheral vision and attention to tactical cues.

- When dribbling past a defender, increase speed and keep the ball as low as possible. Dribble with the outside hand (hand furthest from the defender) and protect the ball from the defender with the body and free arm.

- If a defender tries to steal the ball, make use of dribbling skills to avoid the defender, such as switching hands, cross over, change of pace, behind the back, etc.

Tips for defending the dribbler

- Maintain a low centre of gravity—a prerequisite for defending the dribbler successfully. Avoid contact with the dribbler, as this constitutes a foul. Try to steal the ball when it bounces up from the floor. You must watch and time the rhythm of the dribble. A good time to try to steal the ball is when the dribbler is switching hands or direction and the ball is in front of him or her.

- Try to control the dribbler by forcing him or her towards the sideline or baseline of the court, or force him or her to pick up his or her dribble. Making the dribbler pick up the ball is an important aspect of the overall team defensive strategy.

- When chasing the dribbler from behind, one can try to knock the ball away, hopefully to a teammate.

DRIBBLING

Chart 9

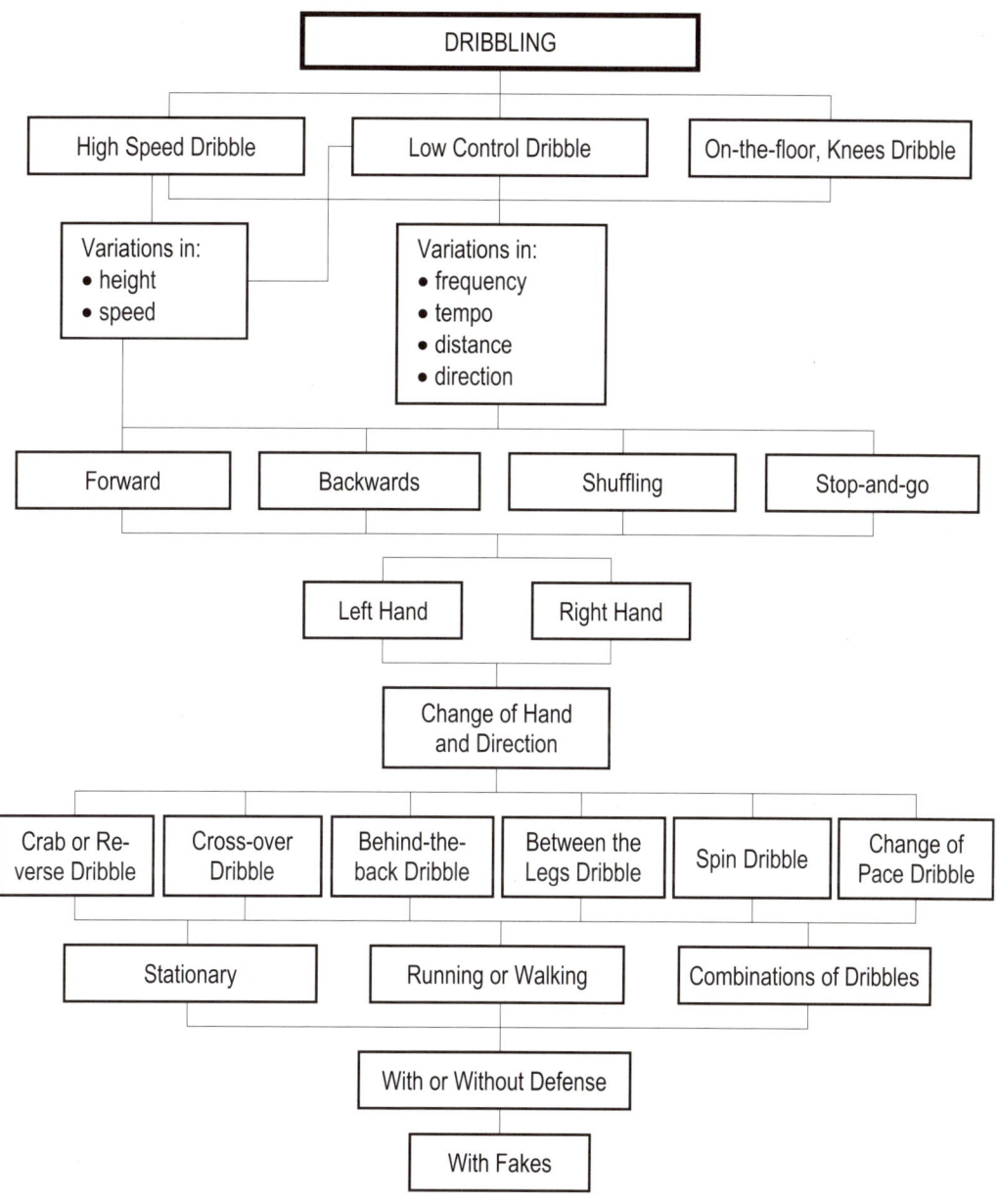

DRILLS

Chart 10

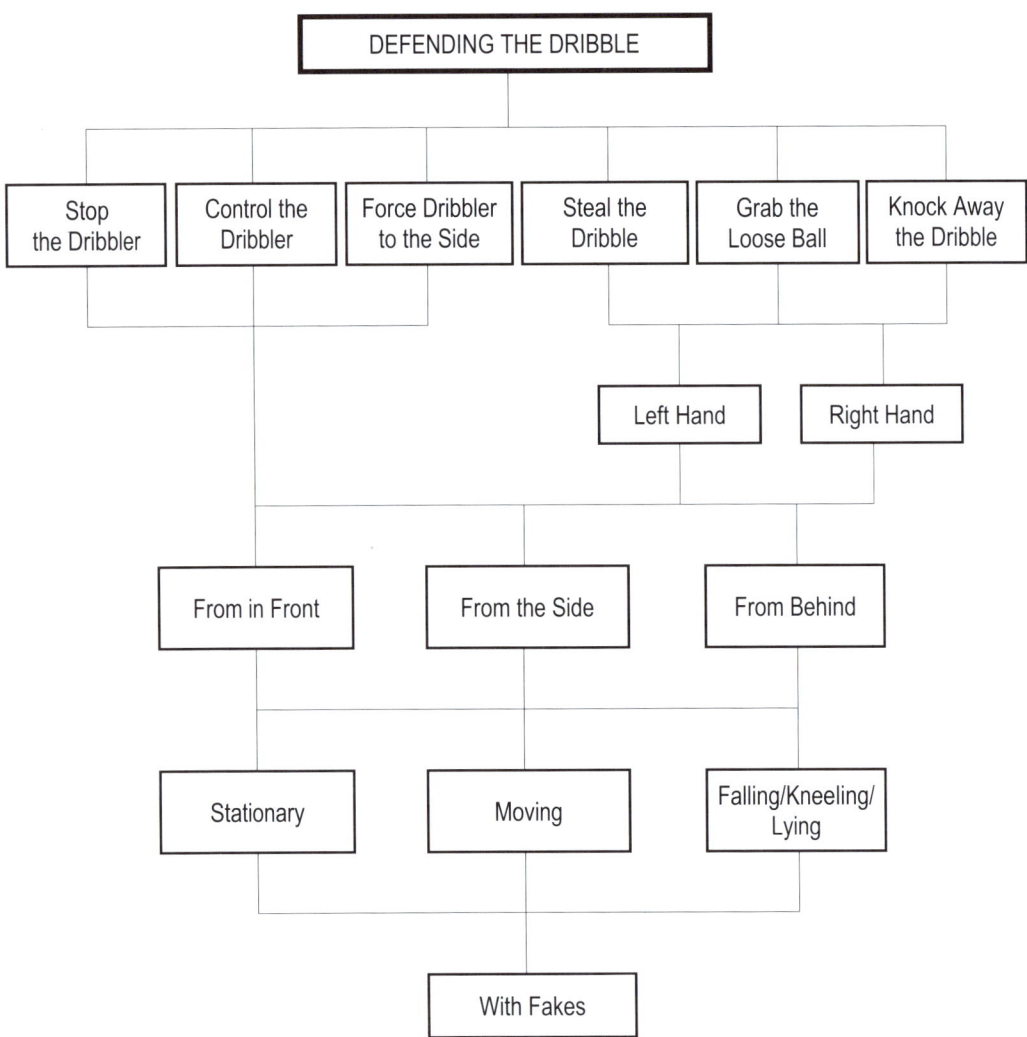

DRIBBLING

D52 Follow the leader Each player is given a ball and practices the various dribbling skills, either stationary or moving around on the court. The coach or another player can give various commands, such as dribble right, dribble left, speed dribble, control dribble, kneeling, lying on your back, squatting, etc. *Variation:* Every player imitates the moves of one leader or demonstrator (this may be a player or coach).

D53 Obstacle dribbling Obstacles are set up on the basketball court (benches, boxes, chairs, pylons, etc.) and the players must dribble around or over them using either a high speed dribble or a low control dribble. Lines on the court may also be used as points to practice switching between various dribbling skills. As the players approach or cross the designated lines, they switch from one dribbling skill to another.

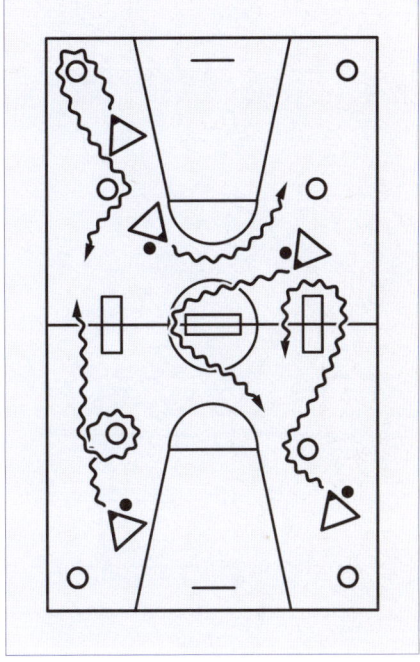

D54 Dribble relay Players are divided into two or more equal groups and line up in rows behind a designated start line. The first player in each row is given a ball. At the signal, the first member of each group dribbles the ball ahead to a designated line, dribbles back to the baseline, passes the ball off to the next player in line, and so on. The first group to return to its original position is the winner. If numbers are uneven to start, one player can go twice.

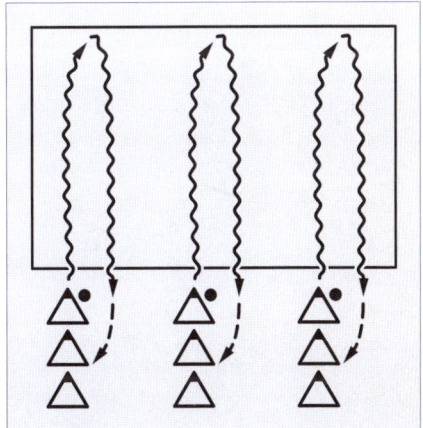

DRILLS

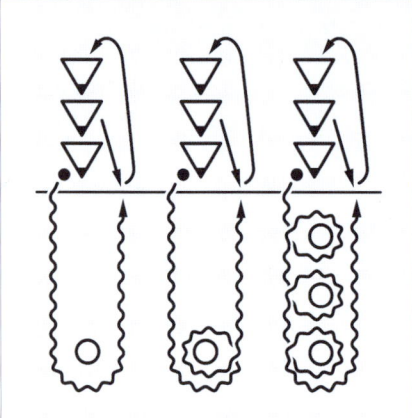

D55 Circling relay Similar to the dribble relay on the previous page (D54), players are divided into equal groups and line up in rows behind a designated start line. In this drill, players must dribble around one or more pylons before returning to the starting line to complete the relay. The first team to have all its members back in their starting positions is the winner. *Variations*: players can alter the dribbling hand, type of dribble, direction of dribble, etc

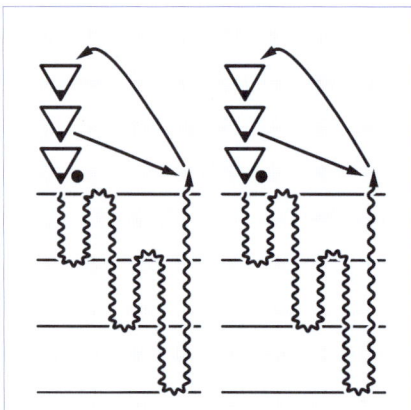

D56 Accordion dribbling The distance each player must dribble is varied and marked with lines or pylons on the floor. For example, the first player in each row dribbles to the first mark, returns to the starting line, dribbles to the second mark, returns to the starting line, dribbles to the third mark, and so on until he or she has dribbled to all marks. At each turning point, the player must switch hands and either dribble backwards or turn and dribble forwards back to the starting line. A change of direction dribble such as a behind the back or between the legs dribble can also be used at each turning point.

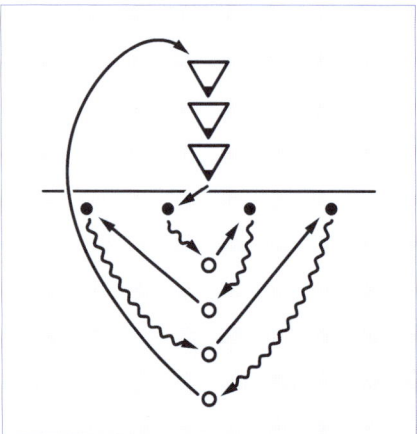

D57 Run—dribble—drop relay The first player in the group must run to pick up the first ball, dribble to a designated spot, put the ball down, run to pick up the next ball, dribble to the next designated spot, put the ball down, and so on. This continues until the player has picked up all four balls, dribbled to the four designated spots on the floor, and returned to the end of the line. The next player in line then does the opposite, returning all four balls to their original spots on the floor, the third player in line repeats what the first player did, and so on. *Variation*: groups can compete against each other in a relay.

DRIBBLING

D58 Dribble and hand off Players are divided into two equal groups and face each other as shown. Player 1 is given a ball to start. At the signal, player 1 dribbles towards player 2 as player 2 simultaneously begins moving towards player 1. When the two players meet half way, the ball is handed off from the dribbler (player 1) to the non-dribbler (player 2). Once the ball is handed off, player 1 joins the end of the opposite row he or she started from. Player 2 then dribbles towards player 3 who is moving to meet him or her, hands the ball off to player 3, and so on. This pattern continues for a set period of time.

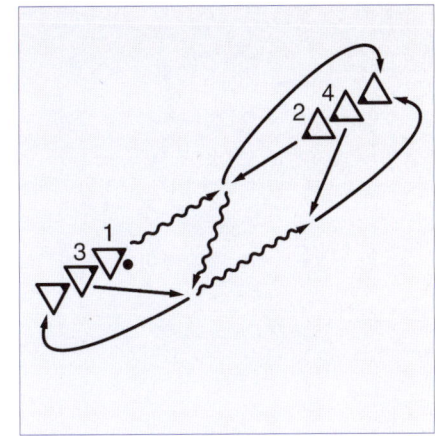

Dribbling patterns on the court Running patterns used for practicing the various dribbling skills on the basketball court may be varied as shown in D59 to D61. Not only can the running patterns be varied (moving forwards, moving backwards, turning), but also the types of dribbles used (speed dribble, control dribble, change of direction dribbles—behind the back, between the legs, cross over) depending on your needs.

D59 Figure eight Players are divided into two equal groups and stand facing each other along one sideline on opposite sides of the half court line. The first player from each group begins dribbling in a figure eight pattern around pylons placed in the four corners of each half of the basketball court. When turning around each pylon or marker, players can practice using different change of direction dribbles, such as behind the back, between the legs, or cross over. When each player has completed the figure eight, he or she rejoins the end of the line and the next player in line follows suit. *Variations*: (a) players must dribble in opposite directions after each turn (i.e., alternating between dribbling forwards and backwards); (b) groups compete in a relay and can try to knock the opposing player's ball away when crossing paths at half court. The first team to have all its players return their original positions is the winner.

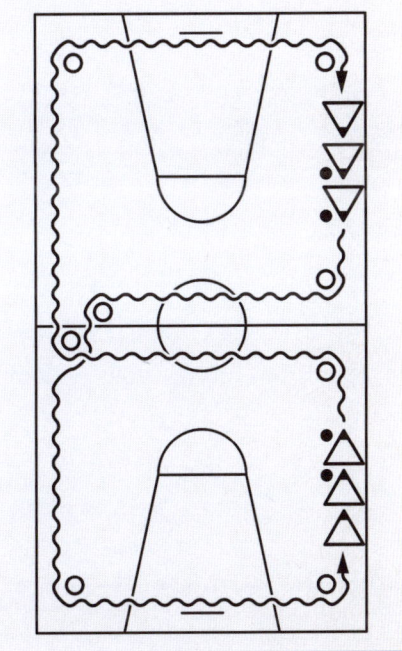

103

DRILLS

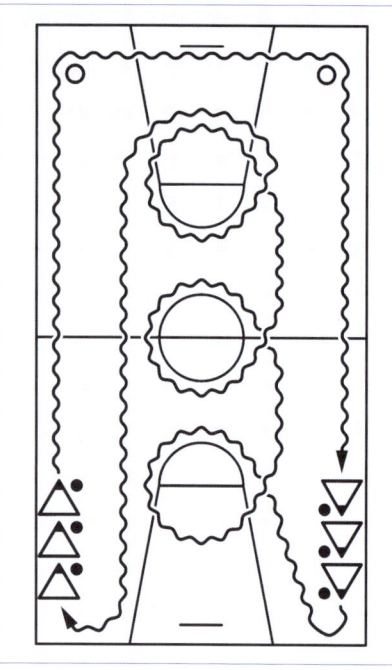

D60 Circling Players are divided into two equal groups and stand along opposite sidelines facing opposite directions at one end of the basketball court. Each player is given a ball and follows the first player in line. One group begins by dribbling the length of the court and continuing around the perimeter until reaching the corner vacated by the other group. The other group begins by circling around the circle at the top of the key, the circle at half court, and the circle at the top of the key at the opposite end of the court, before ending up in the corner vacated by the other group. Eventually, both groups follow the same path around the court, completing a full circuit. This pattern continues for a set period of time or until one group catches up to another.

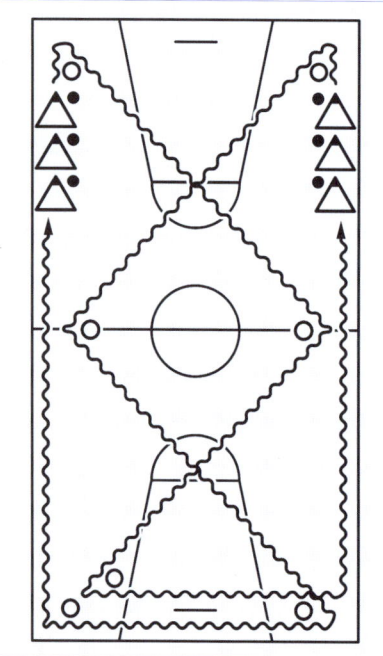

D61 Criss-cross Players are divided into two equal groups and stand facing the same direction along opposite sidelines at one end of the basketball court. Each player is given a ball and must dribble around a set of pylons placed on the court in a zig-zag pattern. At the signal of the coach or instructor, the first player in each group begins dribbling around each pylon, until rounding the final pylon and joining the end of the other group's line. Once the first player has rounded the second pylon, the next player in line can begin dribbling along the same path, and so on. This pattern continues for a set period of time. *Variations*: (a) players can try to knock other players' balls away when crossing paths at any point along the dribbling course; (b) groups can begin dribbling at the same time and must travel together as a group.

DRIBBLING

D62 Team chase Players are each given a ball and divided into two equal teams, each team standing on opposite sidelines at centre court. At the signal of the coach or instructor, both teams begin dribbling around the perimeter of the court (in the same direction), making sure to round each pylon or marker placed in the four corners of the court. The goal of each team is to try to catch up to and tag the last member of the opposing team. When a player is successfully tagged, he or she moves off the court and practices stationary dribbling until the drill is complete. The drill continues for a set period of time or until all players from one team have been tagged.

D63 Changing direction dribble Players are each given a ball and spread out on the basketball court. At the signal, players begin dribbling randomly around the court. When players dribble to the right they must use the right hand and when dribbling to the left must use the left hand. When changing directions, players can use any dribbling skill (behind-the-back, cross over, between the legs, etc.). The switch from one hand to the other occurs during every change in direction.

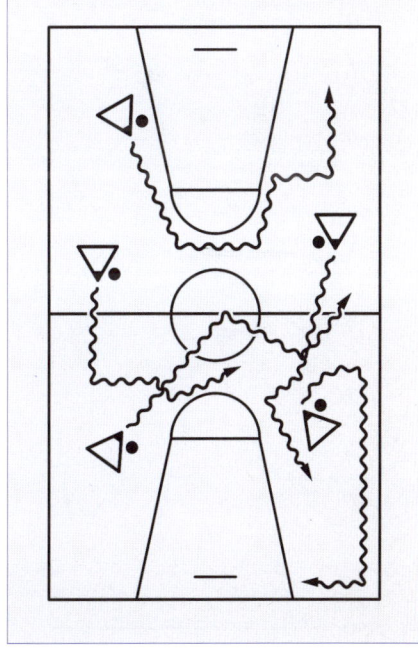

DRILLS

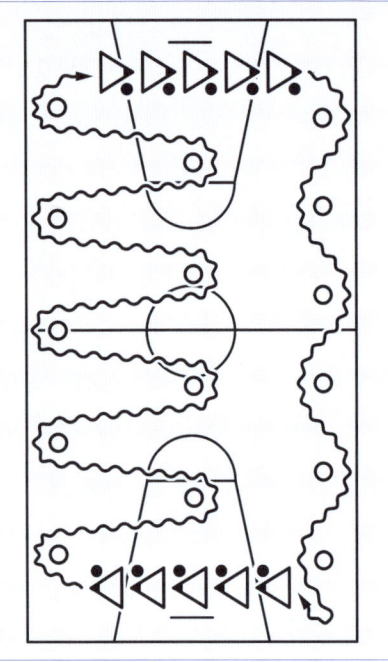

D64 Zig-zag dribbling Players are each given a ball and divided into two equal groups. Each group stands along opposite ends of the basketball court facing opposite directions (both groups move in a clockwise direction). Several pylons or markers are placed along each sideline as obstacles for the dribbling players. At the signal, players must zig-zag their way around the pylons using either a low control dribble (down the left sideline) or a high speed dribble (down the right sideline). When players are dribbling to the right of the pylon they must use the right hand and when dribbling to the left of the pylon must use the left hand. As players round each pylon, the ball is switched to the opposite hand using one of the dribbling skills for changing direction. *Variation*: Defenders can stand in the place of pylons or markers and try knocking the ball away as the dribbler changes directions. This drill emphasizes the importance of maintaining a low dribble during directional changes to protect the ball.

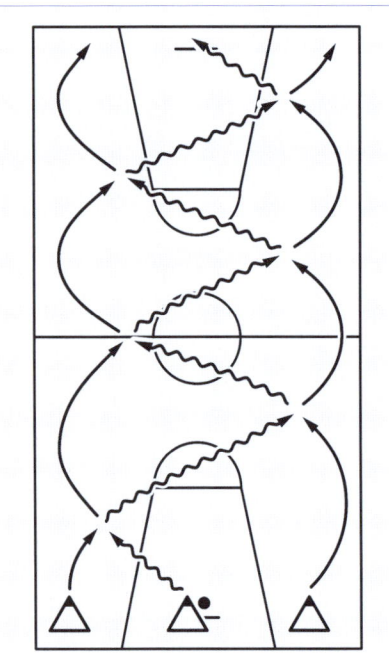

D65 Weave dribble Players line up in three rows at one end of the basketball court. The first player in the middle begins with the ball while the other two stand just inside each sideline. At the signal of the coach or instructor, the three players weave their way down the floor using the dribble-hand-off as shown in the diagram. The player in the middle begins by dribbling up the court angling towards one sideline. The player on that sideline runs ahead to receive a hand off from the dribbler and then dribbles towards the next player on the opposite sideline who takes a hand off from him or her, and so on. After each pass, players always fill the position vacated by the player receiving the pass (pass and go behind). The players weave their way down the court in this manner until reaching the opposite baseline.

DRIBBLING

D66 Dribble knock away Players are each given a ball and line up along one baseline of the basketball court. At the signal, each player must try dribbling from one end to the other without losing his or her ball to the one or more defenders positioned throughout the court. The defenders' job is to try to steal the ball or knock it away and pick up the loose ball. *Variations*: (a) the drill can be performed in a smaller area to add difficulty and emphasize ball control; (b) when a dribbler looses the ball he or she becomes a defender, until only one dribbler is remaining.

D67 Dribbling against a defender Players are divided into two groups and line up along opposite sidelines at one end of the basketball court. Each player in line is given a ball, while several players without a ball line up along each sideline at equal intervals as defenders. The dribbling players must try to get past the series of defenders one at a time by using one of the dribbling skills (change of pace, change of direction, cross over, behind the back, etc.) without crossing into the other half of the court. The dribbling player must try to make it from one end of the court to the other without losing possession of the ball. *Variation*: all players line up in the middle of the court behind one baseline and must get past two defenders at a time using the entire width of the court.

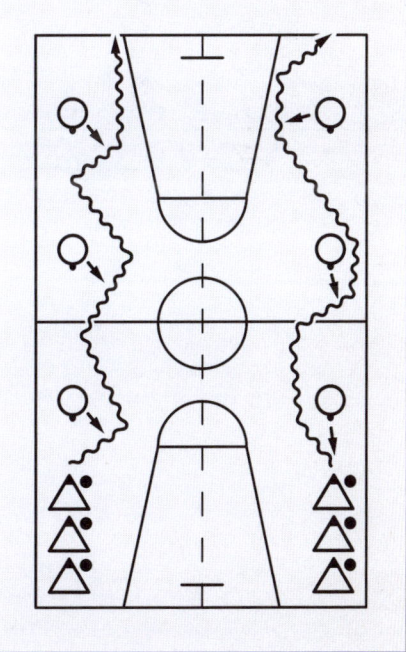

DRILLS

D68 Signal dribbling Players are each given a ball and stand in a large circular formation. At the signal of the coach or instructor, each player begins dribbling around the circle in a clockwise direction. As the players continue dribbling, the coach calls out random instructions – switch hands, change directions, behind the back, between the legs, etc. – which each player must follow. *Variation*: at the given signal, one identified player in the group must dribble around all the other players, still running in the same direction, until returning to his or her original position in the circle.

D69 Dribble tag Similar to D66, several defenders roam around the playing area trying to tag dribbling players entering a clearly bounded area (e.g., half of the basketball court). Tagged players lose the ball to the defenders who tagged them and then become defenders in their place. Two new dribbling players then enter the playing area and the drill continues for a specified period of time or until every player has been tagged at least once. *Variation*: every player is given a ball and must try to tag other players or knock away their balls while maintaining their own dribble.

DRIBBLING

DRILLS

Pivoting

Pivoting refers to a player turning, jab stepping, or stepping away from the defender while keeping one foot in contact with one spot on the floor (pivot foot) (see **Charts 11 and 12**). The other foot can be moved in any direction (turning around the pivot foot). Pivoting is used mainly to avoid a defender while holding the ball in an "attack position" (dribble, shoot, or pass) standing in one spot. It is also used in one-on-one situations as a fake, and serves to get into a better position to pass or shoot the ball. After the jab step, the player can pass, dribble, or attempt a shot at the basket.

Tips for pivoting

- The ball should be held firmly with both hands close to the body away from the defender.

- Do not lift the pivot foot from the floor, as this results in a traveling violation. Do not make large side steps, which may put you off balance.

- Watch the position and movements of the defender closely. This allows you to keep the ball away from the defender and to shoot, pass, or dribble at the right moment.

Tips for defending the pivoting player

- Harass the player with the ball to try to force a stepping mistake or to disrupt their concentration. Do not make it easy for the offense.

- Always be aware of passing lanes and potential passes by the offensive player with the ball. Try to deflect or intercept the pass or try to knock the ball away before a pass is attempted.

- Double-teaming is very effective (i.e., two defensive players approach the offensive player with the ball and try to steal or deflect the ball or force a turnover).

Chart 11

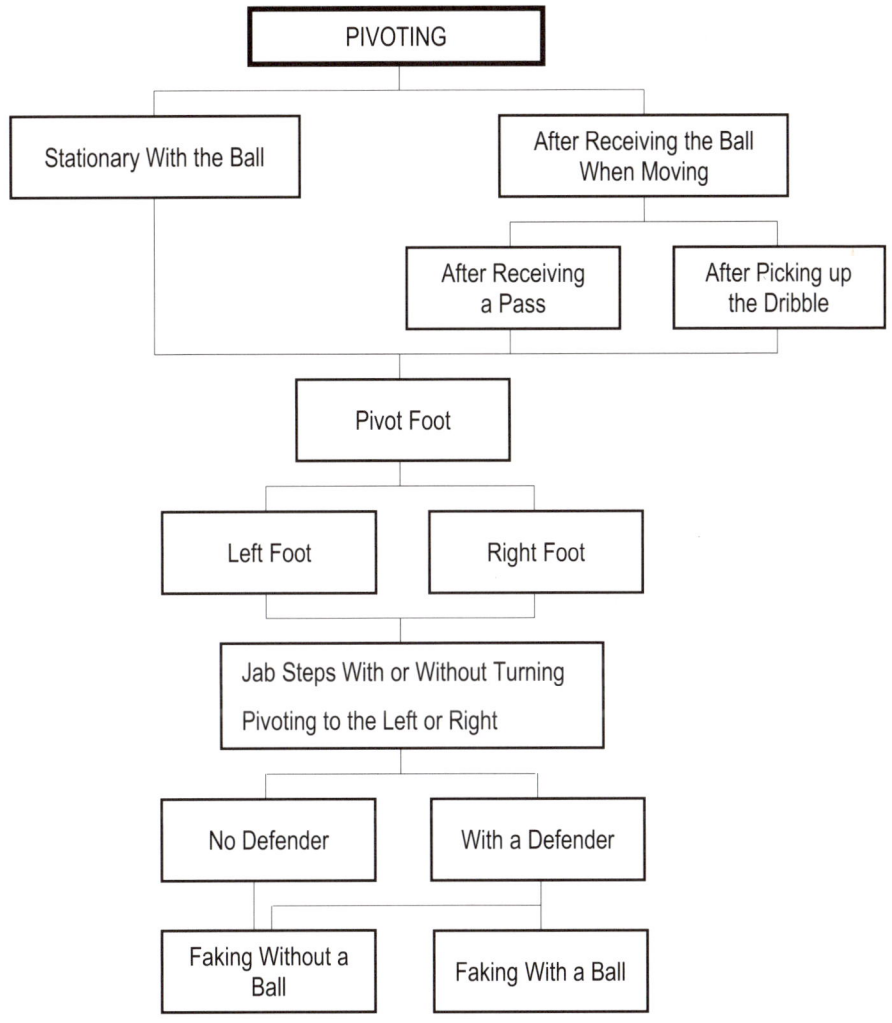

DRILLS

Chart 12

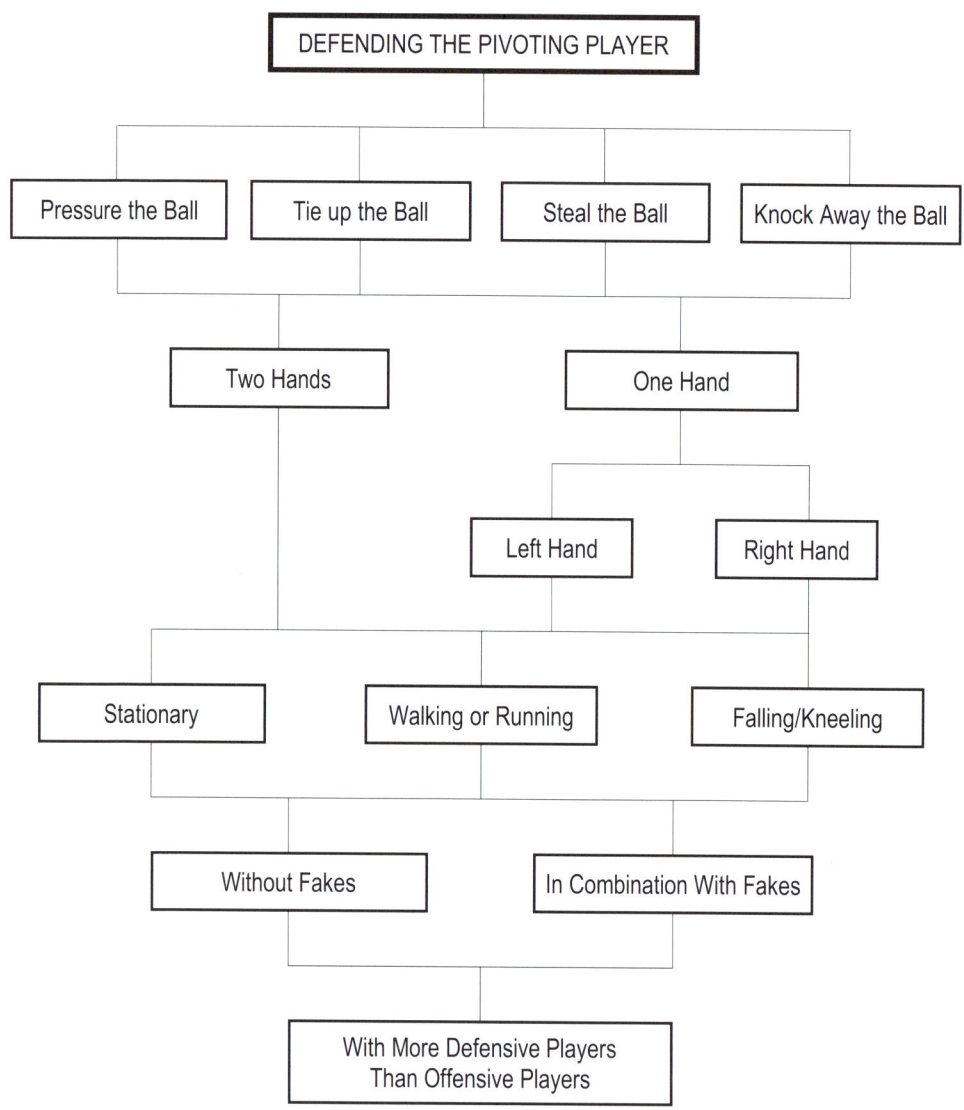

PIVOTING

D70 Pivot and pass Two players stand facing each other from a given distance. One player begins by passing the ball to his or her partner, who catches the ball, performs a series of pivots, passes the ball back to his or her partner, and so on back and forth. Players can perform the same drill with more players, remembering to pivot before passing the ball on to the next player.

D71 Pivoting with a defender Two players face each other—one on defense, one on offense with the ball. The offensive player must secure the ball by pivoting as the defender attempts to steal the ball. When the defensive player is successful in touching the ball, roles are reversed. No foul play! *Variation*: another player is added as a passing option for the offensive player. This extra player can either be stationary or moving, and may be with or without a defensive player guarding him or her.

D72 Pivot, dribble, pass Players form a square, one player in each corner. Player 1 starts with the ball and begins by dribbling towards player 2. After passing the ball to player 2, player 1 moves to replace player 2, who pivots and dribbles towards player 3 in the next corner. The pivot – dribble – pass pattern continues around the square until every player has occupied every corner of the square. *Variation*: using two balls, and two or more players in each corner, one of the players in each corner plays defense against the pivoting player.

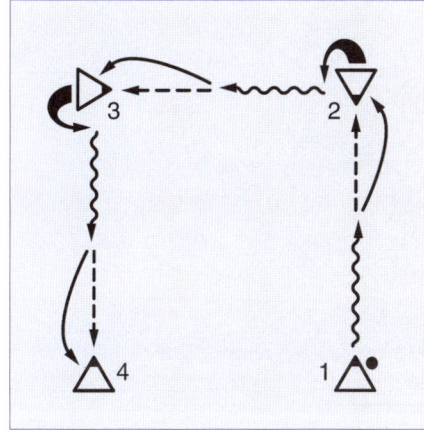

D73 Pivoting out of a double team Two players "double team" the player with the ball. The offensive player with the ball must pivot to elude the double team and try to get a pass to one of two teammates on the court. The teammates may have defenders playing them as well, trying to prevent the pass.

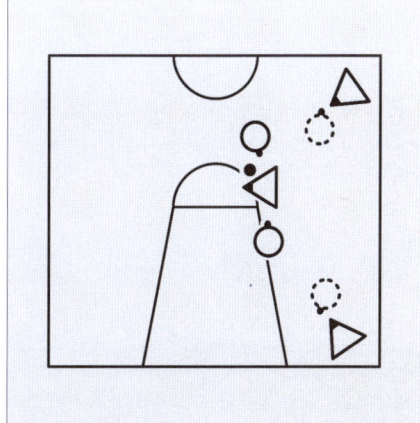

DRILLS

Picking up the dribble and pivoting to pass

In the following drills, the player with the ball will dribble to a spot, pick up the dribble, and make a pivot or series of pivots before passing to a teammate. The various drills should first be practiced without defenders, but may later be practiced with one or more defenders on the dribbler (D74 to D76).

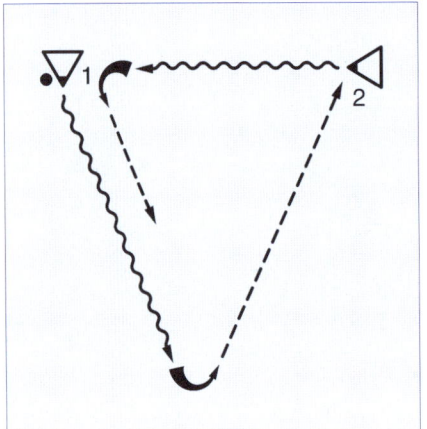

D74 Dribble, pivot, pass Players are divided into pairs and stand a given distance apart. Player 1 is given a ball and begins by dribbling at an angle in the direction of player 2, picks up the dribble when reaching the halfway point between the two starting positions, pivots, and passes the ball to player 2. Player 2 then dribbles across to complete the triangle, picks up the dribble, pivots, and passes back to player 1. The drill continues for a specific amount of time or until a certain number of passes have been completed.

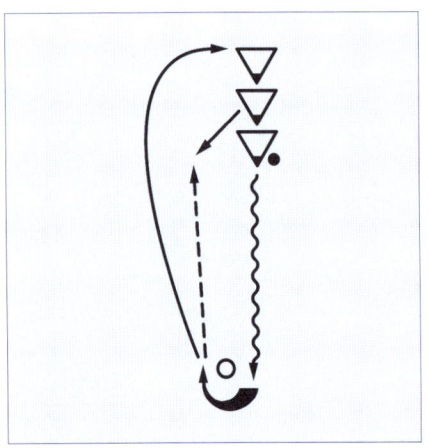

D75a Dribble, pivot, pass back Players line up in a row and the first player in line is given a ball. At the signal, the first player dribbles forwards until reaching a marker (pylon, bench, etc.) some distance ahead, picks up the dribble at this point, pivots, and passes the ball back to the next player in line, who repeats the pattern. Players join the end of the row after completing a cycle.

114

PIVOTING

D75b Dribble to a defender Players are divided into two groups with a defender standing between them. The first player in one group (player 1) is given a ball and begins by dribbling towards the other group. When reaching the defender, player 1 picks up the dribble, pivots to elude the defense, and pivots to pass the ball to the first player in the other group (player 2). Player 1 then takes a spot at the end of the line he or she passed to. The drill continues with player 2 dribbling towards the defender, pivoting, passing, and so on, until players have returned to their original positions. Switch roles periodically.

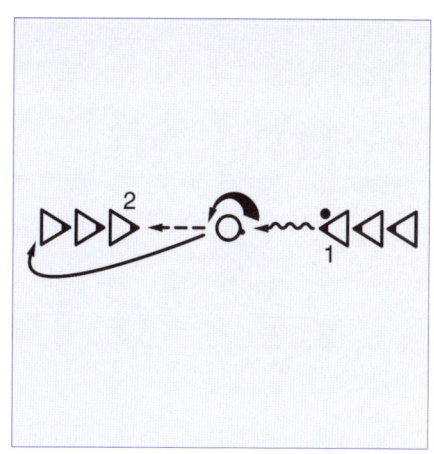

D75c Dribble to a defender, pivot, pass back Players are divided into (offensive and defensive) groups and line up in two rows facing each other from a given distance. The first offensive player is given a ball and begins by dribbling towards the defensive line. When he or she meets the first defender, the dribbler stops, picks up the dribble, pivots, and passes the ball back to the next player in line, who repeats the drill. Offensive and defensive players switch roles after each encounter, joining the end of opposite lines.

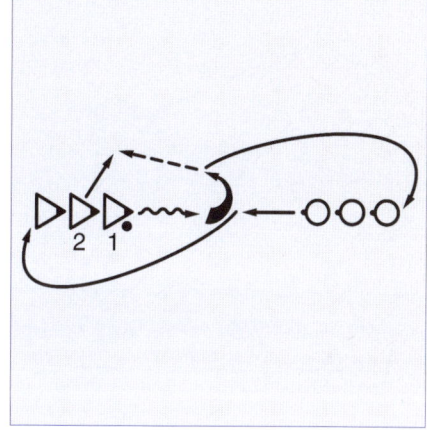

D76a Dribble to a defender, pivot, pass, replace Players begin in two rows facing each other on opposite corners of a square. Two other players stand in the two remaining corners as defenders. The offensive player at the front of each row is given a ball and begins by dribbling towards the defender to the right. When each player reaches the defender he or she stops, picks up the dribble, pivots, and passes to the player at the front of the next line. The player who made the pass becomes the next defender and the defender moves to the next line as an offensive player.

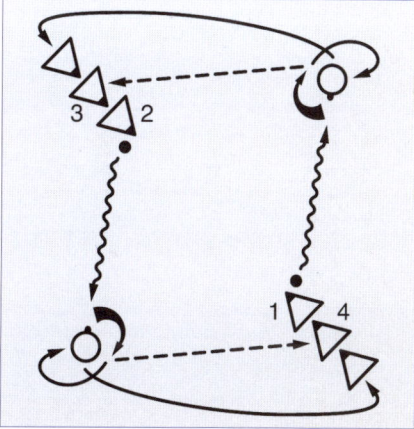

115

DRILLS

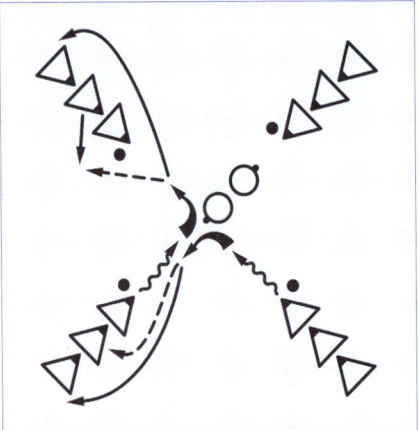

D76b Pivot, pass, and follow Players are divided into four groups and line up in the four corners of a square. Two additional players stand in the middle of the square as defenders. The first players in two adjacent rows begin dribbling towards the middle, pick up the dribble when reaching the defenders, pivot to the left, pass to the next player in the row to the left, and proceed to follow their passes to join the end of that row. The drill continues in this fashion, with players always pivoting and passing to the left. Roles should be switched periodically.

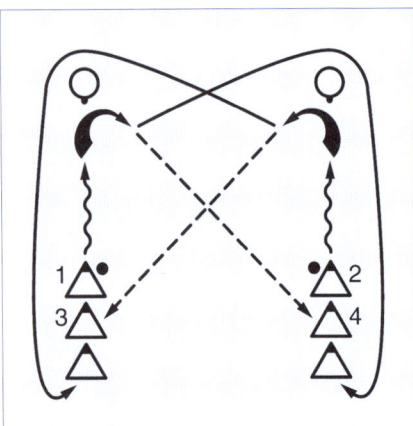

D76c Pivot, pass, switch sides Players are divided into two groups, each lined up in a row facing one defender. The first player in each row is given a ball and begins by dribbling to the defender, picking up the dribble, pivoting, and passing to the next player in the opposite row. After passing the ball, players circle around the defender on the opposite side and join the end of the opposite row.

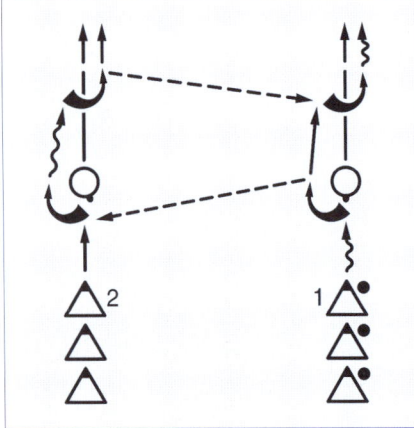

D76d Pivot, pass, and go Two groups each line up facing one defender. Each player in one group has a ball. The first player in line (player 1) dribbles ahead to the defender facing the row, picks up the dribble, pivots, and passes to the first player in the opposite line (player 2) who moves ahead to meet the pass. Player 2 then pivots upon meeting the defender facing his or her row, dribbles ahead to open space, pivots around the defender again, and passes the ball back to player 1 (who has moved up for a return pass). Player 1 makes a final pivot before dribbling past the defender.

116

PIVOTING

D76e Meet the defender Players form two (offensive and defensive) rows on adjacent corners of a square. One other player stands in the corner diagonally opposite the offensive row. The first offensive player dribbles ahead to the vacant corner of the square as the first defender tries to beat him or her to the spot. When reaching the corner, the offensive player stops, pivots, and passes across to the single player, who passes the ball back to the offensive line. The previous offensive player becomes the single player in the corner, the single player joins the defensive line, and the previous defender joins the offensive line.

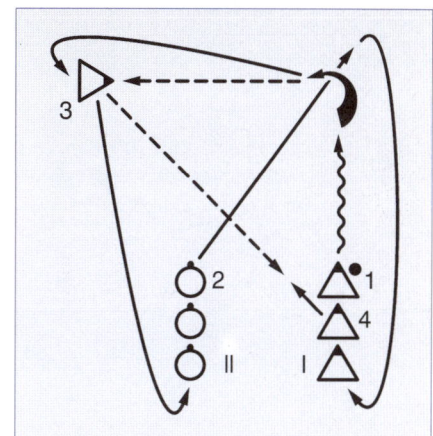

D77 Pivot, dribble, hand-off Two groups line up facing each other. Player 1 begins by passing to player 2, who moves to meet the pass. After receiving the pass, player 2 pivots, dribbles back towards his or her own row, and hands the ball off to player 3. Player 3 then passes to player 4, who moves to meet the pass, pivots, dribbles towards the end of the same row, and hands the ball off to player 5. After passing the ball, players join the end of the closest row. *Variations*: (a) the passer may become a defender before returning to the end of the row; (b) player 2 passes the ball to player 3 after pivoting (without dribbling).

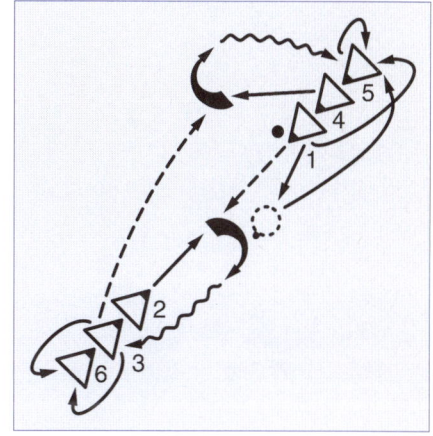

D78 Return pass and pivot Players are divided into two groups and each stand facing one defender from a given distance. One other player (M) stands between the two defenders as a passer. The first player in each row is given a ball and begins by passing (one at a time) to M and moving towards the defender for a return pass. After receiving the return pass, the player pivots away from the defender and passes back to the next player in line. The player making the final pass becomes the new defender and the previous defender moves to the end of the offensive line for the next round.

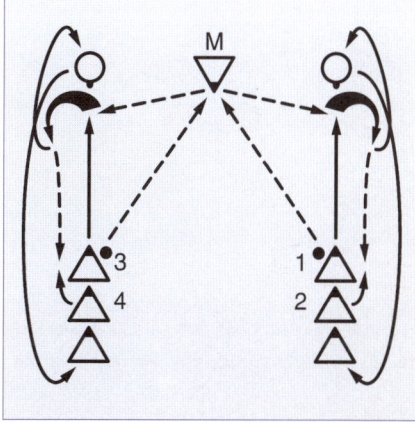

DRILLS

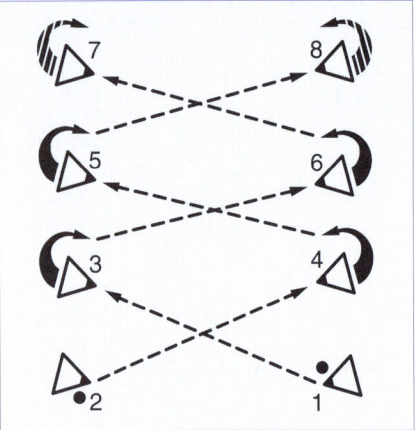

D79 Zig-zag pass and pivot Players line up in two rows facing each other from a given distance. The first player in each row (1 and 2) each start with a ball and begin by passing to the next person in the opposite row. The receivers (3 and 4) pivot after receiving the ball, and pass to the next person in the opposite row (5 and 6), and so on down the line. When the ball reaches the end of the row, the pattern is repeated in the opposite direction. Make eye contact with the intended pass recipient before throwing each pass.

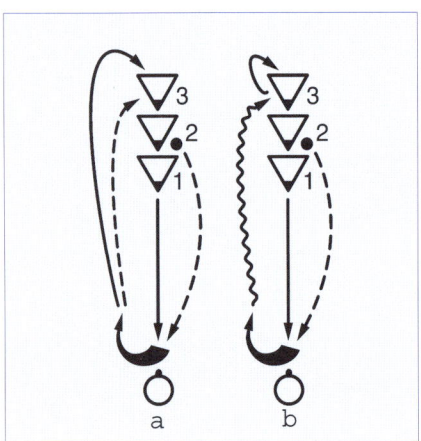

D80 Over the shoulder pass and pivot Players are divided into two groups and line up each facing one defender. The first player in line (1) runs towards the defender looking for a pass over the shoulder from the second player in line (2). After receiving the pass and stopping under control, the player pivots away from the defender and either (a) *passes* the ball back to the next person in line (3), or (b) *dribbles and hands the ball off* to the next player in line (3). After passing or handing the ball off, players join the end of the row.

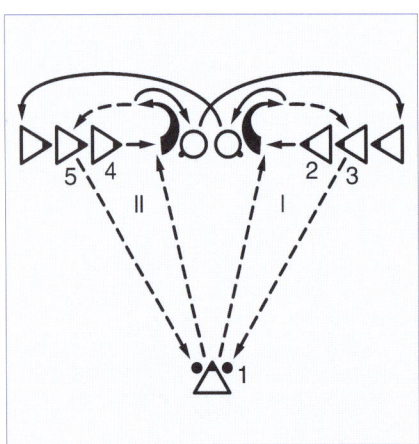

D81 Double pass and pivot Players are divided into two groups and stand facing each other from a given distance. Two defenders stand between the two rows facing each group. One other player (1) is given two balls and stands perpendicular to the rows. Player 1 begins by passing (one at a time) to the first player in each row (2 and 4) who moves forward to meet the pass, pivots away from the defender, passes back to the next player in line (3 or 5), and moves to replace the defender (defenders join the end of the row). The players receiving the pass (3 and 5) then pass back to the starting position (1).

PIVOTING

D82 **Pass, catch, pivot on the move** Players are divided into three groups. Two groups (II and III) stand facing each other with a defender standing between them. The remaining group is given balls and stands perpendicular to the other two groups. Player 1 begins by passing to player 2, who moves forward to meet the pass, pivots away from the defender, passes to player 3, and moves to replace the defender (the defender then joins the end of row III). Player 3 then passes back to the starting line. Passing and player movement follow a I – II – III – I pattern.

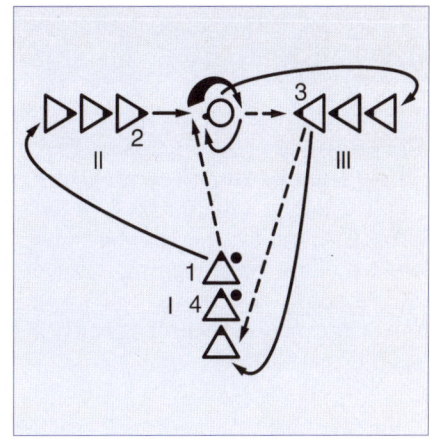

DRILLS

Shooting

Shooting is one of the more difficult technical skills to learn. Since success or failure in a game depends largely on making shots, shooting should be a major focus during training. Initially, a high number of repetitions of the various shots should be practiced, later progressing to practicing the same shots in game-like situations. The drills utilized should allow for practicing a variety of shot types, distances from the basket, locations on the court, etc., and at some point should include defenders. Practicing shots in scrimmage games and recording the results increases the concentration level and performance level of the players.

A special focus should also be placed upon defending the shooter. Almost every drill presented here can be practiced with defenders. The positions for possible defenders are noted in the diagrams. The intensity of defence applied for each drill can be altered depending on skill level as follows:

Passive defender:
The passive defensive player applies only token defence. He or she maintains a defensive position but does not try to prevent or block the shot. The offensive player is forced to shoot the ball over or dribble past the defender.

Semi-active defender:
The semi-active defensive player plays at 50% full speed. They try to make it difficult for the player to shoot the ball, but will not prevent it.

Active defender:
An active defensive player tries to prevent the shot by using all the defensive skills possible. Alternately, the offensive player must try to take the best possible shot. If a good shot is not available, the ball should be passed to a teammate.

Aggressive defender:
The aggressive defensive player not only tries to prevent a shot but also tries to block the shot or steal the ball.

Several defenders:
Two or three defensive players try to prevent a shot by the offensive player and gain possession of the ball. Rebounding can also be practiced in this case.

The overview diagrams (**Charts 13 and 14**) outline the variety of shots and defensive strategies used with shooters. The illustrated drills incorporate only standard drills that may be used. The coach should arrange variations in all drills with regard to types of shots, distance from the basket, positions on the floor, etc.

SHOOTING

Chart 13

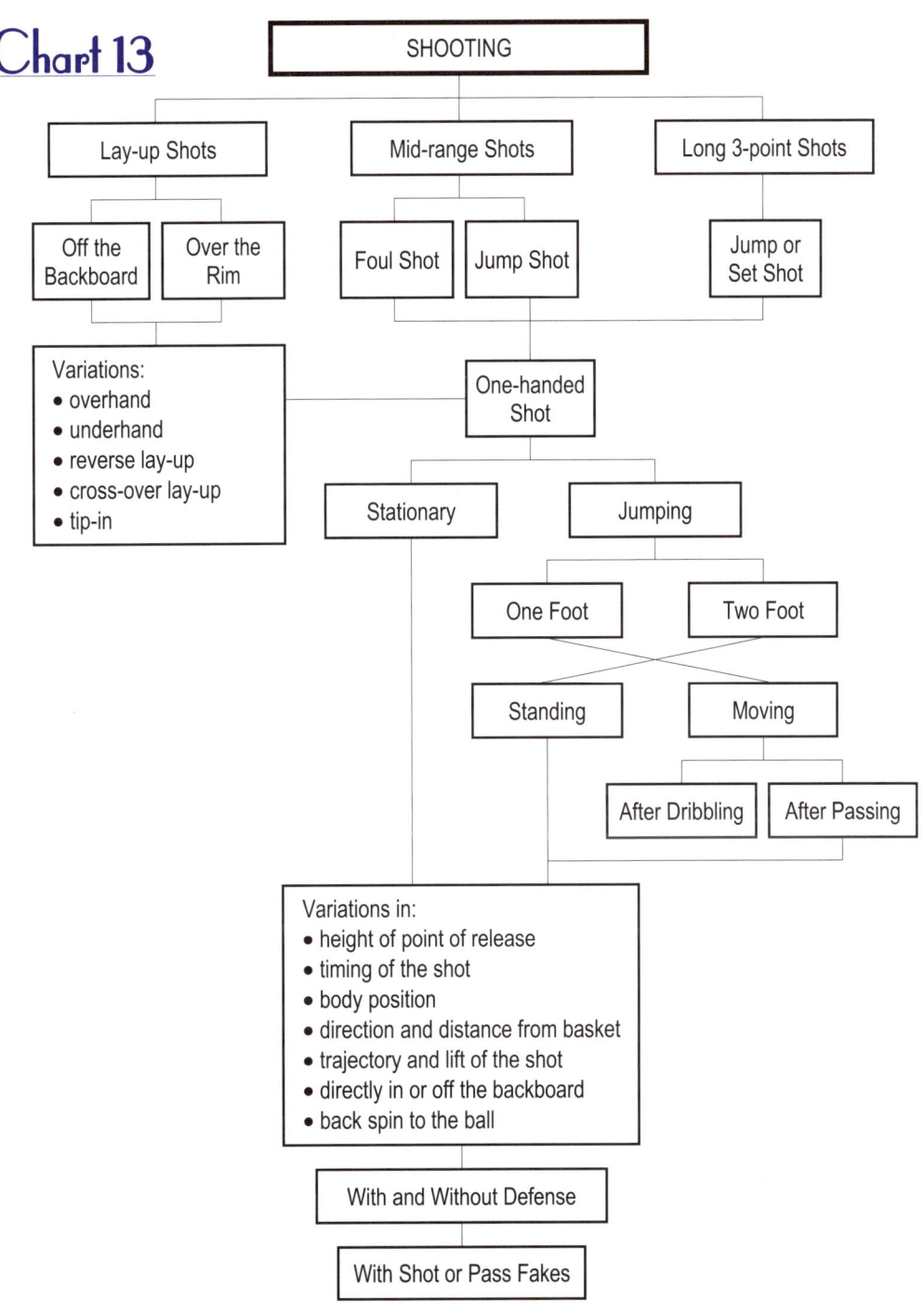

DRILLS

Chart 14

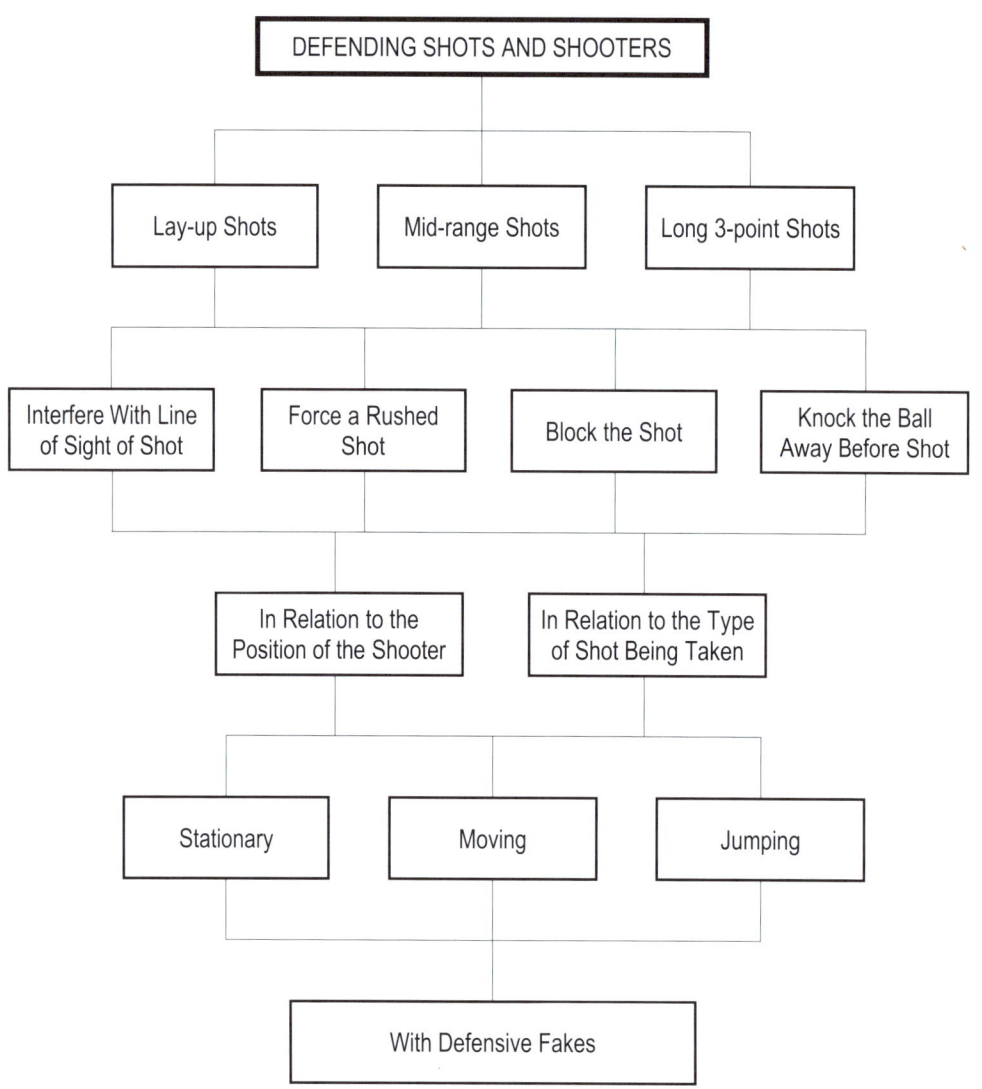

SHOOTING

Tips for shooting

- Learn the proper technique and mechanics of shooting the basketball. Using correct mechanics leads to greater shooting consistency and percentages, especially for three-point and mid-range jump shots.

- Always pay close attention to game situations before shooting the ball (teammates and defenders). If you have an open shot, concentrate on the shot and try not to be distracted by other players.

- Only shoot from beyond the three-point line when there is no better shot available or if the shot is part of the offensive play for the team.

- Use shooting practice to also practice (offensive and defensive) rebounding.

Tips for defending the shooter

- Successfully defending the shot requires quick reaction speed and movement, jumping ability, as well as knowledge of the offensive player (tactical experience). Every shot prevented is as valuable to the team as a basket scored. Remember, offense wins games, but defense wins championships.

- Stay on your feet when defending a jump shooter. The offensive player may be faking the shot trying to draw a foul.

- Do not jump directly into the opponent, but more sideways (towards the shooting arm) to avoid fouling the shooter upon landing.

- Do not try to blindly knock the ball away while it is still in the opponent's hands. You may hit the hands or wrists instead of the ball and this is often called a foul. The reaction of the defense should always be directed by the ball.

DRILLS

Lay-ups

A lay-up is a shot taken a few feet away from the basket. Prior to shooting a lay-up, the player usually dribbles or receives a pass (from a teammate) while running or cutting to the basket. The one-handed overhead shot should be practiced before practicing the lay-up shot in full motion. The first three drills below (D83 to D85) provide examples of pre-shooting drills for practicing the one-handed overhead shot.

D83 **Stationary shot** Players stand to the right of the basket (about one metre away) and practice one-handed shots from a standing position with the right hand. Players may jump off the left foot and lift the right knee while shooting to mimic a lay-up in motion. For practicing left-handed shots, players move to the left of the basket, jumping off the right foot and lifting the left knee.

D84 **One-step approach** Players stand one-and-a-half to two metres away from the basket on either side. For a right-handed lay-up the player stands to the right of the basket, taking one step with the left foot and lifting the right knee during the shot. For a left-handed lay-up the player stands to the left of the basket, taking one step with the right foot and lifting the left knee during the shot.

D85 **Two-step approach** Players stand two to two-and-a-half metres away from the basket. For a right-handed lay-up players begin by taking a step with the right foot, followed by a step with the left foot, before shooting the ball with a right-handed overhead shot. Again, players drive off the left leg and lift the right knee during the shot. The technique is the same for performing a left-handed lay-up, except players begin by taking a step with the left foot, followed by a step with the right foot. A left-handed lay-up therefore involves driving off the right leg and lifting the left knee during the shot.

LAY-UPS

Lay-ups off the dribble

D86 Random dribble and shoot Players are each given a ball and spread out over the basketball court. Players dribble randomly around the court, shooting lay-ups at the various baskets and rebounding their own shots. They continue dribbling and shooting for a specified period of time or until they have made a certain number of shots. If there are not enough balls for every player, players can pair up and alternate shooting.

Variations:

- Defenders are located at each basket or randomly throughout the court to defend shooters and/or dribblers.

- Players must dribble around obstacles or pylons on their way to shooting the lay-up.

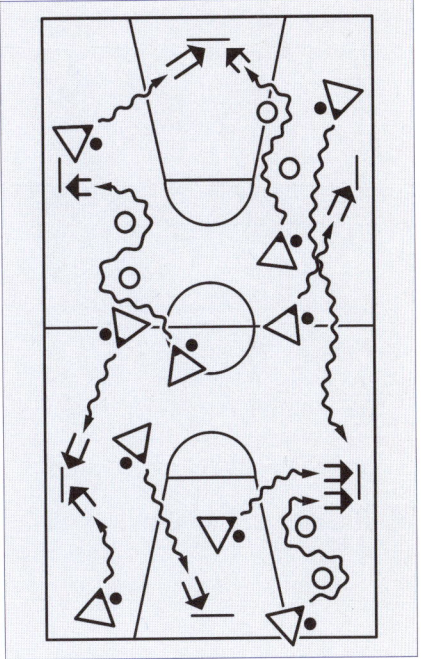

D87 Lay-up lines Players form two lines along opposite sidelines at centre court and alternate dribbling to the basket and shooting a lay-up. Players rebound their own balls and dribble back to join the end of the opposite line.

Variations:

- A defender is positioned near the basket to try to disrupt the shot. Players switch positions after each shot.

- Players cut to the basket and shoot the lay-up off a pass from the opposite line. The passer rebounds the shot and passes to the opposite line.

- One player defends a two-on-one situation. The lay-up is taken if it is available; otherwise, the ball is passed to the other player for a better shot.

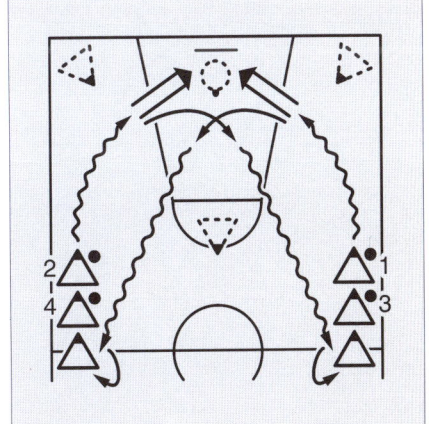

125

DRILLS

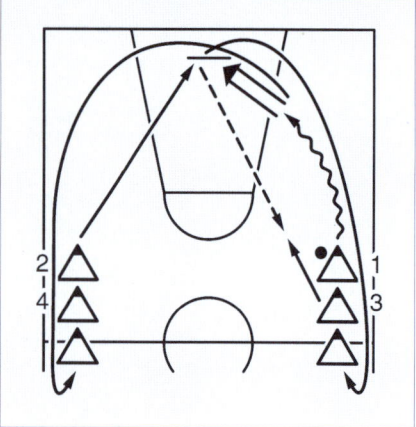

D88 Dribble, shoot, switch Players are divided into two lines and stand on opposite sidelines at centre court. Player 1 begins with the ball (in the shooting line) and dribbles to the basket from the right side for a lay-up. Player 2 in the opposite line (rebounding line) rebounds the ball and passes it to the next person in the shooting line. Shooters join the end of the rebounding line after each shot, while rebounders join the end of the shooting line after each rebound. The drill continues for a specified period of time or until every player has attempted a certain number of shots.

Variations:

- The shooting line starts on the left side to practice left-handed lay-ups.

- More than one player in the shooting line has a ball.

- Rebounders may also try to defend the shot attempt.

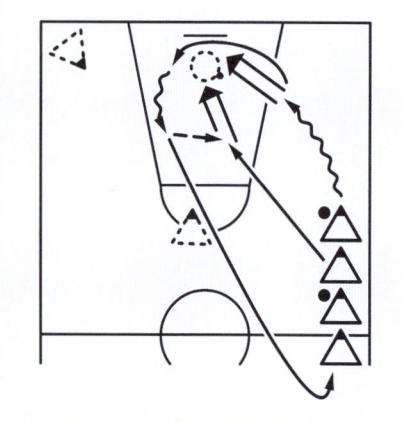

D89 Lay it up and pass it off An uneven number of players form a shooting line along one sideline at centre court. Every other player in line is given a ball. The first player in line dribbles to the basket for a lay-up, rebounds the ball, dribbles back towards the shooting line, and passes the ball off to the second player cutting to the basket for a lay-up. *Variation*: the drill can be carried out with defenders who try to prevent an easy shot at the basket.

LAY-UPS

D90 **Dribble lay-up relay** Players are divided into two equal teams and stand on opposite sidelines at opposite ends of the court. At the signal, the first player on each team dribbles to the basket at the other end of the court, shoots a lay-up, rebounds the ball, dribbles back to hand off the ball to the next player in line, and joins the end of the line. The drill continues until every player on the team has made two lay-ups.

Variations:

- Additional teams compete in several rounds and points are tallied to determine a winner.

- After shooting the lay-up, the ball is passed to the next player in line without dribbling. The pass distance can be varied (e.g., next player cuts to the basket once the shot is made).

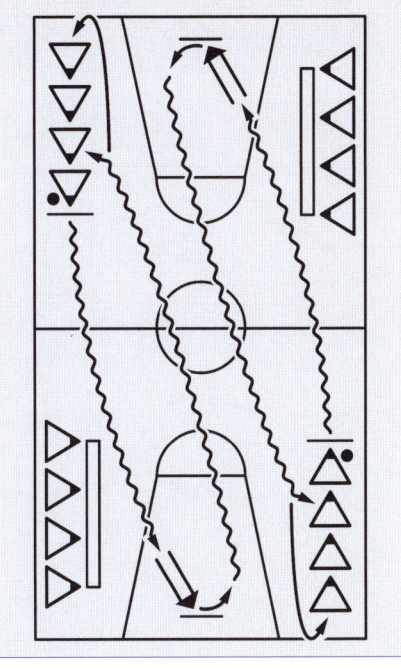

D91 **Dribble and shoot the lay-up** Using every available basket, players dribble to a basket for a lay-up and return to the shooting line for another shot. As players dribble to the basket, they must use offensive dribbling skills to avoid a collision with other players as they cross paths. This drill can be carried out as a competition among teams. The team making the most shots in the allotted time is the winner.

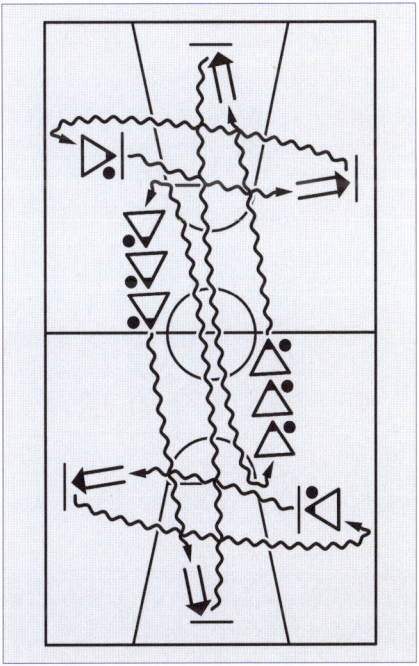

DRILLS

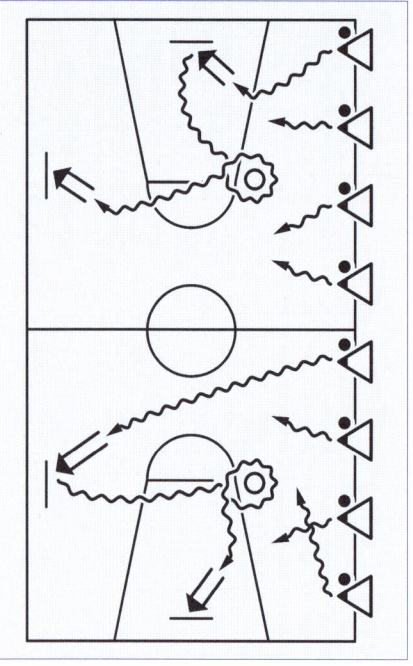

D92 Shoot around Players are divided into two groups, each occupying half of the basketball court. Every player is given a ball to dribble and shoot at every available basket on their side of the court. Players must circle around a pylon or obstacle after each lay-up, before attempting another shot at another basket. Only one shot may be attempted at each basket before moving on, so make every shot count!

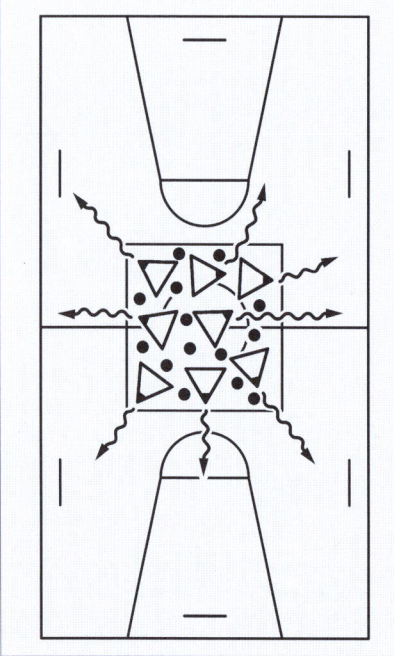

D93 Lay it up at the signal Each player is given a ball and dribbles randomly within a bounded area on the basketball court. The coach gives directions on how to dribble (e.g., right hand, left hand, standing, sitting, etc.), and at the signal of the coach, players must dribble as quickly as possible to the nearest basket to shoot a lay-up until they score. After a shot is made successfully, players dribble back into the marked area. To make the drill more competitive, the first player returning to the marked area earns three points, the second two points, and the third one point. After several rounds, a winner is determined. *Variation*: defenders may be positioned within the marked area or in a zone marked under each basket.

LAY-UPS

Lay-ups off the pass

D94 Pass for a shot, rebound, and pass Players form two lines, one along the right sideline at centre court (shooting line) and one in the middle of the key (passing line) (D94a). Note: the passing line may be set at the top of the key, in the corner, etc. Players in the passing line have a ball and pass to players in rhythm cutting to the basket from the shooting line. The player receiving the pass shoots a lay-up (without dribbling the ball), rebounds the ball, passes to the next player in the passing line, and joins the end of the passing line. The player throwing the pass then moves to join the end of the shooting line. The drill continues for a specified period of time or until every player has had a certain number of attempts at the basket.

Variations:

- The player passing the ball becomes a defender against the shooter, but the shooter is given the option of passing to a teammate if a better shot is available.

- The pass comes from the corner rather than the key area (D94b). A defender may be positioned under the basket to make the shot more difficult.

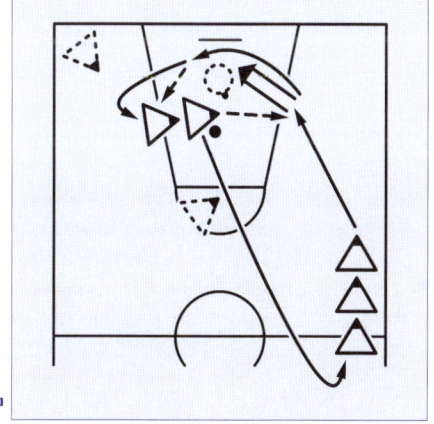
D94a

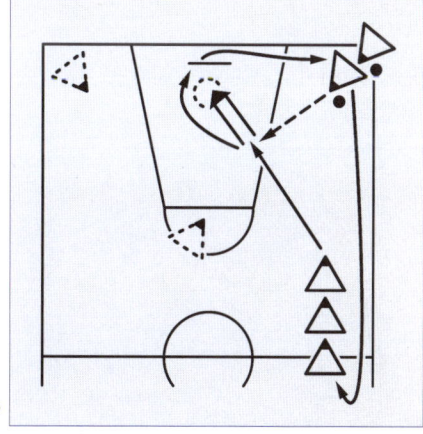
D94b

DRILLS

D95 Circular lay-ups Players form a circle at one end of the basketball court and move in a counterclockwise direction (clockwise when practicing lay-ups from the left side) around the basket. One player begins by shooting a lay-up, rebounding the ball, and passing to the next player coming around the circle, who shoots, rebounds, and so on, until every player has shot at least once. *Variations*: (a) the "circle" extends the entire length of the court with one ball at each basket; (b) the player rebounding the ball becomes a defender against the next shooter.

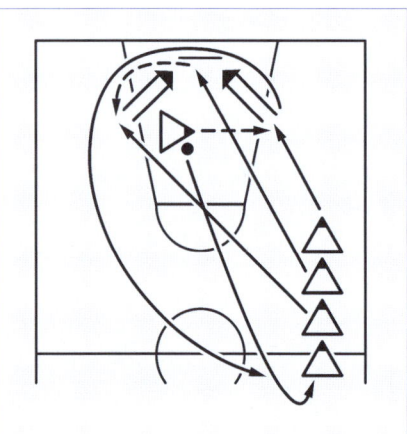

D96 Shoot, rebound, and pass Players line up along the right sideline at centre court and one player stands with a ball in the key as a passer. The first player cuts to the basket, receives a pass from the key, shoots a lay-up, and runs back to the end of the shooting line. The second player in line, who follows closely behind the first shooter, rebounds the ball and passes to the third player, who cuts to the basket behind the passer in the key for a shot at the basket from the left side. *Variations*: (a) the passing player becomes a defender after the pass; (b) the drill spans the entire length of the court.

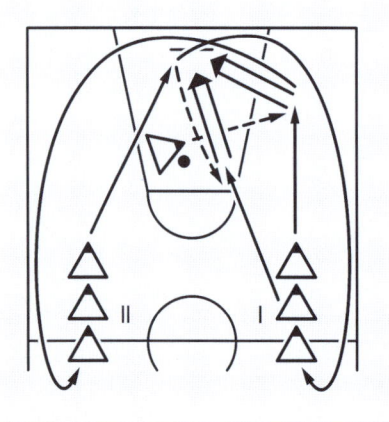

D97 Key passer Players form two lines along each sideline at centre court. Line I along the right sideline is the shooting line and line II along the left sideline is the rebounding line. One other player stands with a ball in the key as a passer. The first player in line I cuts to the basket, receives a pass from the key, shoots the lay-up, and runs to the end of line II. The first player in line II rebounds the ball and passes to the second player in line I (who has cut to the basket behind the first shooter) for another lay-up, before running to the end of line I. Players switch lines after each shot or rebound.

LAY-UPS

D98 Pass, shoot, rebound Players stand in two shooting lines along each sideline at centre court. Two other players stand with a ball in the key as passers for each line. The first player in each line cuts to the basket, receives a pass from the key, shoots a lay-up, rebounds the ball, and passes to the second player in line, who has cut to the top of the key to replace the passer. Shooters and passers move to the end of the opposite line after each round.

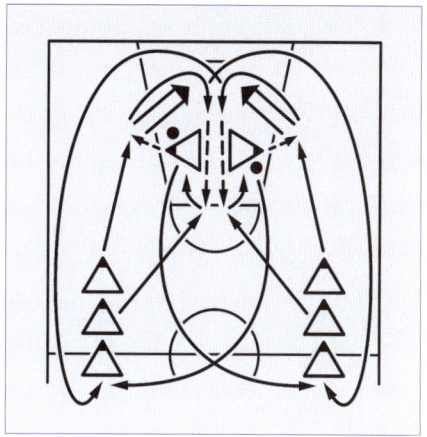

D99 Lay-up off a lead pass Players form two lines along each sideline at centre court. Line I along the right sideline is the shooting line and line II along the left sideline is the rebounding line. Player 2 in line I has a ball and throws a lead pass to player 1 as he or she cuts to the basket for a lay-up. Player 3 in line II rebounds the ball and passes to the next player in line I (player 4), who throws a lead pass for player 2, and so on. Shooters and rebounders switch lines after each shot or rebound.

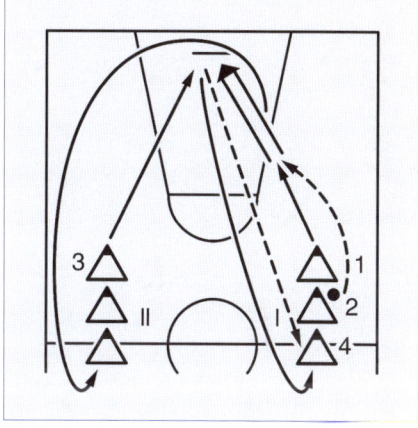

D100 Return pass for a lay-up Players form a shooting line along the middle of the court beyond the top of the key. The first player in line (1) passes the ball to the player in the corner (2) and cuts to the basket to receive a return pass for a lay-up. Player 2 rebounds the ball, passes to the next player in the shooting line, and joins the end of the shooting line, while the shooter (player 1) replaces player 2 as the passer in the corner. *Variation*: if a defender is positioned under the basket, player 2 becomes a pass option for the shooter.

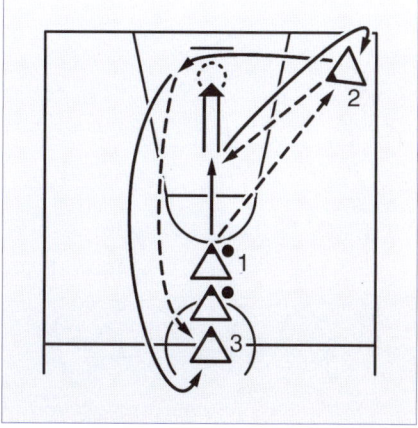

DRILLS

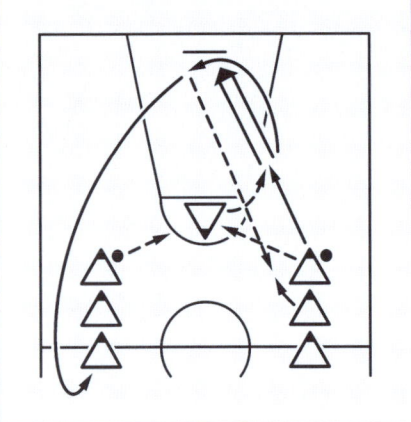

D101 Pass from the high post for a lay-up
Players stand in two shooting lines along each sideline near centre court. One other player stands in the high post (at the foul line) as a passer. The first player in the shooting line to the right passes to the player in the high post, cuts to the basket for a return pass, receives the pass, and shoots a lay-up. After rebounding the ball and passing to the next player in the same line, the shooter runs to join the end of the opposite shooting line. The drill is then repeated on the left side of the court. The passer in the high post can be exchanged at any time.

D102 Alternating shots off the pass Players stand in two lines along each sideline near centre court. The first player in line I and the second player in line II are given a ball to start. The first player in line II cuts to the basket (without the ball) and receives a pass from the first player in line I for a lay-up. The first player in line I then cuts to the basket (now without the ball) and receives a pass from the second player in line II for a lay-up. Shooters rebound their own balls, pass to the next player in the line they came from, and then join the end of the opposite line. *Variation*: a defender is positioned under the basket.

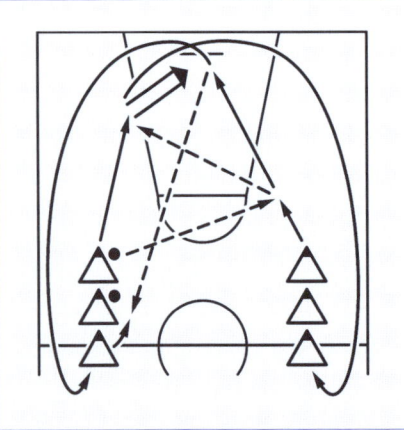

D103 Pass, pass lay-up drill Players stand in two lines along each sideline near centre court. The line along the left sideline is the shooting line and the line along the right sideline is the rebounding line. The ball starts with the first player in the shooting line, who passes ahead to the first player in the rebounding line, and cuts to the basket for a return pass and lay-up. The other player rebounds the ball and throws a pass to the next player in the shooting line. Both shooter and rebounder switch to opposite lines after each shot. *Variation*: the player from the rebounding line becomes a defender after making the pass.

LAY-UPS

D104 Into the key for a lay-up Equal players stand parallel to the baseline in two shooting lines (I and II) facing each other on opposite sides of the key. The remaining players form a passing line (III) at the top of the key perpendicular to the shooting lines. The first two players in the passing line are given a ball and alternately pass to the first player in each shooting line, who cuts into the key for the pass and a quick lay-up. The shooter rebounds the ball and passes to the next player in the passing line. After shooting or passing the ball, players move to join the end of the line they passed to.

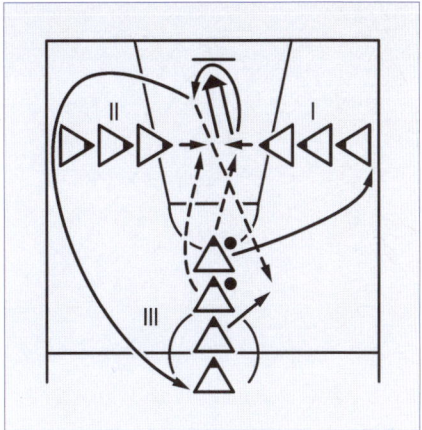

D105 Back to the basket Players form two lines, one on the left wing (passing line) and one along the right sideline (shooting line). Players in the shooting line run across the key towards the passing line to receive a pass just the outside the key with their back to the basket. After receiving the pass, players then shoot a quick lay-up or a short turn-around jump shot.

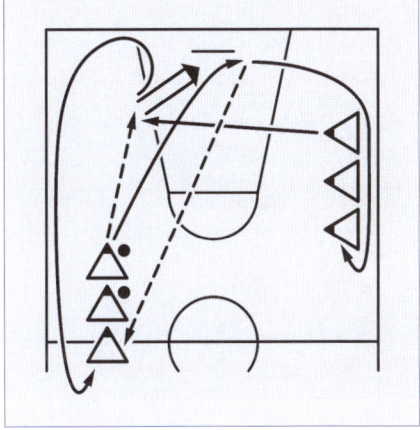

D106 Triangle pass and shoot Players are divided into two lines, one positioned in the left corner (passing line) and one diagonally opposite the passing line near half-court (shooting line). One other player stands in the circle at centre court as a passer. Player 1 begins by passing to player 2 in the centre circle, who in turn passes to the first shooter (player 3) cutting to the basket for a lay-up. Shooters rebound their own balls and pass to the last player in the passing line. All players follow their passes to join the end of the line or position they passed the ball to.

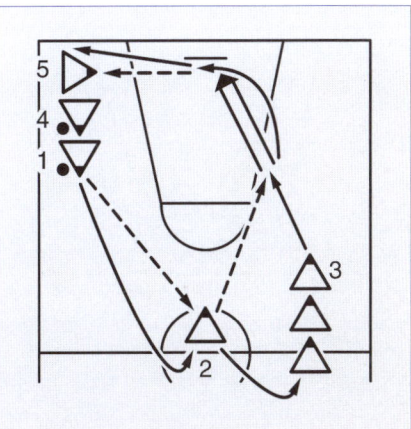

133

DRILLS

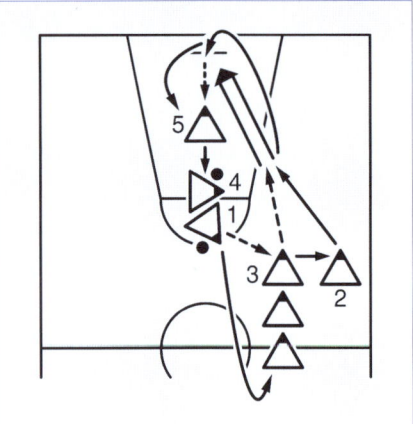

D107 Tight triangle pass and shoot Similar to the previous drill (D106) on a different area of the court, players throw two passes in a triangular pattern leading to a lay-up. Player 1 begins by passing to player 3 on the wing, who passes to the first shooter (player 2) cutting to the basket for a lay-up. The shooter rebounds the ball and passes to the last player in the passing line. All players follow their passes to join the end of the line or position they passed to. *Variation*: after making the pass to player 3, player 1 can defend player 3, making the pass to player 2 more difficult.

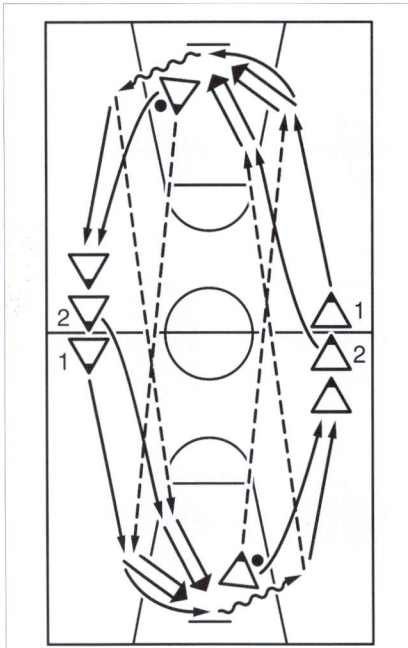

D108 Baseball pass for a lay-up Players are divided into two groups and line up on opposite sidelines at the half-court line. Two additional players stand with a ball under opposite baskets at each end of the court. Each passer throws a long lead baseball pass to the first player in each group who cuts to the basket, receives the pass, and shoots a lay-up. After rebounding the ball, the shooter dribbles the ball outside the key and becomes the passer for the next player in line on the other side of the court. After passing the ball, all players move to join the end of the line they passed to. This pattern continues for a specified period of time or until every player has attempted two shots at each basket.

LAY-UPS

D109 Throw it up and tip it in Players are each given a ball and line up in a row behind the foul line at one basket. One at a time, each player gently throws the ball up against the backboard and tries to tip in the rebound, either with one hand or two. *Variations*: (a) players form two rows on either side of the basket and take turns trying to tip the ball in the basket. After several attempts from one side, players switch sides; (b) players line up on either side of the basket. At a given signal, the coach (or another player) stands at the foul line and tosses the ball up off the backboard. The first players in each line both try to tip the ball in. The rebound is returned to the coach.

D110 Pass and tip drill Players stand in two lines on each side of the basket. Player 1 in the passing line passes a ball off the backboard to be tipped in by player 2 in the tipping line. Player 2 then rebounds the ball and passes to the next player in the passing line (player 3). Players switch lines after each tip-in attempt. *Variations*: (a) the player throwing the ball up off the backboard for the tip can become a defender against the tipper; (b) a defender stands at the foul line and may move as soon as the ball is released by the passer to challenge player 2 for the tip in.

D111 Tip-in lay-up drill Players line up in two rows on opposite sides of the basket. Player 1 begins by gently throwing the ball against the backboard from the side for player 2, who attempts to tip the ball in. Player 3 rebounds the ball and passes it to player 4, who throws the ball up against the backboard for player 5, and so on. Players switch sides after each pass or shot.

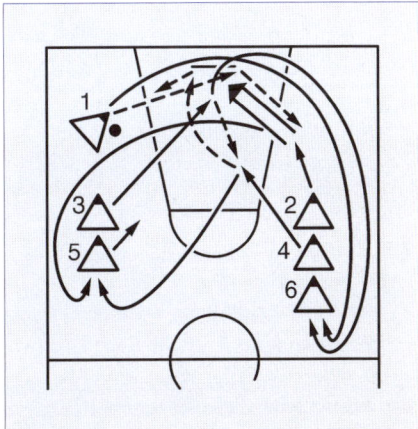

DRILLS

Mid-range shots

Mid-range shots are defined as shots taken two to six metres away from the basket. This includes free throws, jump shots, and in some cases lay-ups (from this distance often referred to as "runners").

Free throws (foul shots)

We can distinguish among three types of foul shots: two-handed shot from the chest, two-handed shot from below the waist (underhand), and the one-handed push or set shot from above the chest or head. The most common shot used today is the one-handed set shot. Depending on the practice goals, free throws can be practiced in fast succession, or in a competitive context (two shots after a foul). But these shots should also be practiced in high stress situations (under high psychological pressure, after high physical exhaustion, etc.) to mimic game-like situations.

Examples for competitive free-throw practice

- Each player tries to hit as many shots as possible. Who or which group makes the most baskets in a specified amount of time?

- Each player must score one more basket than the player before him or her. If unsuccessful, he or she earns a minus point or is out of the competition.

- Each player has to make two shots in a row. If a player is unable to sink consecutive shots, he or she is out of the competition and works on a different skill. The last player remaining is the winner.

- Only two or three shots in a row count as one point. Who or which group accumulates the highest score?

- The more shots scored in a row, the higher the points awarded (e.g., one shot made earns one point; two consecutive shots earns four points, etc.). Who or which group accumulates the highest number of points?

MID-RANGE SHOTS

D112 **Free throws in pairs** Players are divided into pairs and practice shooting free throws at one basket. One player (1) begins shooting free throws while the other player (2) rebounds and passes the ball back for the next shot. After shooting a given number of shots the two players switch positions.

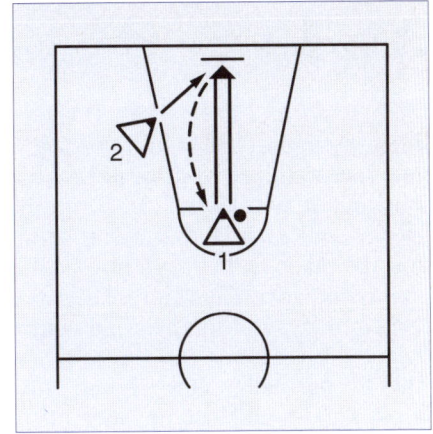

D113 **Around the key** Players line up around the key in the free-throw slots and take turns shooting free throws. After the first player shoots, the ball is rebounded and passed to the next player in line for a shot. Players rotate one position to the right (counterclockwise) after each attempted free throw. *Variations*: (a) players shoot a specific number of shots (e.g., five) before rotating positions; (b) practice challenging for the rebound as well. The player rebounding the ball is awarded the next shot. If a shot is made, the player shoots again (no more than three consecutive shots).

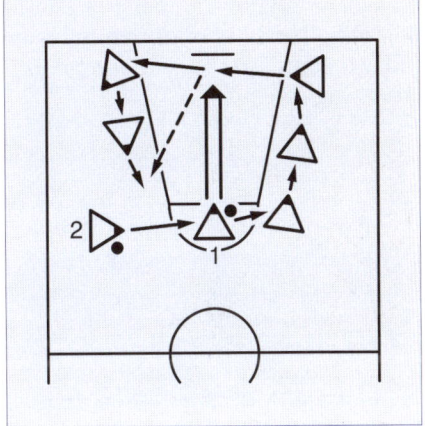

D114 **Rebound the missed free throw** Players form groups of two or more. One group starts with a ball at the free-throw line and shoots at the basket. The remaining players line up around the key ready to rebound any missed shots. Players successfully rebounding a missed shot become the next shooters. The team accumulating the most points in a given time is the winner. (See rebounding section, pp. 194-195)

DRILLS

Jump shots

Since being introduced into basketball, the one-handed jump shot has become the dominant shot utilized by players in the game. The jump in a jump shot is performed by pushing off with both legs. Jump shots can be taken from varying distances on the court (from close range to perimeter shots five or more metres away from the basket), and may be taken from a standing (stationary) position, off a pass reception, or following a dribbling move. Therefore, keep in mind that the shooting exercises to follow can be varied by incorporating these elements into the various drills.

Ideally, perimeter shots should only be used in a game when the player has an open look. This should also be taken into account when performing the various drills—shoot only when you are open and balanced.

Jump shots should be practiced from several positions on the floor—initially close to the basket, and later on further from the basket—with and without defenders on the shooter. The level of difficulty should increase as players become better and more technically sound. It is also possible to practice (offensive and defensive) rebounding during shooting drills.

Examples for competitive shooting practice

- *Kick out*: players are divided into pairs and each given a ball. Shooting one at a time, each player has two attempts to try to score a basket from each position on the court (five to seven designated spots). Both players begin at the same position and if a player misses both shots attempted, he or she must wait for his or her turn to come up again. When a player scores from a spot already occupied by another player that person gets "kicked out" of the spot and returns to the first shooting spot. The winner is the first player to make a basket at all the positions on the floor.

- Played as a one-on-one or team competition, a made jump shot counts as two points and a rebound (ball cannot touch the ground) counts as one point. If the ball is slam dunked into the basket, that also counts as two points. This competition between shooter and rebounder is over when an individual (or team) reaches a specified number of points.

MID-RANGE SHOTS

D115 **Pair spot shooting** Players are divided into pairs and work on shooting from various positions on the floor. One player begins as the shooter and the other as the rebounder. After each shot, the ball is rebounded and passed back to the shooter for the next shot in rhythm. After a specific number of shots have been attempted (or made), players switch roles—shooter becomes rebounder, rebounder becomes shooter. Several pairs can practice at the same basket. *Variation*: after passing to the shooter, the passer can passively defend the shot.

D116 **Individual work** Each player shoots, follows his or her shot, rebounds the ball, dribbles back to another spot, and shoots again. Try several positions.

D117 **Jump shots in a row** Players line up in rows (no more than three players per row) around a basket each with a ball. Several rows can play at one basket at the same time. Similar to the drill above (D116), players shoot, follow, and rebound their own shots. After rebounding the ball, players pass to the next player in line, and so on. *Variation*: after taking a shot, players become passive defenders against the next shooter.

D118 **Three-person pass and shoot** Players arrange themselves in a triangular formation and execute a three-way passing play, with a shot in between. Player 1 under the basket passes the ball to player 2 on one wing, who passes to player 3 on the other wing for a shot. Player 3 follows his or her shot to rebound the ball and passes back to player 1, who has run around to take the position previously occupied by player 3. The ball is then returned to the starting point and the drill is repeated on the other side of the court. After each pass, players move in the opposite direction of the pass.

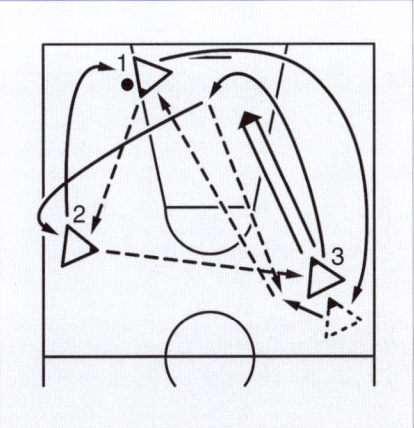

DRILLS

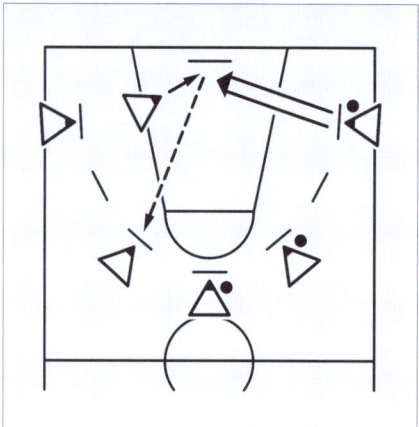

D119 One after the other Players stand at designated spots on the floor along a semi-circle around the basket. Half or more of the players are given a ball to start and one player begins as a rebounder. The first player shoots the ball, which is rebounded by the rebounder and passed to another shooter on the semi-circle. The shooter then becomes the rebounder for the next shot and the rebounder moves to an empty spot on the semi-circle. The drill continues until each player has attempted at least five shots.

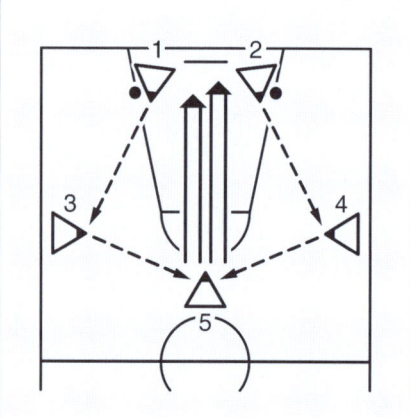

D120 Groups of five Five players arrange themselves on the court as shown. Two players stand with a ball under the basket on each side of the key (players 1 and 2), two players stand on each wing (players 3 and 4), and one player plays the point at the top of the key (player 5). Each ball is swung around to the point (one at a time) for a shot from the top of the key. Players 1 and 2 rebound the ball after each shot and repeat the drill until player 5 has made at least five baskets. Players then rotate positions until every player has had an opportunity to be the shooter.

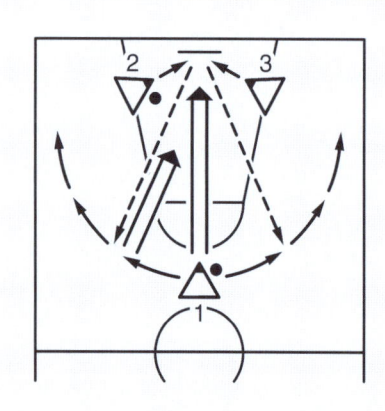

D121 Groups of three Players arrange themselves in a triangular formation, with two players under the basket (2 and 3) and one player at the top of the key (1). Player 1 begins as the shooter and moves along a semi-circle around the basket (first to the left, then to the right), taking several shots from various spots on the floor. After each shot is taken, players 2 and 3 rebound the ball and pass back to player 1 for another shot. Player 1 continues shooting until he or she has made at least five baskets. Players then switch roles and the drill is repeated.

MID-RANGE SHOTS

D122 Switch shooters Players stand in a triangular formation at one end of the basketball court. Player 1 is given a ball and begins by shooting from the wing. Player 2 moves from the top of the key to rebound the ball, passes out to player 3 on the opposite wing for a shot, and replaces player 1 on the wing. Player 1 (who has moved to the position previously occupied by player 2 at the top of the key) rebounds the shot taken by player 3, and so on, until every player has attempted a certain number of shots.

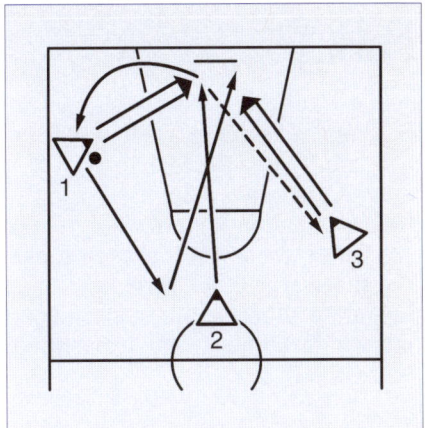

D123 Two passes and a shot Players stand in a triangular formation at one end of the basketball court, with one player under the basket (1) and one player on each wing (2 and 3). Player 1 begins by passing to player 2 on one wing and runs out at player 3 with his or her hands up. After receiving a pass from player 2, player 3 attempts a shot from the wing and follows his or her shot to rebound the ball. Player 3 then passes back out to player 1 (now in the position previously occupied by player 3), who quickly passes across to player 2 for a shot, as player 3 runs at him or her with his or her hands up, and so on.

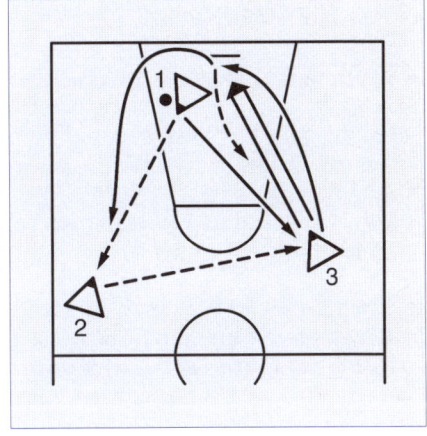

D124 Spot shooting Ten shooting positions are marked on the floor as shown. Players move from one position to the next, practicing shooting from various areas on the court. This drill can be performed either in pairs (with passing) or individually (dribbling), with up to four players shooting at one basket at a time. Positions 1, 3, 5, 7, and 9 focus on perimeter or 3-point shooting, positions 2, 4, 6, and 8 focus on mid-range jump shooting, while position 10 focuses on free-throw shooting. Players may shoot one or more shots randomly at each position or make it a competition.

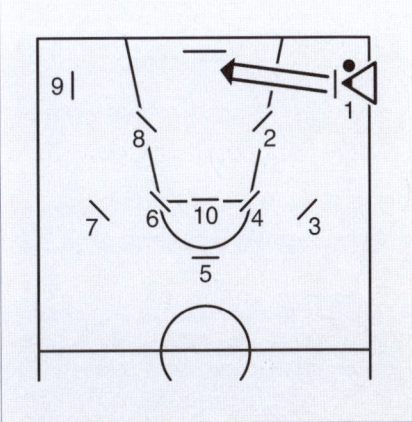

DRILLS

Faking

Faking is a useful individual tactical skill that may be used to gain an advantage over the defense. To be effective, the transition from fake to intended action must be smooth and quick; otherwise, a defender can usually distinguish between a deceptive movement (fake) and an intended action.

There are several fakes in basketball that can be used in different situations, which are summarized in **Chart 15**. Some of them again have several possibilities (e.g., passing fakes, shooting fakes, etc.). Some examples are given in the following section. A summary of how players can learn and practice defending against the fake is also provided (**Chart 16**).

Tips for faking

- When practicing faking, be sure to practice both to the left and to the right.

- Faking should be learned and perfected, but then only applied when necessary during a game situation.

- Players should have a variety of fakes in their repertoire and should be able to utilize them at various times so defending players cannot get used to a certain pattern.

- Practice faking first with a passive defender to learn the faking movements properly. Later, practice with a fully active defender to simulate game situations and choose the right fake for the given situation.

Tips for defending against the fake

- Try to anticipate the actions of the offensive player by observing details very closely (body position, where he or she is looking, leg position, etc).

- A fake can be made less effective when the defender backs off or tries to knock the ball away during the fake attempt. Stay active and don't get caught flat-footed.

- Fake when you are on defense also—this keeps the offensive player off balance.

- Do not react too quickly to movements of the offensive player.

FAKING

Chart 15

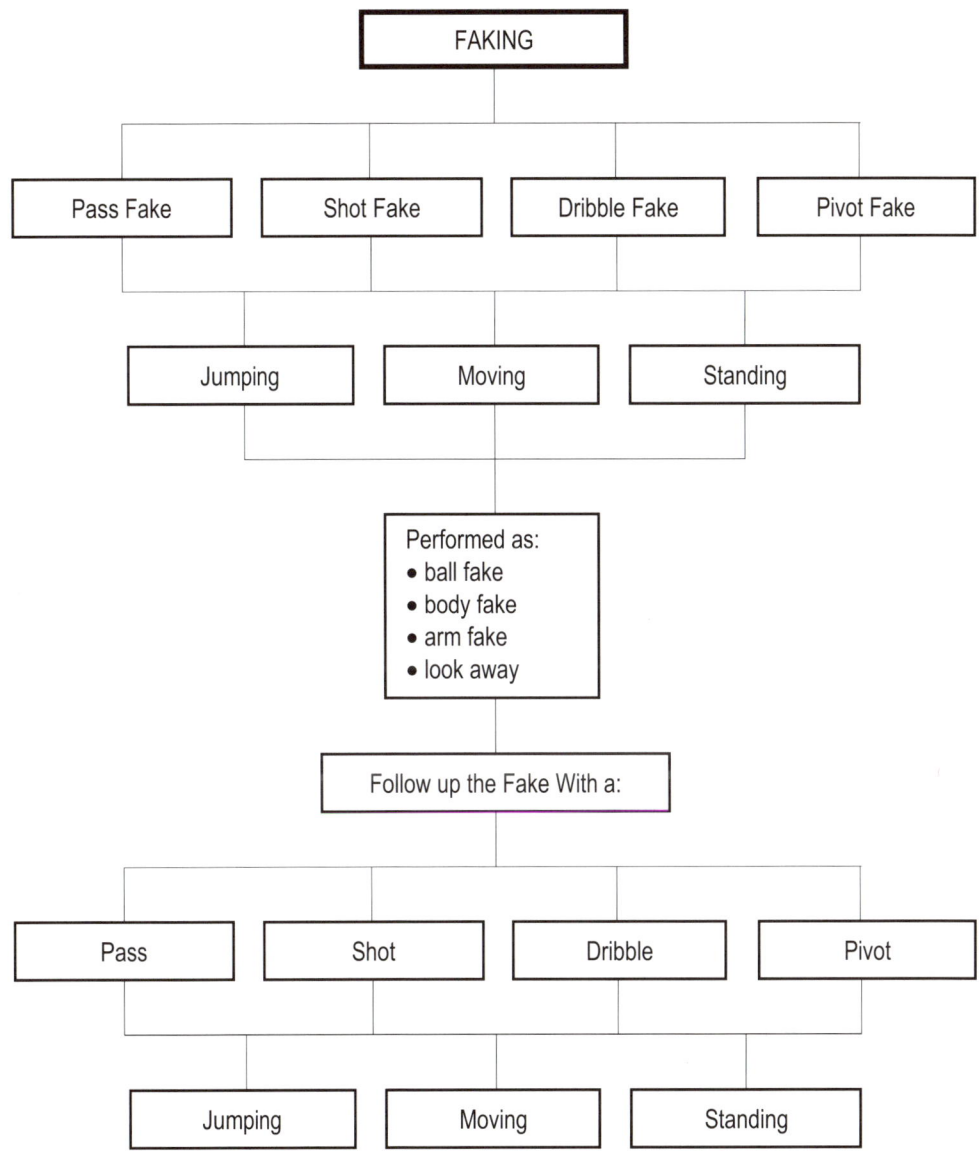

143

DRILLS

Chart 16

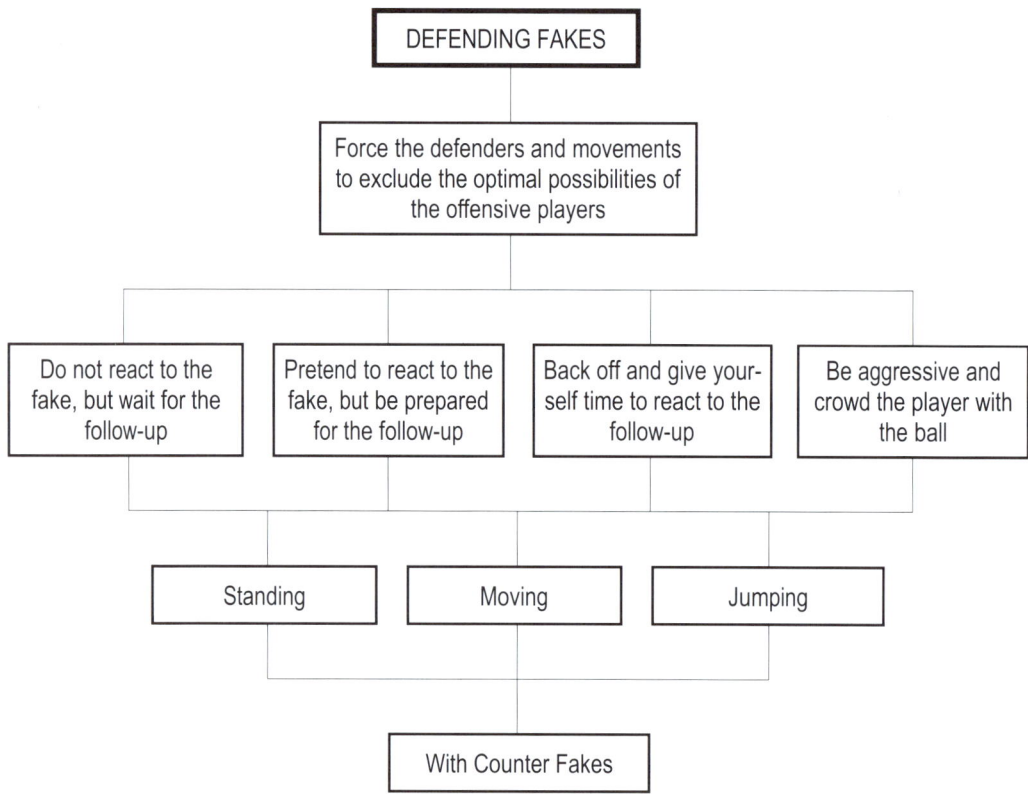

Apart from a few typical situations that can be practiced, learning to fake well requires experience and knowledge of how and when to utilize fakes. The most important factor to consider when faking is to make them realistic. You want the defender to believe you are going to do what you are faking to do. In other words, a fake should approximate the actual movement (speed, positioning, and direction) as closely as possible. The faking drills presented here offer a few suggestions for coaches and players, but may also be utilized to develop general player skills. In the following examples, the *fake movement* is the skill you use to try to get the defender to react, while the *follow-up movement* is the actual skill you perform after the fake.

FAKING

Faking a pass

Fake movement: Pass • Pass in one direction • Direct pass	Follow-up movement: Pass • Pass in the other direction (D125) • Bounce pass (D125)
Fake movement: Pass • Bounce pass • Pass • Pass after two steps	Follow-up movement: Shot • Perimeter shot (D126a) • Jump shot (D126a) • Lay-up (D126b)
Fake movement: Pass • Pass to one side • Pass over the head	Follow-up movement: Dribble • Dribble around opponent (D127) • Dribble around opponent

D125

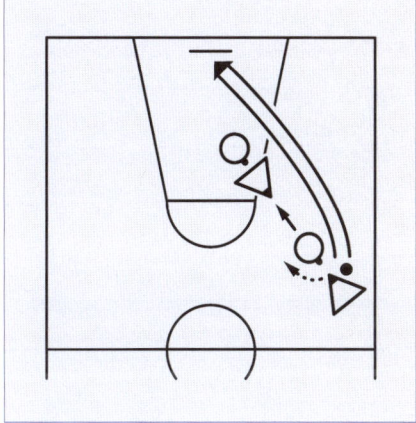

D126a

D126b

D127

DRILLS

Faking a shot

Fake movement: Shot	Follow-up movement: Pass
• Perimeter shot • Jump shot • Lay-up	• Pass to centre (D128a) • Pass (D128a) • Pass backwards (D128b)
Fake movement: Shot • Jump shot • One-handed overhead shot	**Follow-up movement: Shot** • Delayed jump shot • Underhand shot
Fake movement: Shot • Perimeter shot • Jump shot	**Follow-up movement: Dribble** • Dribble around opponent • Dribble around opponent

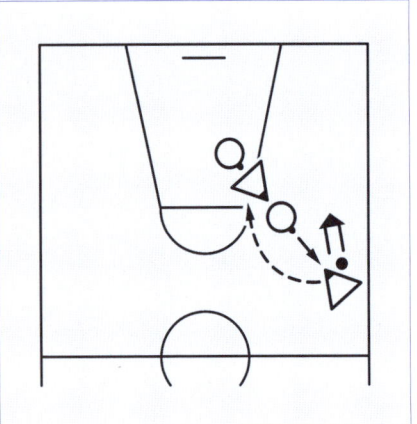

D128a

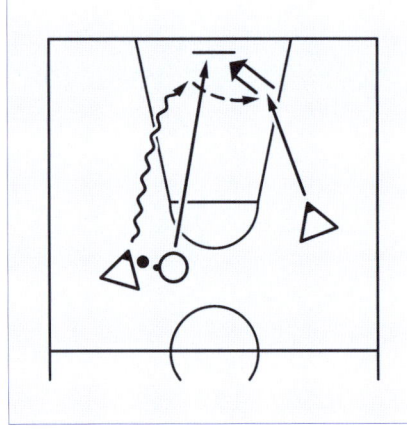

D128b

FAKING

Faking a pivot or dribble

Fake movement: Pivot/Dribble	Follow-up movement: Pass
• Pivot sideways forward • Dribbling	• Draw back and pass • Stop and pass (D129)
Fake movement: Pivot/Dribble • Pivot sideways forward • Back to basket—pivot to side • Dribbling	**Follow-up movement: Shot** • Delayed jump shot • Move back and turn to basket, jump shot • Stop—shot
Fake movement: Pivot/Dribble • Pivot sideways forward • Slow dribbling • Dribbling • Dribbling • Fast dribbling	**Follow-up movement: Dribble** • Break through other side • Fast dribbling past opponent • Switch hands behind or in front of the body and dribble past opponent • Stop—dribble past opponent • Stop to rub off opponent, then dribble

D129

147

DRILLS

Combination Drills

Combination drills include several technical and tactical components, incorporating elements of both offense and defense. The drills presented here (D130 to D159) represent just a small collection of exercises and should serve only as an inspiration for coaches and players. The drills can be varied (type of shot, pass, shot distance, dribble, and shot direction, with and without defense, etc.) or new ones may be created. These drills can also be run as small competitions to motivate the players. Since the exercises are adequately explained by the diagrams, and these are intended mainly to inspire, descriptions are not provided in this section.

Tips for combination drills

- Performing these drills without a defense serves to improve the performance of the players, especially with technical movements.

- Combination drills performed with a defense serve to practice and train individual tactics, i.e., getting open with (dribbling) or without the ball, passing and shooting against active defenders using various fakes, etc.

- Combination drills with active defenders should allow attacking players to use alternatives to proposed actions, depending on what the defense gives them.

- The status of the defense should be set before the drill begins (i.e., passive, semi-passive, active, etc.) to ensure everything runs smoothly. When using an active defense, be sure to practice defensive skills as well.

- To ensure peak efficiency, make sure players have ample time to relax and recover between drills.

COMBINATION DRILLS

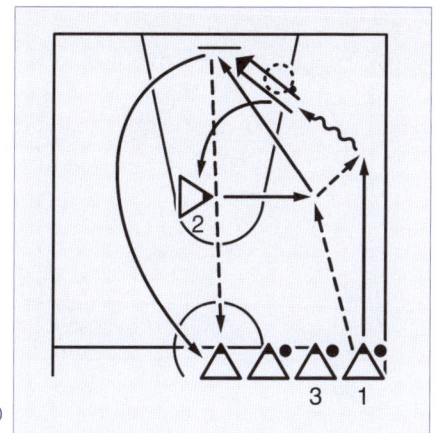
D130

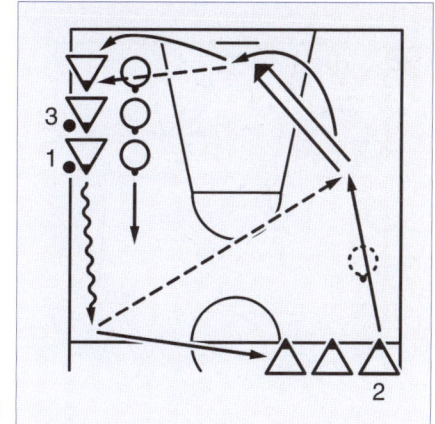
D131

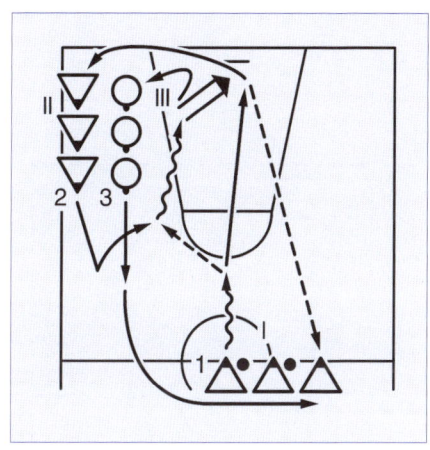
D132

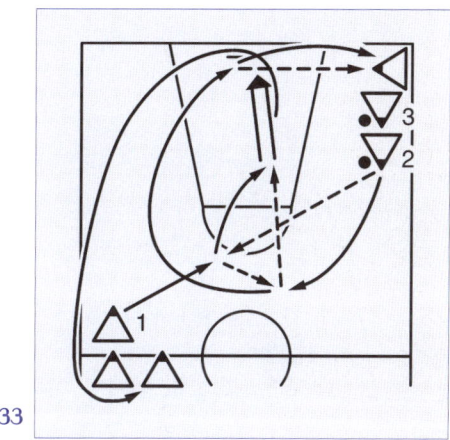
D133

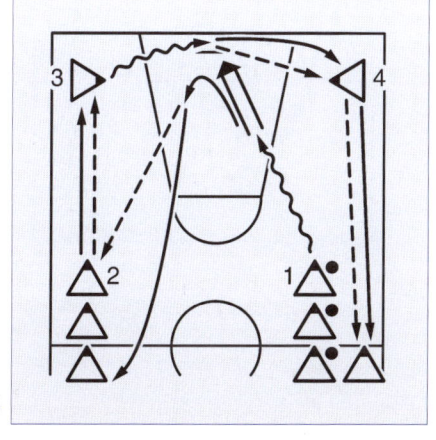
D134

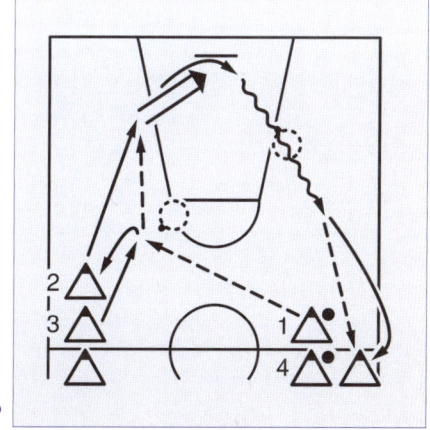
D135

149

DRILLS

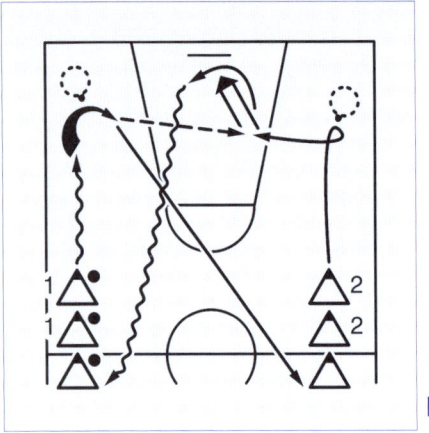
D136

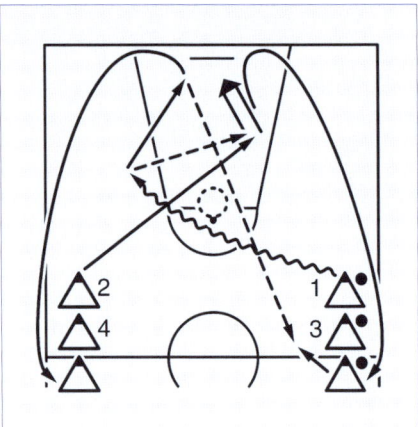
D137

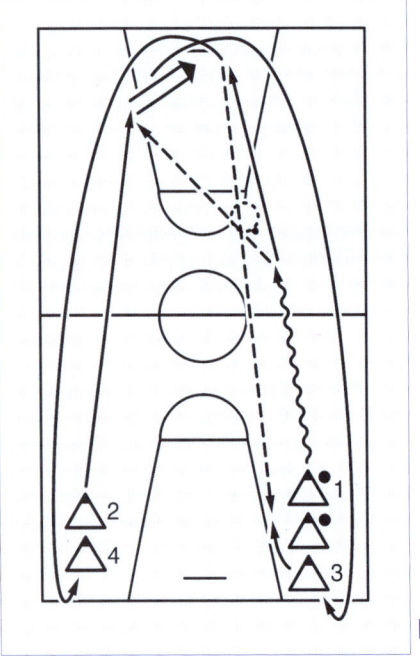
D138

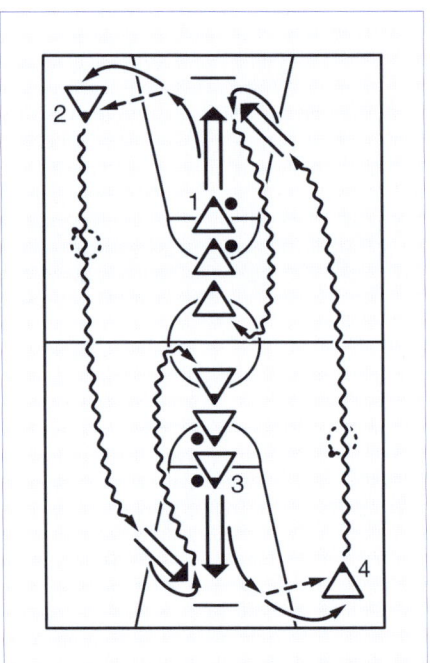
D139

COMBINATION DRILLS

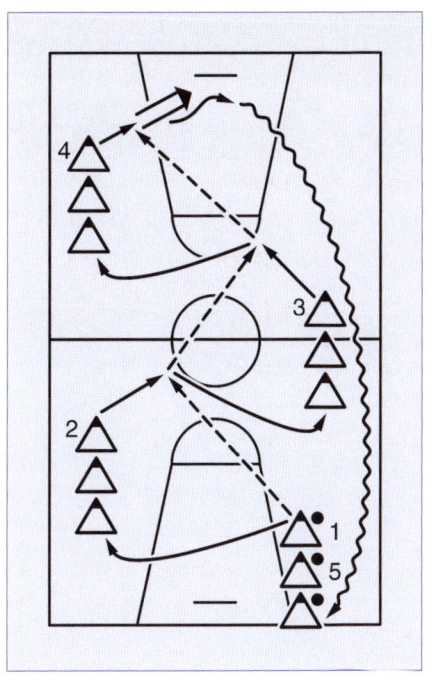

D140

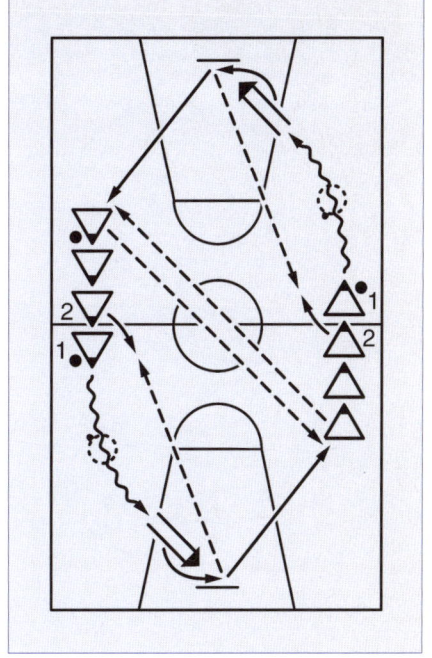

D141

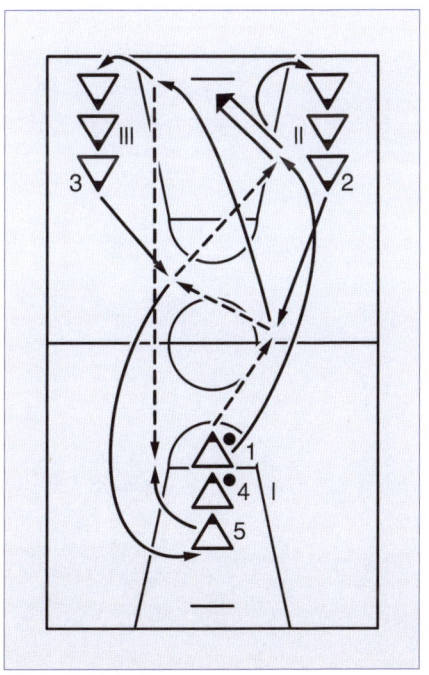

D142

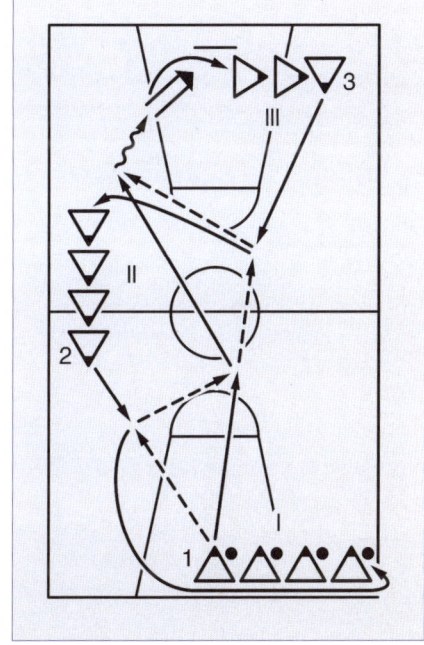

D143

DRILLS

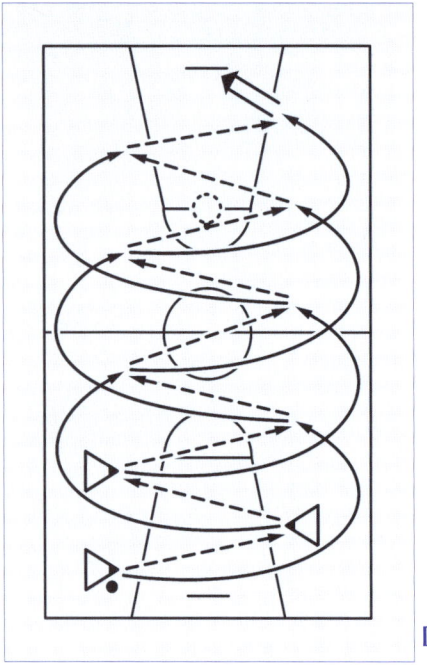

D144

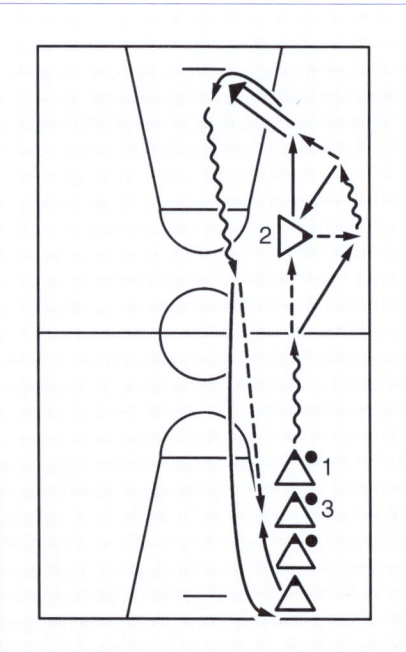

D145

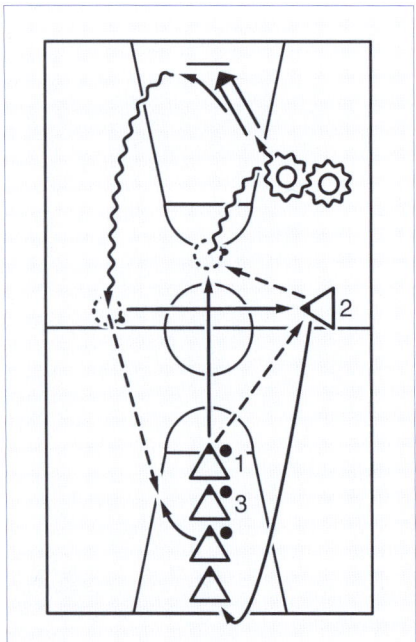

D146

D147

COMBINATION DRILLS

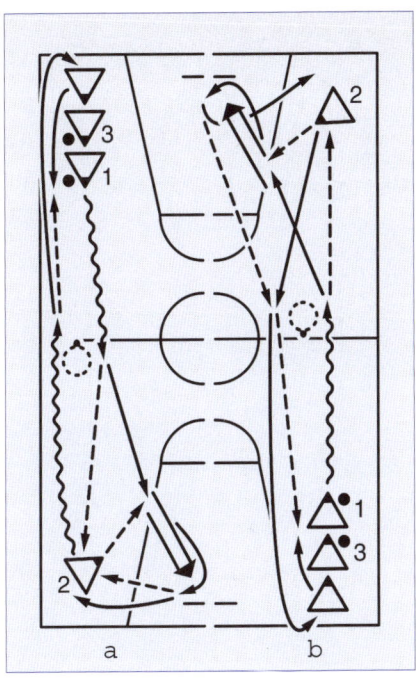

D148 a b

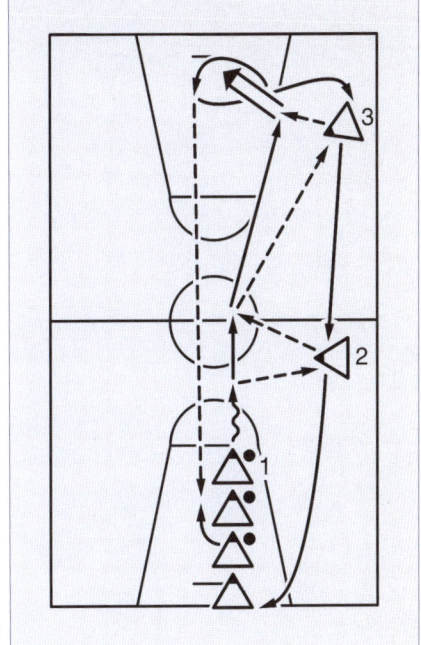

D149

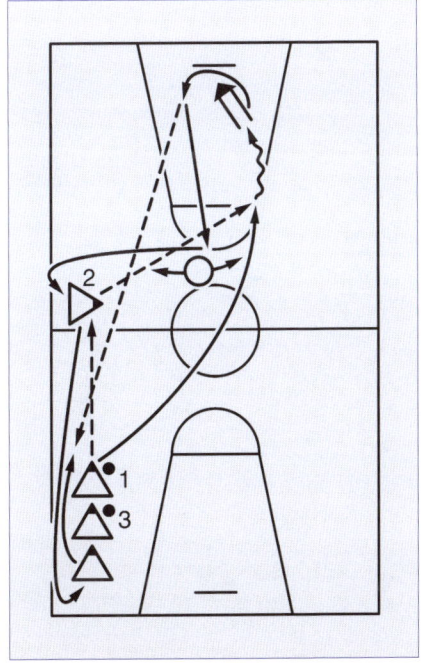

D150

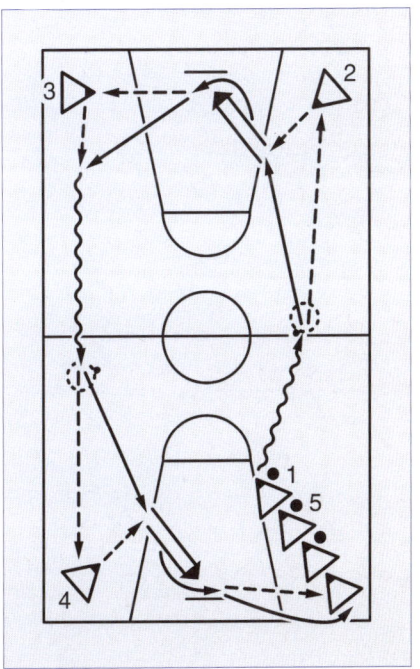

D151

153

DRILLS

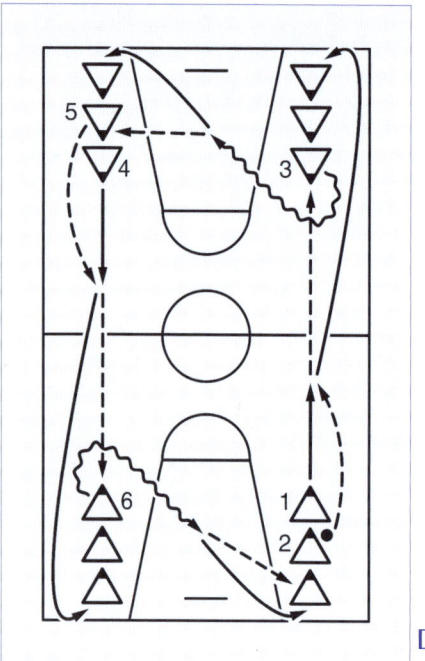
D152

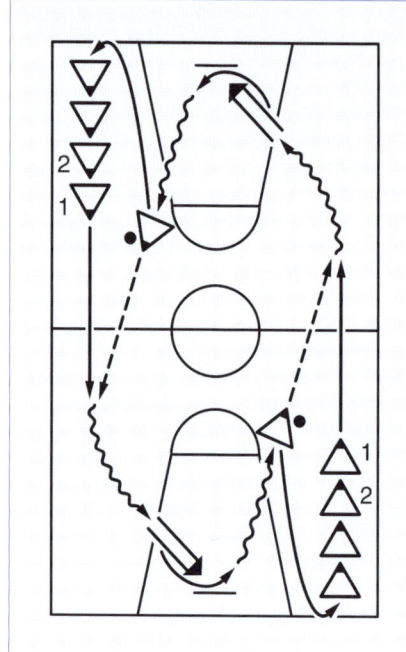
D153

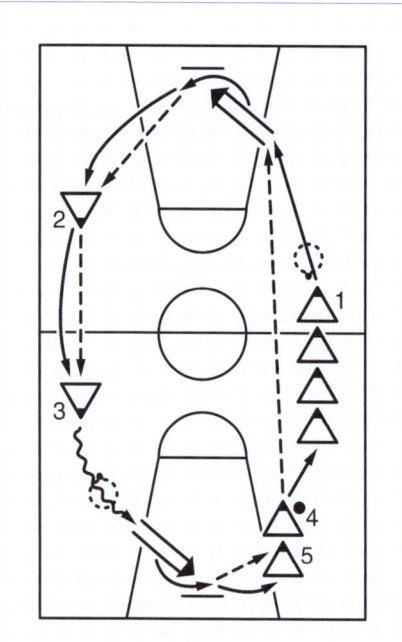
D154

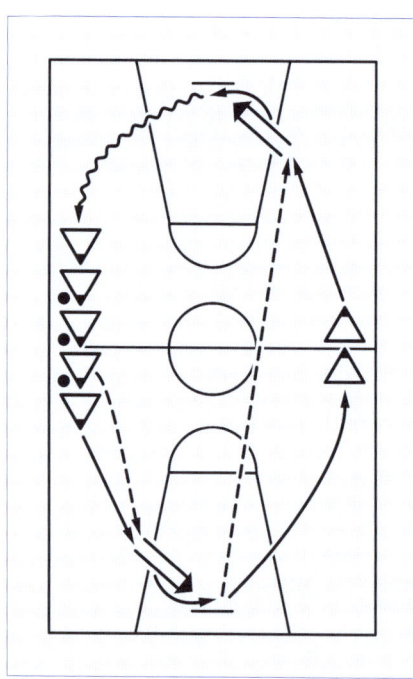
D155

COMBINATION DRILLS

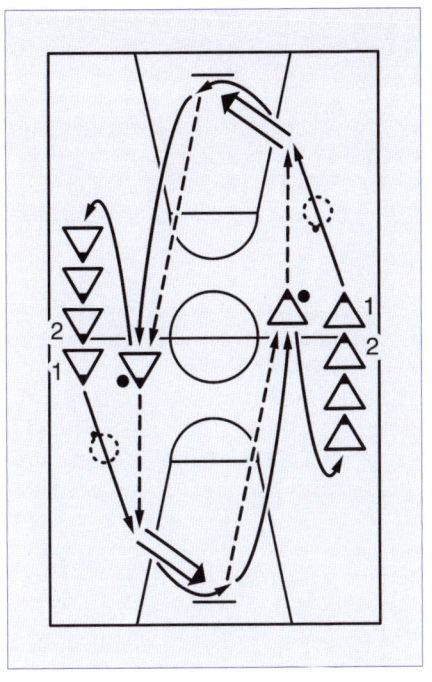
D156

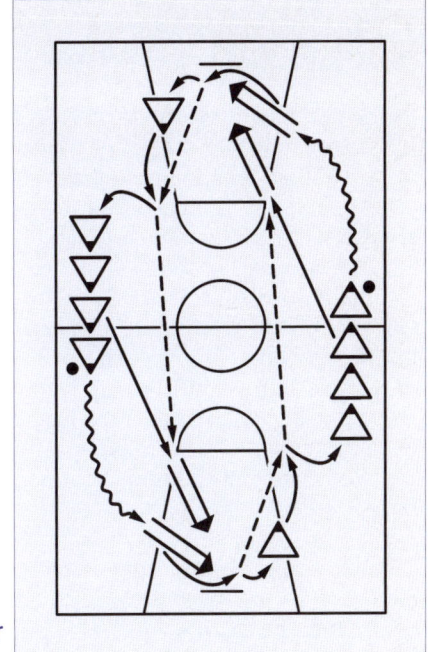
D157

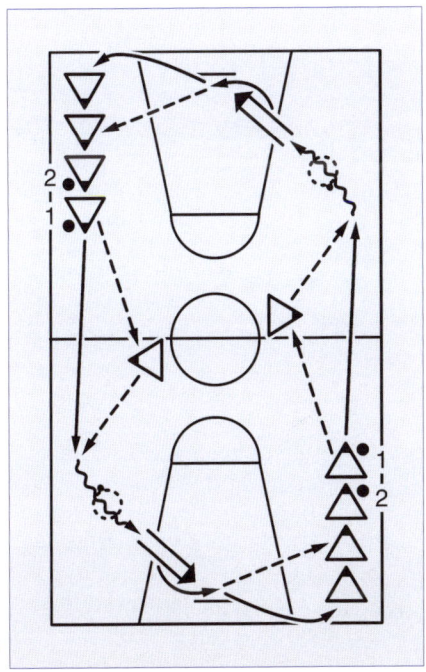
D158

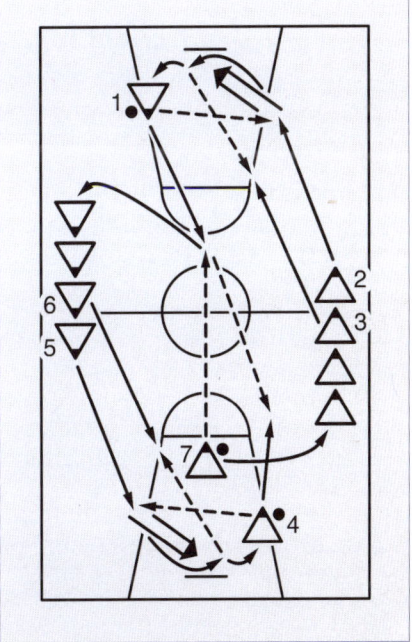
D159

155

DRILLS

Odd-person advantage situations

In the game of basketball, creating odd-person advantage situations (where offensive players outnumber defensive players by one or more players) often leads to easy scoring opportunities for the offence. Beating the defence down the court with quick transition offence and fast breaks offers the best opportunity to take advantage of odd-person situations when executed effectively.

In a half-court set offensive situation, an odd-person situation can be created by using various offensive tactics (e.g., passing the ball quickly to an open teammate, utilizing fakes, screening, etc.) to generate good scoring opportunities. Players must learn to quickly recognize odd-person advantage situations when they arise and take advantage when good scoring opportunities present themselves. These offensive sets must be practiced systematically to be effective, first mastering the correct techniques in a controlled practice environment and then increasing the pace until players are practicing at game speed.

The higher percentage shots created by odd-person advantage situations for the offence dictates that defensive strategies must also be practiced to prevent these situations from occurring. If a team wants to become effective at stopping odd-person advantage situations, defensive players need to practice the same drills with emphasis on defending against the advantage situation (see **Charts 17 and 18**).

Tips for executing odd-person advantage situations

- Players must be very conscious of floor spacing. The space between players should be enough to prevent one defender from playing two offensive players.

- Players attacking or driving the middle should hold on to the ball as long as possible to draw the defense (until the defense has committed), unless a better shot is available or a teammate is in a better scoring position.

- If a defender does not challenge the dribbler in the lane, he or she should attempt a shot him- or herself. If the attacking player is challenged by the defense, a pass to an open teammate is the most effective strategy. Always be ready for the pass.

- Do not run towards the attacking player with the ball to receive a pass. This makes it easier for the defense to defend the attack.

- Do not pick up the dribble too early without a good pass or shot opportunity. This effectively negates the attack and presents fewer scoring opportunities.

ODD-PERSON SITUATIONS

Chart 17

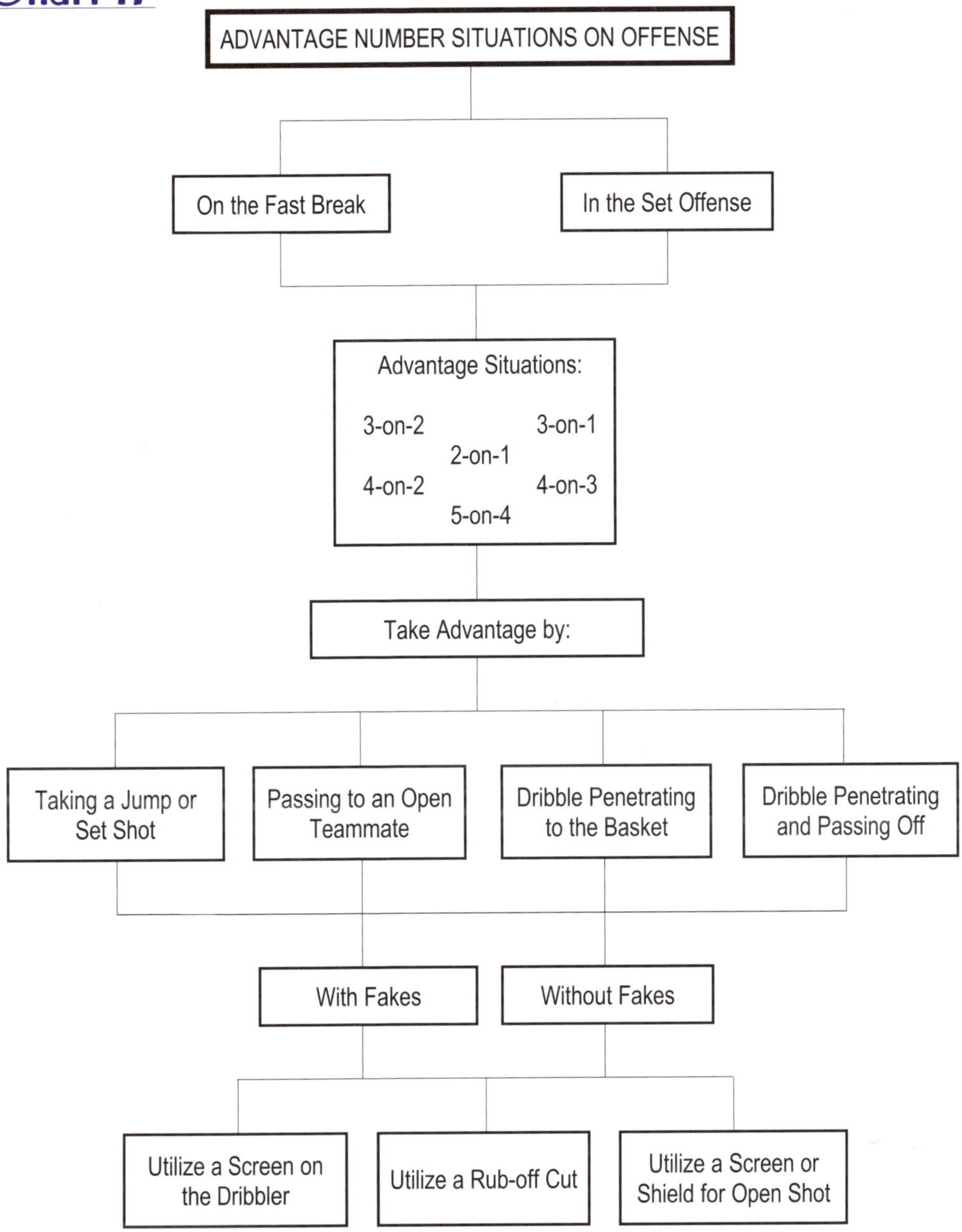

ADVANTAGE NUMBER SITUATIONS ON OFFENSE

- On the Fast Break
- In the Set Offense

Advantage Situations:

- 3-on-2
- 3-on-1
- 2-on-1
- 4-on-2
- 4-on-3
- 5-on-4

Take Advantage by:

- Taking a Jump or Set Shot
- Passing to an Open Teammate
- Dribble Penetrating to the Basket
- Dribble Penetrating and Passing Off

- With Fakes
- Without Fakes

- Utilize a Screen on the Dribbler
- Utilize a Rub-off Cut
- Utilize a Screen or Shield for Open Shot

DRILLS

Chart 18

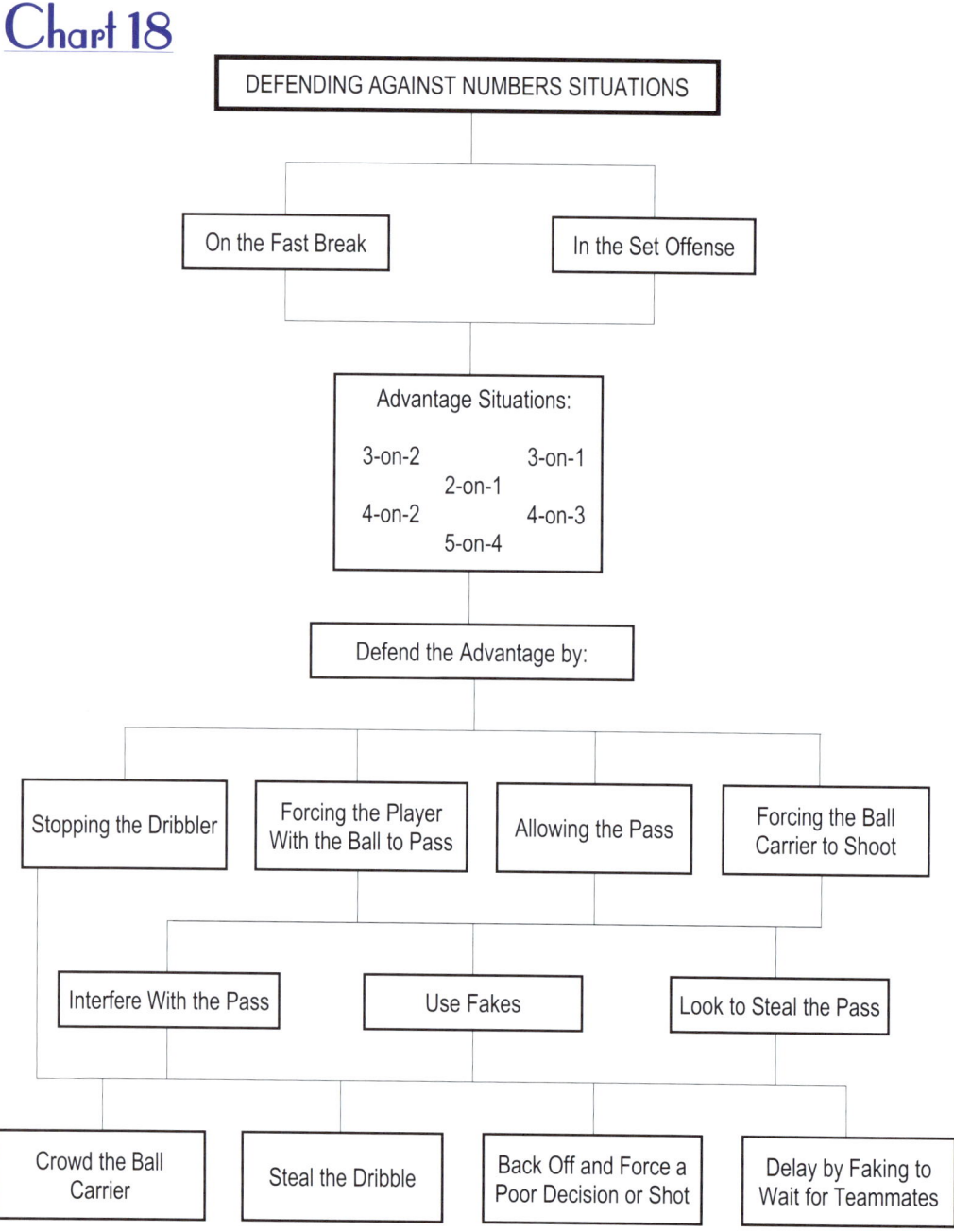

158

ODD-PERSON SITUATIONS

Tips for defending against odd-person advantage situations

- Try to stall or delay the offensive attack to allow defensive teammates to recover and help.

- The offensive team can be induced into making errors (forced passes, traveling violations, rushed shots, etc.) through skilful position play or effective faking.

- The attacking player with the ball is always the most dangerous player. Stopping the ball and denying a free path to the basket is important to defending against numbers.

- Always be aware of potential passing lanes and pass options when defending the player with the ball. This is sometimes the best opportunity to prevent the offensive team from scoring.

- When facing an odd-person advantage, concentrate on the best tactical methods for defending these situations and attempt to utilize this knowledge.

- Observe the offensive players very closely and try to recognize their intentions early.

Two-on-one situations

D160a **Simple two-on-one** The player with the ball dribbles towards the basket, and when the defender makes an attempt to stop the ball, the ball is passed to a teammate for a lay-up. If the defender does not challenge the dribbler, the ball should be taken all the way to the basket for a lay-up.

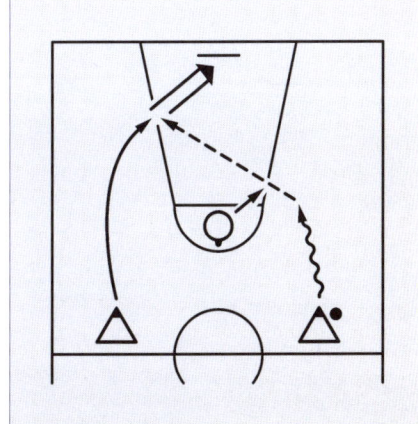

DRILLS

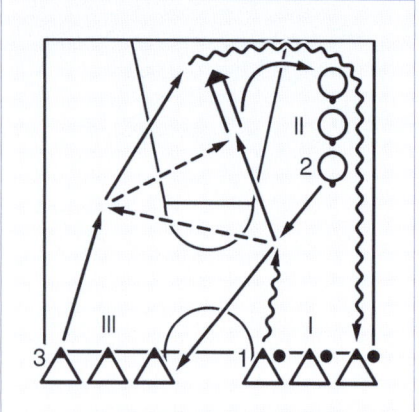

D160b Three groups Players are divided into three groups, two offensive (I and III at centre court) and one defensive (II in the corner). The ball always starts with group I. Player 1 begins by dribbling towards the basket and is met by player 2 on defense. Player 1 then passes to player 3 on the opposite wing, continues towards the basket, and receives a return pass for a lay-up. Player 3 rebounds the ball and dribbles to join the end of group I, the shooter (player 1) joins the end of group II, and the first defender (player 2) joins the end of group III.

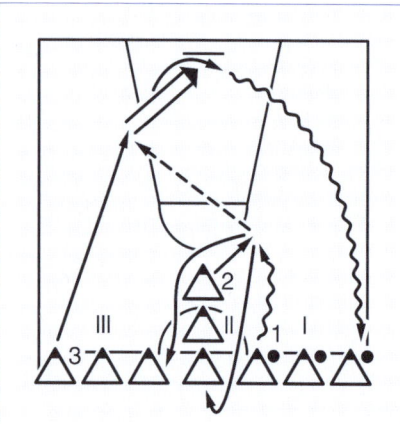

D160c T-line two-on-one Players are divided into three groups and stand along the centre court line in a "T" formation. The ball always starts with the first player in group I. Player 1 begins dribbling towards the basket and is met by player 2 from group II, who forces a pass to player 3 on the opposite wing cutting to the basket for a lay-up. Player 3 rebounds his or her own shot and dribbles to join the end of group I, player 1 joins group II, and player 2 joins group III. Players rotate after each series, group I to group II, group II to group III, and group III to group I.

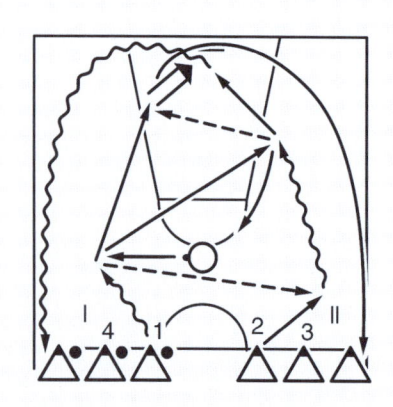

D160d Back and forth for a lay-up Players are divided into two groups and line up along opposite sidelines at centre court. One other player stands at the top of the key as a defender. Player 1 begins by dribbling towards the basket, until met by the defender, and passes to player 2 on the opposite wing. Player 2 then also begins dribbling towards the basket, until cut off by the defender, and passes the ball back to a cutting player 1 for a lay-up. Player 2 rebounds the ball and dribbles to join the end of group I, while player 1 joins the end of group II. The defender can be exchanged at any time.

ODD-PERSON SITUATIONS

D160e **Two-on-one break** Offensive players line up in a corner at one end of the basketball court, facing the offensive basket at the opposite end of the court. Another offensive player stands at the centre court line on the same sideline as the offensive line. A defensive player stands at the top of the key guarding the basket. The first player in line (1) begins by passing the ball to player 2 at half-court and runs ahead to create a two-on-one situation against the lone defender. When the defender has committed to the ball, player 2 passes back to player 1, who dribbles to the basket for a lay-up. After each shot is taken, the shooter becomes the defender, the defender replaces the offensive player at half-court, and the offensive player at half-court rebounds the ball, passes to the next player in the offensive line, and joins the end of the same line.

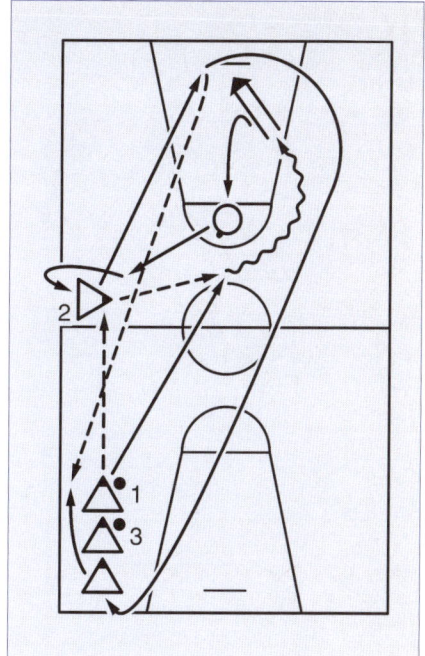

Three-on-one situations

D161a **Simple three-on-one** Offensive players line up in three rows along the half-court line and a single defender stands at the foul line guarding the basket. Player 1 in the middle row is given a ball and begins dribbling towards the basket. Players 2 and 3 mirror player 1, staying wide to keep passing lanes open. When the defensive player commits to the ball, or to one side, player 1 passes to the appropriate wing player for a lay-up. The ball is rebounded by the shooter and passed back to the next player in the middle row for the next round. The defender can be exchanged at any time.

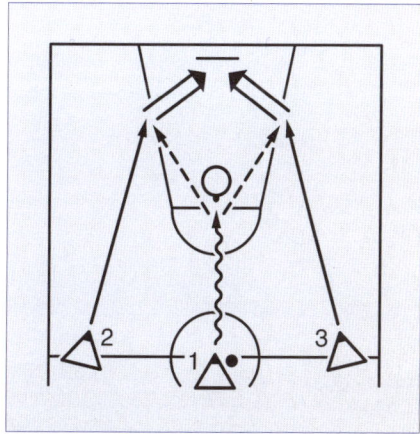

DRILLS

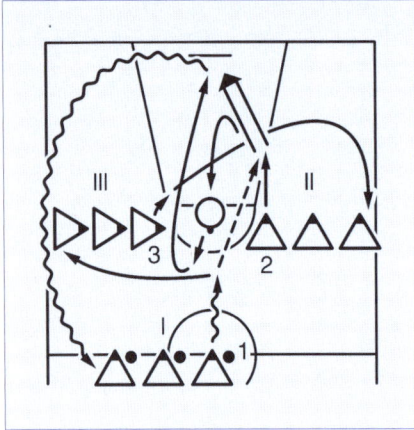

D161b Pick a pass Players are divided into three groups, one with balls at centre court (I) and two others on opposite sides of the key (II and III). Another player stands at the foul line defending the basket. Player 1 begins by dribbling towards the basket until confronted by the defender. Players 2 and 3 make themselves available for a pass and player 1 decides which player to go to. The player receiving the pass goes in for a lay-up and becomes the defender for the next round. The defender rebounds the ball and dribbles to join group I, player 1 joins group III, and player 3 joins group II.

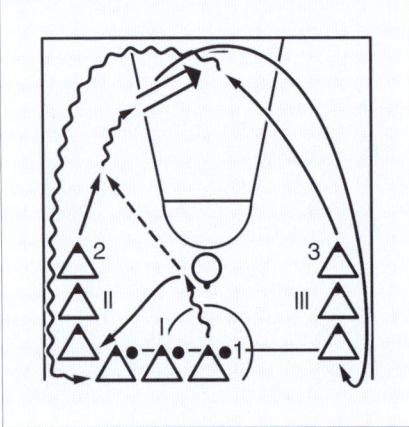

D161c Drive from the wing Players are divided into three groups, one with balls at centre court (I) and two others on opposite wings (II and III). A defender stands at the top of the key defending the basket. Player 1 begins by dribbling towards the basket and, when confronted by the defensive player, passes to either wing player (in this case, player 2) for a drive to the basket and a lay-up. Player 3 rebounds the ball and dribbles to the end of group I, player 2 joins the end of group III, and player 1 joins the end of group II. The defensive player can be exchanged at any time.

D161d Wing options Players line up at the top with two wing players and one player in the middle. A single defender stands at the foul line defending the basket. In this drill, the ball starts on the wing with player 2, who dribbles towards the basket with the option of passing to player 1 coming down the middle or across to player 3 cutting in from the opposite wing. In this case, the ball is passed to player 3 for a lay-up on the opposite side of the basket. The defender should be changed periodically.

ODD-PERSON SITUATIONS

Three-on-two situations

In the following drills, the player dribbling the ball has two main options: (1) when not challenged by the defense on his or her path to the basket, the player should continue and attempt a shot at the basket; (2) if the player is challenged and the path to the basket is defended well, the dribbler should be looking to pass the ball to an open teammate in a better position to score.

D162a **Simple three-on-two** The player in the middle begins with the ball and dribbles towards the basket. When challenged by a defensive player, he or she must look to pass to the player in the best scoring position. Players should switch roles frequently.

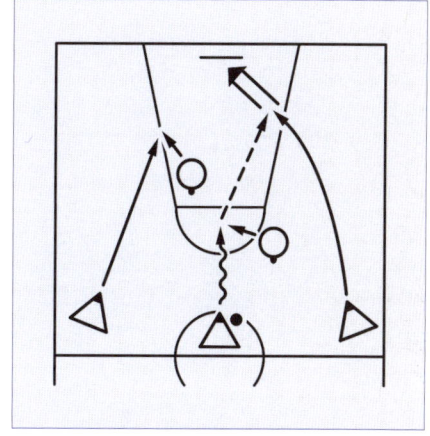

D162b **From the right wing** In this drill, the ball starts on the right wing with player 3, who dribbles towards the basket with the option of passing to player 2 coming down the middle or across to player 1 cutting in from the opposite wing. In this case, the defense commits to players 1 and 3, so the ball is passed to the open player (2) down the middle for a lay-up.

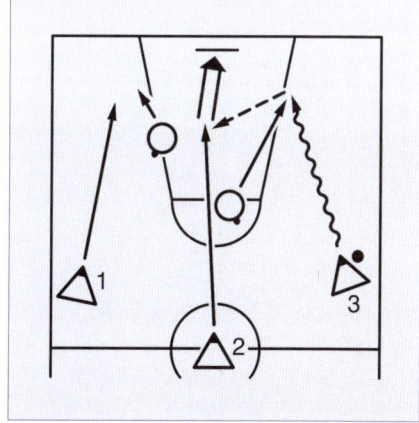

163

DRILLS

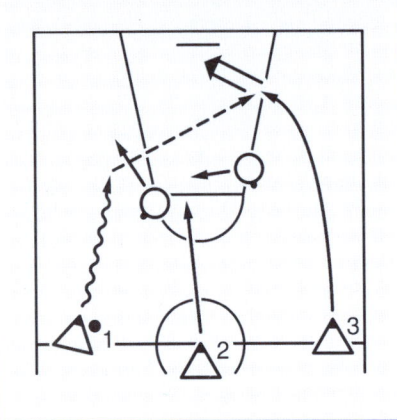

D162c From the left wing In this drill, the ball starts on the left wing with player 1, who dribbles towards the basket with the option of passing to player 2 coming down the middle or across to player 3 cutting in from the opposite wing. In this case, the two defenders choose to guard players 1 and 2, leaving player 3 open on the opposite wing for a quick lay-up.

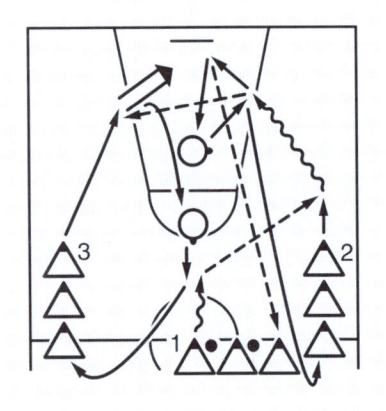

D162d From the middle Players are divided into three groups, one with balls at centre court and two others on opposite wings. Two defenders stand in the key area. Player 1 begins by dribbling towards the basket and, when challenged by the first defender, gives the ball up to player 2 on the wing. Player 2 continues dribbling towards the basket and when confronted by the second defender, passes across the lane to player 3 on the opposite wing for an open lay-up. The two wing players become defenders and the defenders become wing players. The middle players can be exchanged at the discretion of the coach.

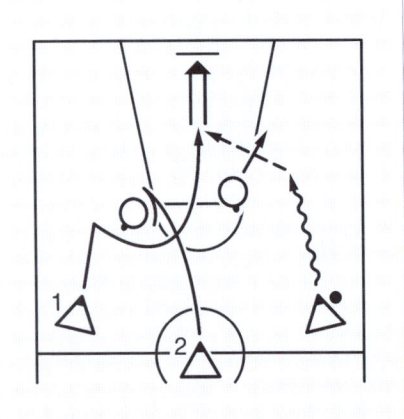

D162e Screen off the ball Players line up at the top with two wing players and one player in the middle. A pair of defenders stand at the foul line defending the basket. The ball starts with a player on the wing. This player dribbles towards the basket and, when challenged by one of the defenders, passes to player 1, who cuts to the basket for a lay-up with the help of a screen set by player 2 off the ball. This drill should be practiced on both sides of the court.

Four-on-two situations

D163 Simple four-on-two Players work similarly to the drills for practicing three-on-two situations. The ball starts in the middle and is passed to an open player with the best scoring opportunity. In this drill, there should always be two players open, as long as players maintain good floor spacing.

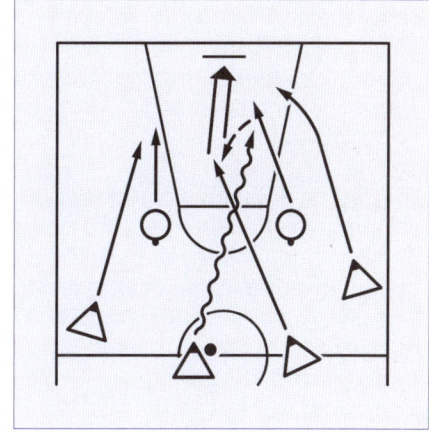

Four-on-three situations

D164 Simple four-on-three Just as in the previous drills, a fourth player is used to follow the offensive play to create an odd-person advantage situation. The player dribbling the ball must always be aware of where his or her teammates are and quickly determine which one has the best scoring opportunity. This is usually dictated by the defense.

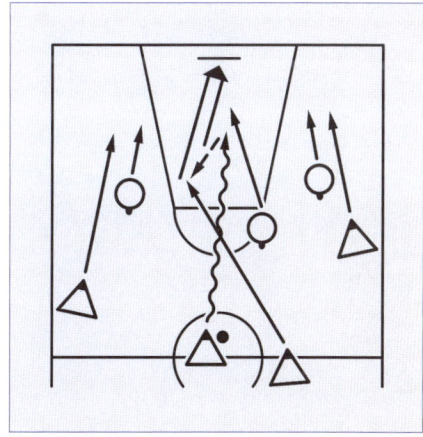

DRILLS

Motion offense

Achieving adequate spacing among teammates, and maintaining that spacing while changing positions or moving on the court, are some of the most important offensive skills a player can possess. These skills are important building blocks for creating an offensive system and are important tactical prerequisites to establishing an effective team offence. Player movement (with or without the ball) allows players to get open by temporarily shedding their defenders.

Moving or changing positions is more effective when combined with screening. An offensive player setting a screen on a defensive player blocks the defender, allowing an offensive teammate to cut to the basket or change positions (simple screen). Without a ball involved in the screening action, it is called an *off-the-ball screen*; with a ball, it is called an *on-the-ball screen*. If the defender guarding the screener switches to the open offensive player, the screener can roll or cut off the screen and open up going to the basket. If the defensive player tries to avoid being blocked by the screener by moving away from the screen, the player setting the screen can become a *shield*. The "shielder" is positioned so the defensive player is shielded from the person he or she was guarding, allowing the offensive player with the ball an easy shot or pass. Player movement, screening, and shielding are all important offensive skills to be learned, but defending these actions must also be practiced (see **Charts 19 and 20**).

Tips for player movement, screening, and shielding

- When a screen is set on the player guarding the ball, the player with the ball has the option of driving to the basket, passing to the screener who rolls after setting the screen (screen and roll), or shooting as the screener becomes a shielder.

- Always screen or shield players so you can still see the game. Best position: back to the defending player.

- Always screen on the side that gives the offensive player most space to maneuver.

- Player movement and screening/shielding should be part of every offensive set. Not every screen or cut will lead to a basket, but it will improve scoring opportunities.

- When using a screen by a teammate, wait for the screen to be set— do not cut off the screen too early. You may even prepare to use the screen by first using a fake. The less prepared the defense is, the more successful your action will be.

- When setting and using screens both on and off the ball, wait for a good opportunity to screen and roll.

MOTION OFFENSE

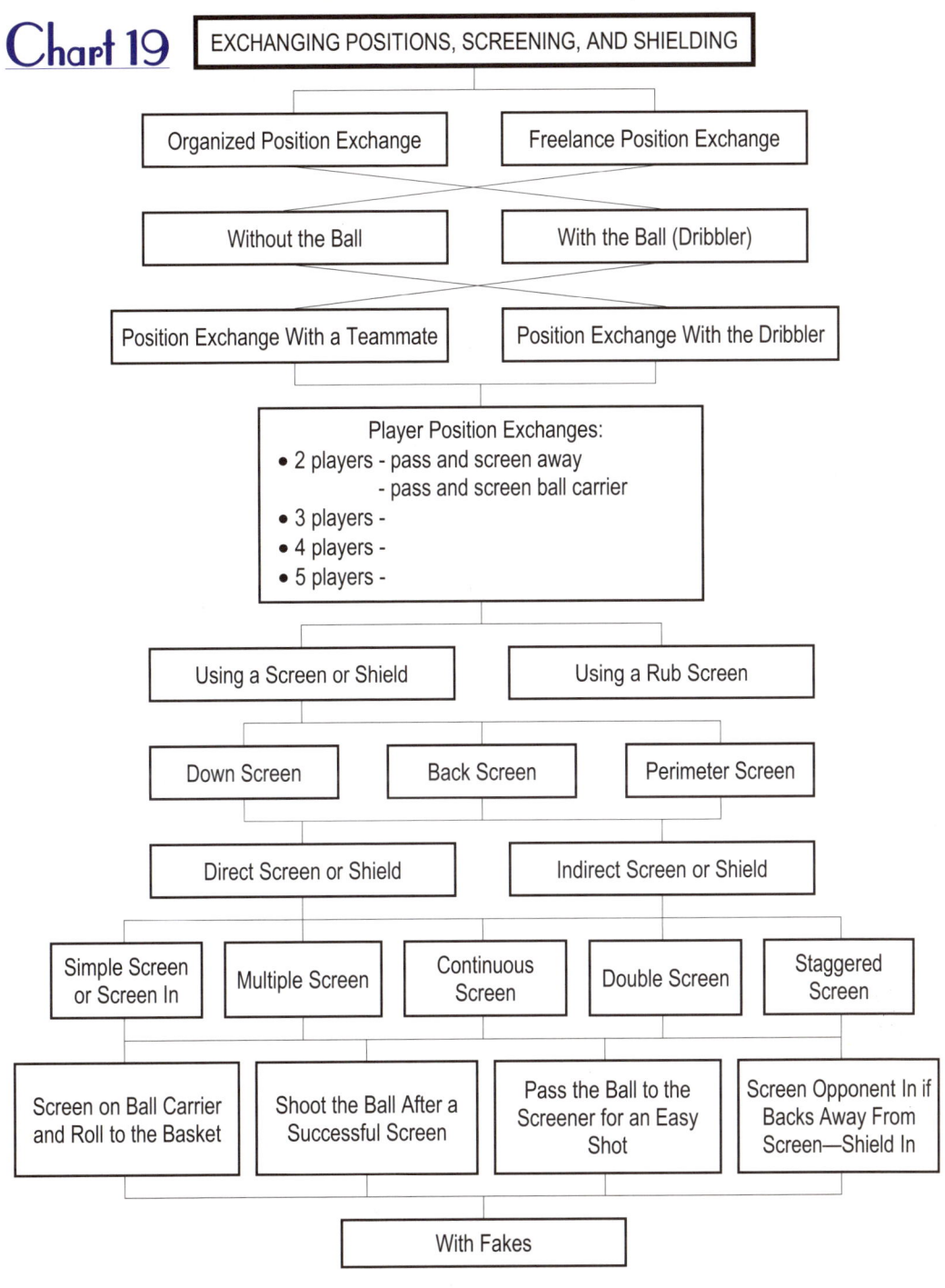

DRILLS

Chart 20

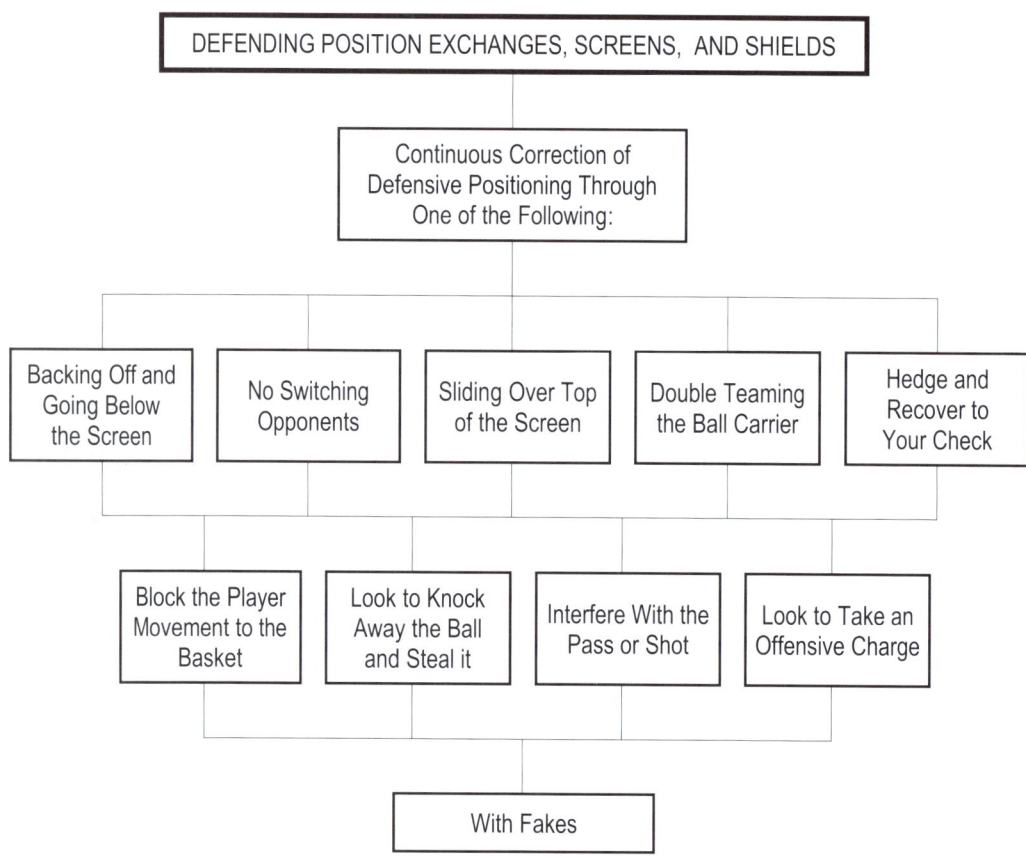

MOTION OFFENSE

Tips for defending against player movement, screening, and shielding

- Adjust your defensive position as the player you are guarding moves around the court.

- Always be aware of players setting screens or shielding you from another player. It is possible to avoid screens by anticipating them and using skillful defensive maneuvers to avoid them.

- It is sometimes possible to slide between two opposing players to prevent being screened successfully.

- When defending against a screen, if a teammate switches to the player you were guarding, be sure to switch to the player he or she was guarding (requires good communication) to avoid leaving the opponent open for a scoring opportunity.

- Always stay in line with the ball so the player you are guarding cannot receive a pass.

- A shield can only be avoided with a strong defensive effort. If you are shielded by another player, a teammate must try to pick up the player you were guarding and you switch to pick up the player he or she was guarding.

The following drills should be practiced for standard situations. After practicing the offensive screening and shielding actions with a passive or semi-active defense, emphasis should then be placed on practicing how to defend against the same situations.

Basic forms of screening

_____ are screens set on the defender of the player with the ball. These are also referred to as "on-the-ball screens" because the screen is set on the defender guarding the ball. Again, the offensive player with the ball has three options available to him or her: (1) use the screen and drive to the basket; (2) dribble around the screen and pass to the rolling screener or another open teammate; or (3) use the screener as a shield against his or her defender and shoot the ball.

_____ are screens set between two players when neither player has the ball. These screens are also referred to as "off-the-ball screens" because they are set away from the ball. The screener is the offensive player setting the screen, and the person "using" the screen is the offensive player cutting past the screener to get open or lose his or her defender to create a scoring opportunity.

DRILLS

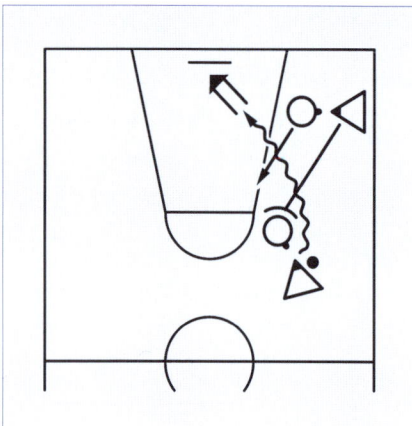

D165 On-ball screen In a two-on-two situation, the offensive player without the ball sets a screen on the player defending the ball. The player with the ball "uses" the screen to dribble past the screener to the basket for a lay-up. The player with the ball can fake one way and drive in the opposite direction to use the screen more effectively. Timing is crucial in executing a successful screen on the ball. The defense applied during the drill should initially be passive or semi-active.

D166 Roll off an on-ball screen In a two-on-two situation similar to the drill above (D165), the offensive player without the ball sets a screen on the player defending the ball. In this case, the screener cuts or "rolls" to the basket for a potential pass. As the player defending the screener switches to take the dribbler coming off the screen, the player with the ball passes to the screener cutting to the basket for a lay-up.

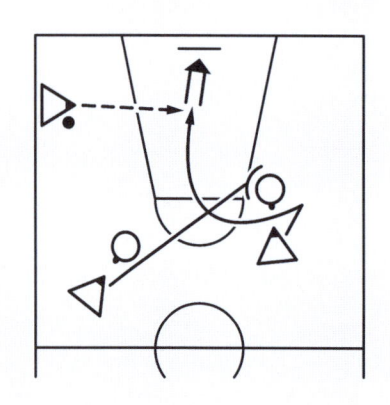

D167 Off-ball screen Players are set in a two-on-two situation with a fifth player positioned in the corner as a passer. One player sets a screen on his or her teammate's defender away from the ball. The player using the screen fakes one way, then cuts closely past the screener in the opposite direction looking for a pass from the player in the corner for a lay-up.

MOTION OFFENSE

D168 Roll off an off-ball screen Similar to the drill above (D167), players are set in a two-on-two situation with a fifth player positioned in the corner as a passer. One player sets a screen on his or her teammate's defender away from the ball. In this case, as the teammate cuts off the screen, the player defending the screener switches to guard the cutting player. As soon as this defensive switch occurs, the screener rolls to the basket looking for a pass from the corner. The screener must be sure not to roll off the screen too late.

Basic forms of shielding

D169 On-ball shield Players set up in a two-on-two situation on one side of the floor. A pivot fake by the offensive player with the ball causes his or her defender to take a step back, allowing the screener to step between his or her teammate and the defensive player. This opens up a shooting opportunity for the player with the ball. This usually does not work without a fake or a quick dribble before the screen is set.

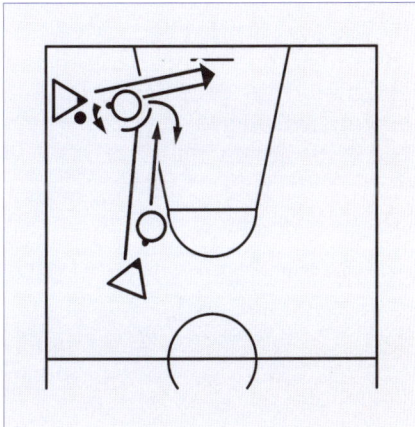

171

DRILLS

D170 Off-ball shield Players set up in a two-on-two situation with another player positioned in the corner as a passer. One offensive player sets a screen on his or her teammate's defender. The teammate fakes a cut to the basket using the screen. When the defender tries to go behind the screen, the screener shields his or her teammate from the defender, allowing a pass from the corner for a shot. The offensive player must receive the pass in a position ready to shoot. The pass must be on time!

Using basic screening and shielding techniques combined with player movement

D171a,b Pass and screen away Screening occurs in a triangular three-on-three game-like situation, with all screens being set as indirect off-the-ball screens (away from the ball). Constant screening by the offense allows players to receive open passes by preventing defenders from effectively defending the passing lanes. This form of triangular play (pass and screen away) often creates several good scoring opportunities by not allowing the defense to get set.

D171a

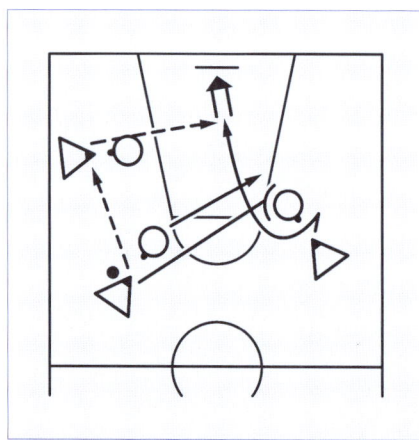

D171b

MOTION OFFENSE

D171c Three-on-three direct screen In this drill, players utilize the triangular offensive play to set a direct screen on the ball. The player with the ball uses the screen and dribbles to the basket for a lay-up.

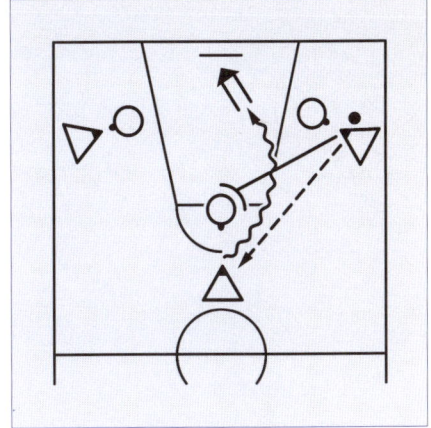

D171d,e,f Three-on-three motion offense Players practice various options learned to this point regarding screening and shielding in a three-on-three game situation. In D171d, the offensive player with the ball passes and moves to screen away. His or her teammate fakes using the approaching screen and cuts behind (back cuts) the defender to the basket looking for a pass and a quick lay-up.

D171d

D171e

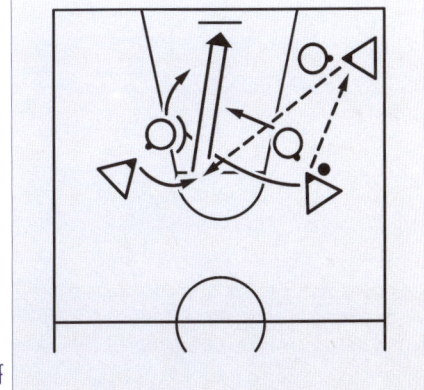

D171f

DRILLS

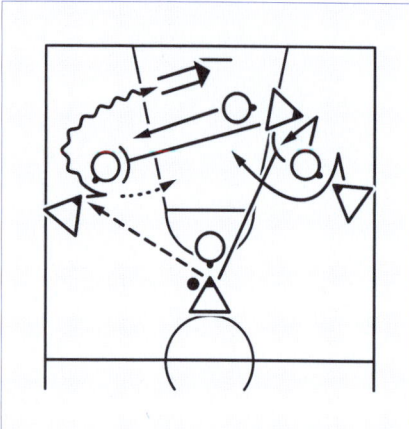

D172a,b,c Four-on-four exchange with centre or forward Player movement, passing, and screening among perimeter players and the centre or forwards must also be practiced systematically. Driving and passing lanes open up for the offense with player movement and screening both on the perimeter and down low (D172a,b). The screen and roll between the centre and a perimeter player off the ball is also very effective (D172c).

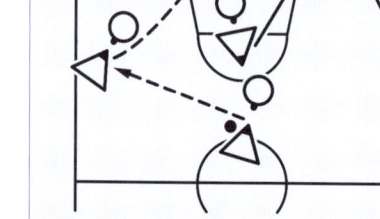

D173a Interior screens for centres and forwards Two offensive players without the ball are positioned on either side of the key in the low post. The player with the ball stands above the foul line as a passer. One player screens across for the other and the ball is passed to the cutter for a quick shot. If the screener is open the ball may go to him or her as well.

MOTION OFFENSE

D173b,c,d Interior screens for a shot The offense sets up with one player in the low post area (outside the key close to the basket) and one player in the high post area (above the foul line). Following a screen on or off the ball, the player with the ball can pass to the player coming off the screen, pass to the screener, or take the ball him- or herself to the basket for a shot.

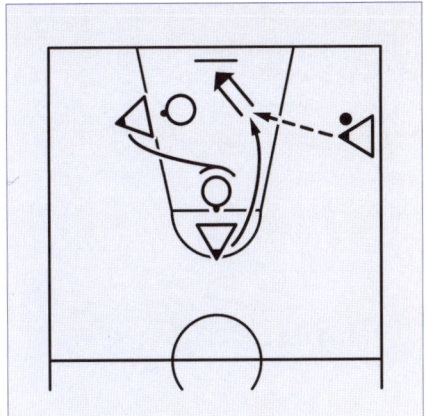
D173b

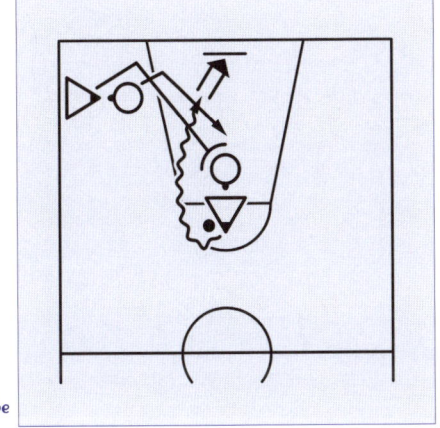
D173e

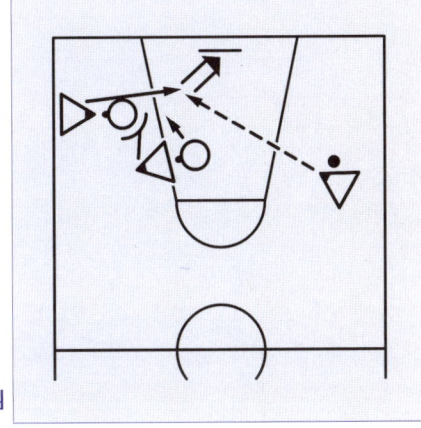
D173d

D174a-g Four-on-four pass and screen away This follows the same principle as the triangular three-on-three pass and screen away. Players passing the ball in one direction run in the opposite direction to set a screen for a teammate. This can be done continuously (D174a-c) to practice passing, screening, and player movement, or can end with a shot inside following perimeter passing (D174d-g).

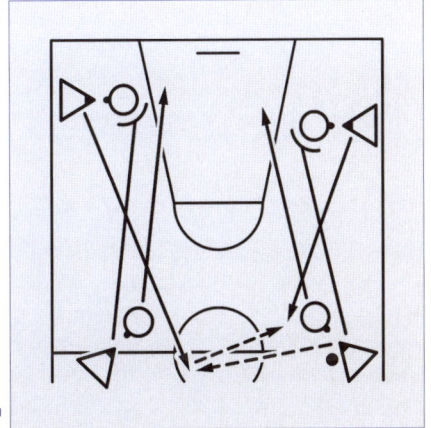
D174a

DRILLS

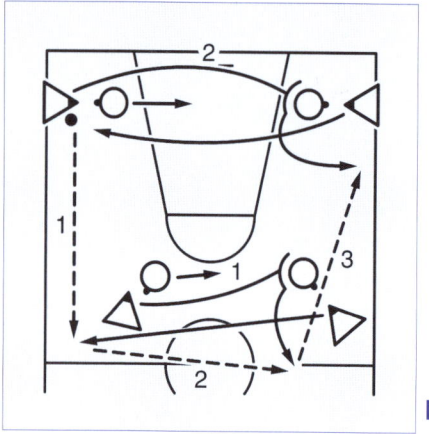
D174b

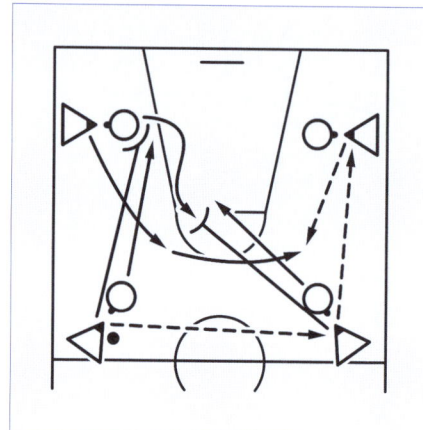
D174c

D174d

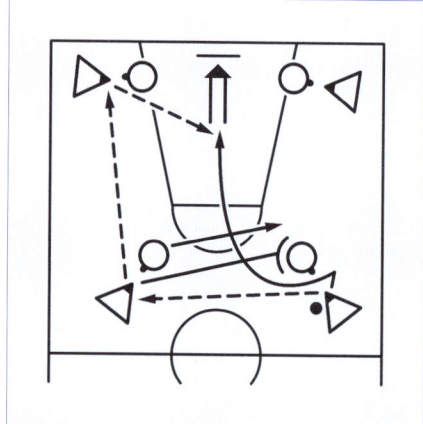
D174e

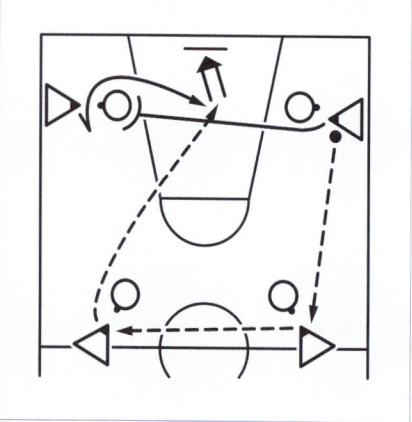
D174f

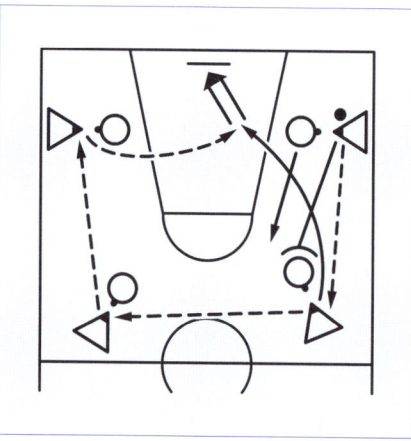
D174g

MOTION OFFENSE

D175a-e Five-on-five player movement and screening This follows the same principle as the triangular three-on-three and rectangular four-on-four pass and screen away. The interior is kept open and available for cutting to the basket. The pentagonal five-on-five pass and exchange can occur continuously (D175a), or can end with a shot using various passing, screening, and cutting maneuvers to the basket (D175b-e).

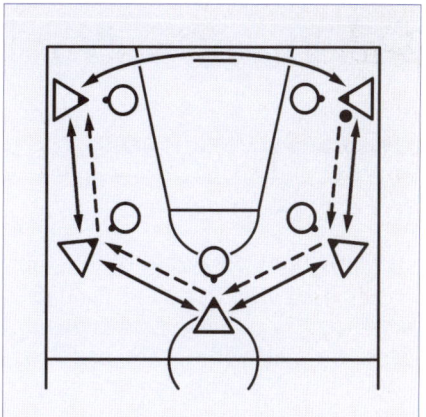

D175a

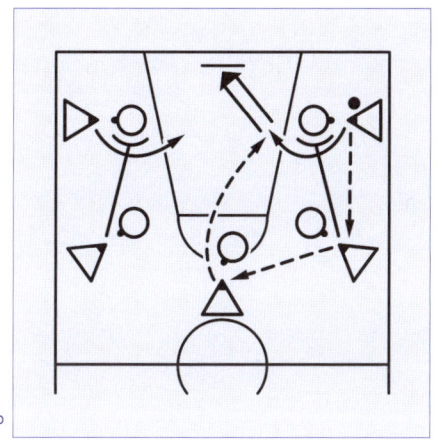

D175b

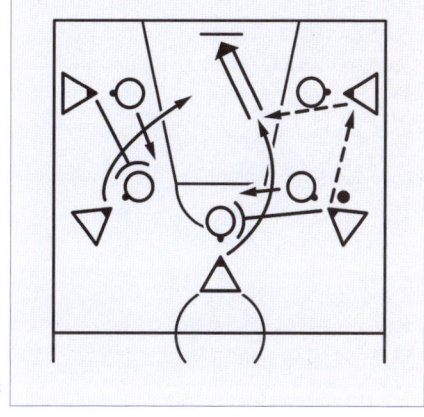

D175c

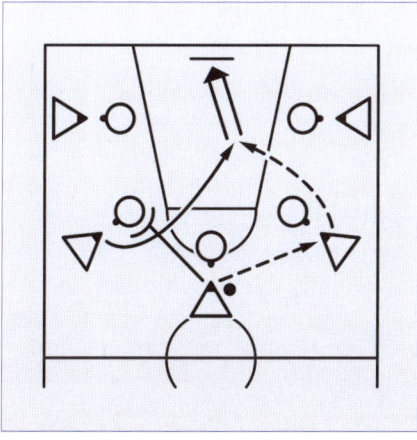

D175d

D175e

177

DRILLS

Rub screens—with and without the ball

A *rub screen*, or *rubbing off* your defender on a teammate or another defender, is an effective and often used technique to free up an offensive player for a scoring opportunity or to receive a pass.

Rubbing off may be described as two teammates or players trying to pass each other so closely that at least one of the defensive players is cut off (simple rubbing off or rub screen). When the defensive player tries to avoid contact and getting rubbed off, the offensive player without the ball can shield the defender and give the player with the ball a good shot or scoring opportunity. If the players on the defensive team switch defensive assignments when an offensive player uses the rub screen, the second offensive player can open up to the ball as another offensive option. Because this all happens very quickly, the defence can become confused and suffer a defensive breakdown. Good concentration and communication among teammates is necessary for both the offence and defence, and must therefore be practiced systematically. See **Chart 21** for a summary of rub-screen skills.

Tips for rubbing off a screen

- Always be aware of your defensive player and the game situation. Try to guide your defender into a teammate or another defender to free yourself up on offense for a better scoring opportunity.

- The successful action of rubbing off must occur very quickly. Waiting too long to make a move will give defenders time to adjust their positions and negate the effectiveness of the screen.

- Pass the ball very quickly and accurately, being sure to pass the ball when your teammate is ready to receive it.

- Using directional changes and change of pace to surprise the defender are very effective and keep the defense off balance. Don't let the defense get set! Keep defenders moving and lead them into a rub-off situation.

RUB SCREENS

Chart 21

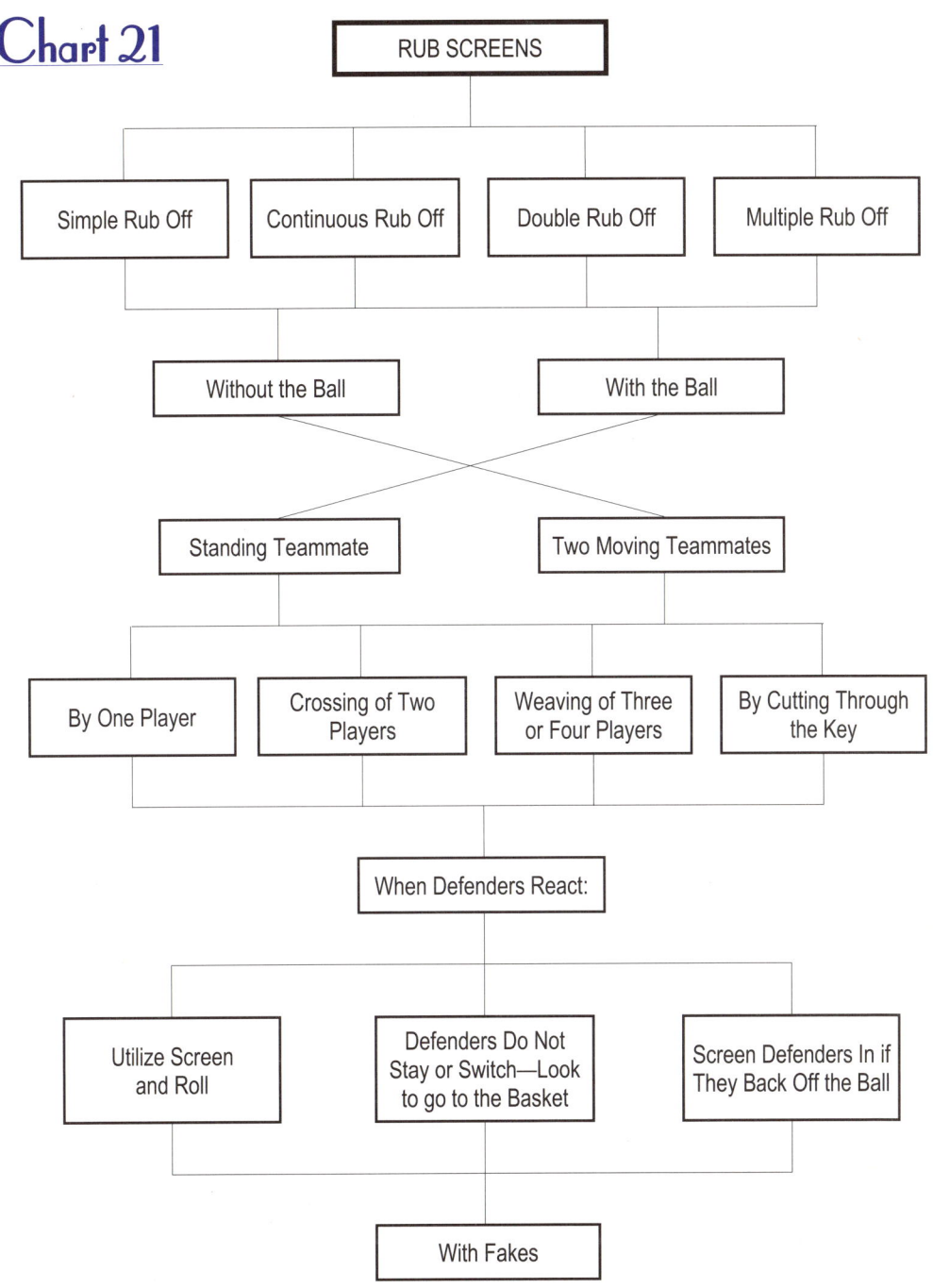

DRILLS

Tips for defending players rubbing off a screen (see also Chart 20)

- The best defense against rubbing off is to be very aggressive defensively.

- Decide ahead of time how the team will play against the rub screen defensively and communicate during the game to avoid confusion about defensive player assignments.

- Move backwards away from an offensive player who tries to rub you off so you can slide past the screening player.

- If it is not possible to move away and slide behind the screen, try to slip through between the two offensive players to remain in a good defensive position.

Rubbing off a stationary player

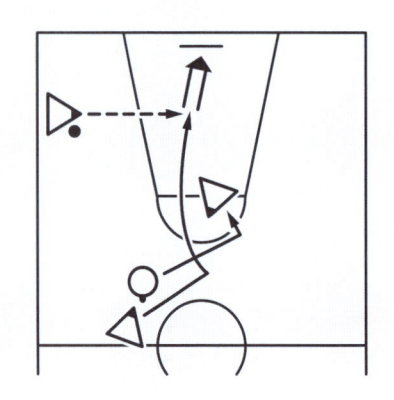

D176a

D176a-h **Rubbing off without the ball** The offensive player guides the defensive player into a teammate with change of pace and direction to rub him or her off. D176a-e show common situations which should be practiced and perfected in this way. D176f-h depict drills for practicing rubbing off in groups using several balls at one basket.

180

RUB SCREENS

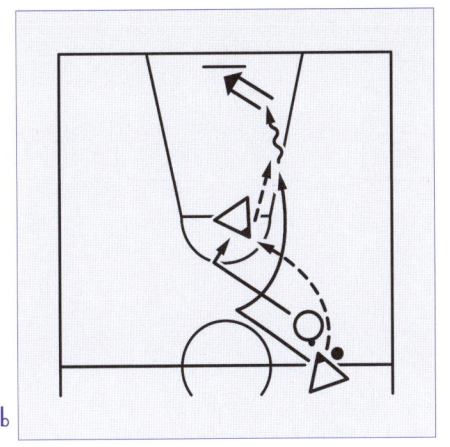
D176b

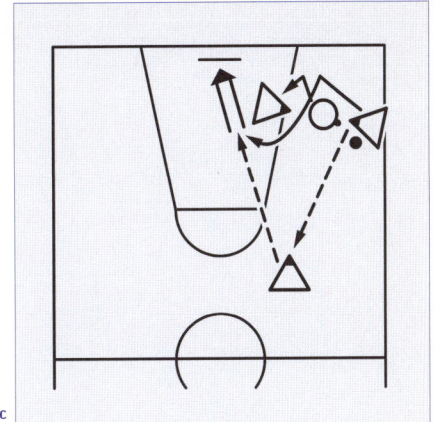
D176c

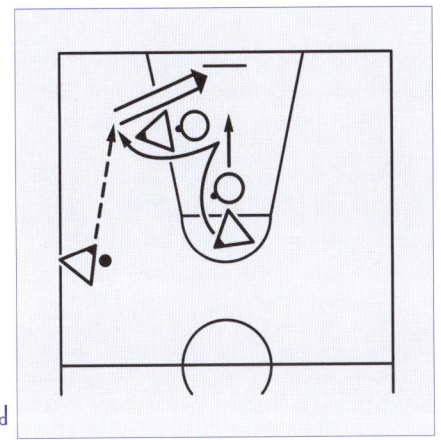
D176d

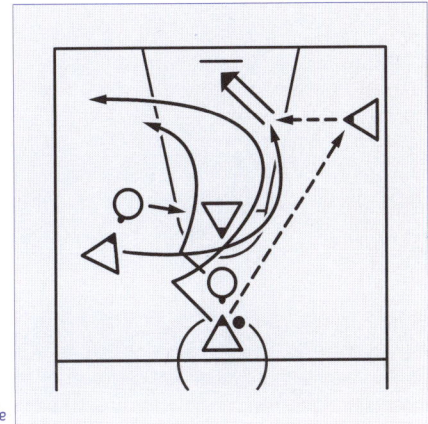
D176e

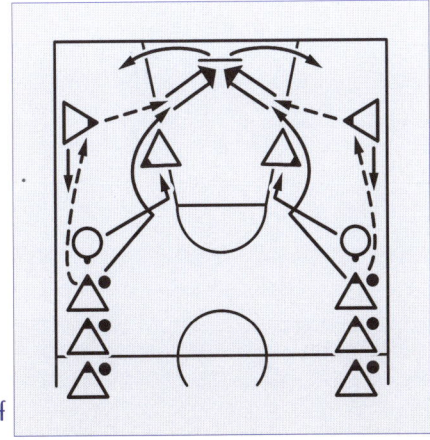
D176f

D176g

DRILLS

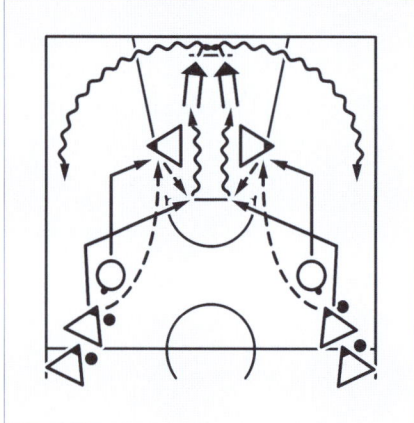

D176h

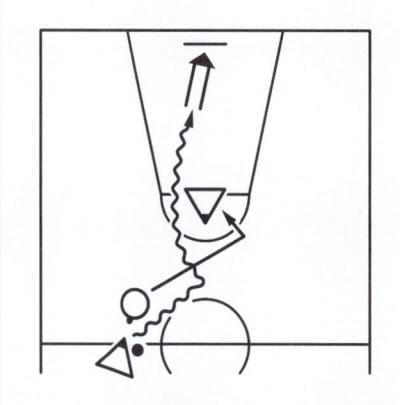

D177a

D177a,b,c Rubbing off using the dribble The dribbler leads the defender into a teammate or another player (using change of pace and direction, keeping the ball close to the body), rubbing off the defender on the way to the basket (D177a). If the defender is able to avoid being rubbed off, the offensive player without the ball can shield the defender to allow a shot from the outside (D177b). If the offensive player with the ball is guarded closely or picked up by another defender, the screener can roll to the basket for a pass or shot (D177c).

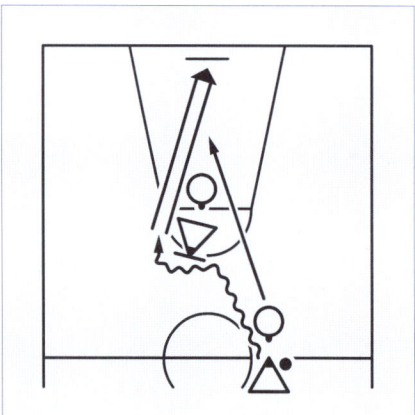

D177b

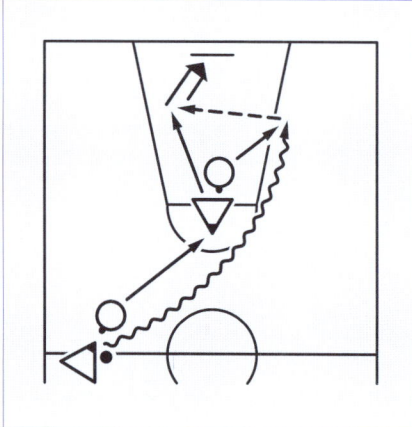

D177c

182

RUB SCREENS

Rub screens between moving players

D178a,b Rubbing off by running towards each other Two offensive players run towards each other and pass each other so closely (shoulder to shoulder) that they are able to rub off their opponents. This can be done without the ball (D178a) or with the ball (D178b). An advanced version of this is called *weaving*, in which the offensive players dribble and pass until one of them successfully rubs off their defensive player and cuts through to the basket for a good scoring opportunity.

D178a

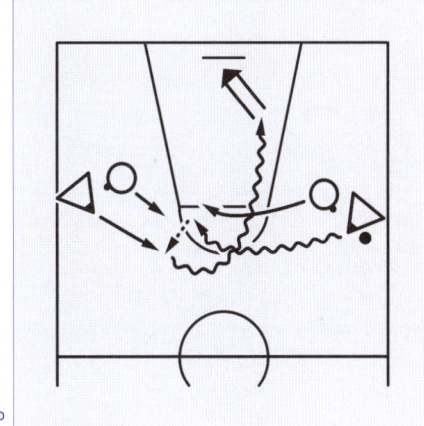
D178b

D179a,b,c Rubbing off by crossing Two offensive players cross paths while running to rub off their defenders. This can be done without the ball (D179a) or with the ball (D179b,c). When performing a rub screen with the ball for a teammate it is often called a ***dribble pick*** or ***dribble rub off***. A player dribbles towards a teammate, passing the ball off to the teammate as he or she cuts past, and provides interference against the defensive player. If defenders switch defensive assignments (D179c), the other offensive player can cut to the basket to receive a pass back for an easy scoring opportunity.

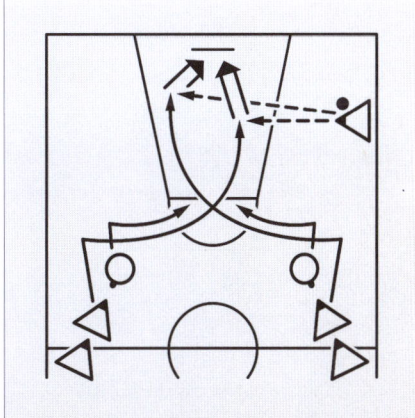
D179a

DRILLS

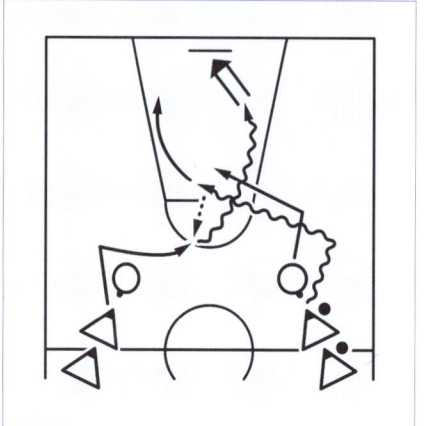
D179b

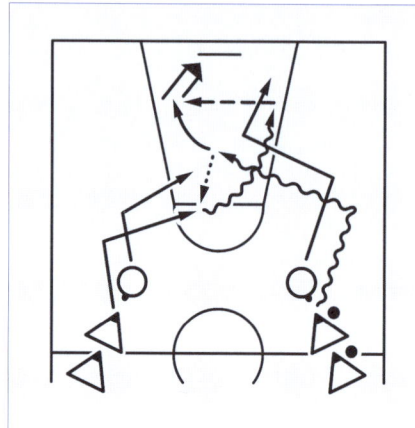
D179c

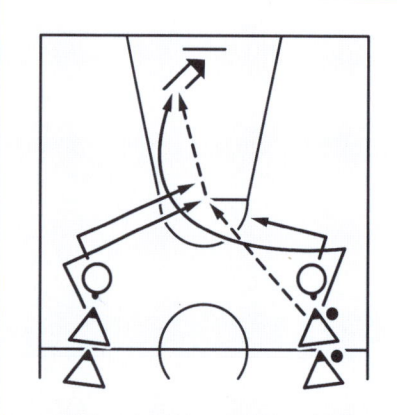
D179d

D179d-g Around for the pass In these drills, players put an emphasis on timing when utilizing rub screens to come around for a pass and a shot. These drills can be performed in two-on-two, three-on-two, or four-on-four situations.

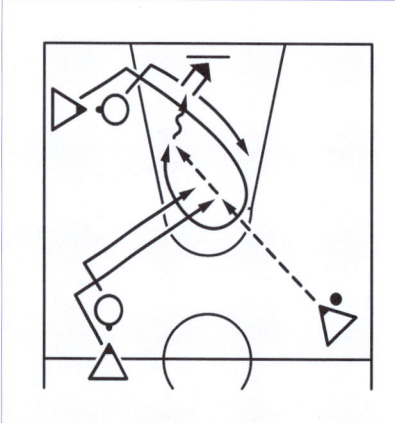
D179e

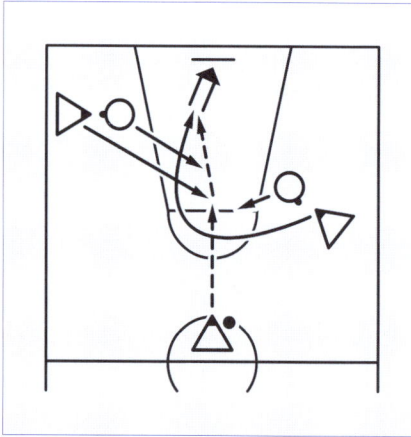
D179f

184

RUB SCREENS

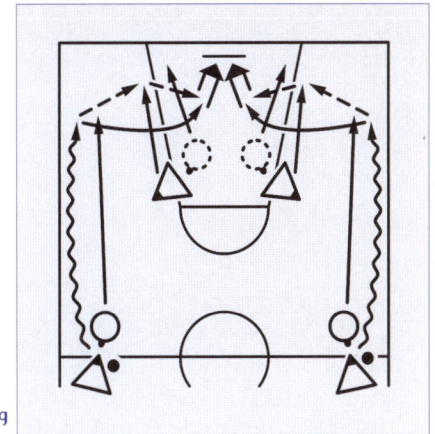

D179g

D180a-d **Crossing in the high post** Crossing can also occur between perimeter and high post players. High post players stand with their backs to the basket and in turn pass to their teammates who practice rubbing off the high post.

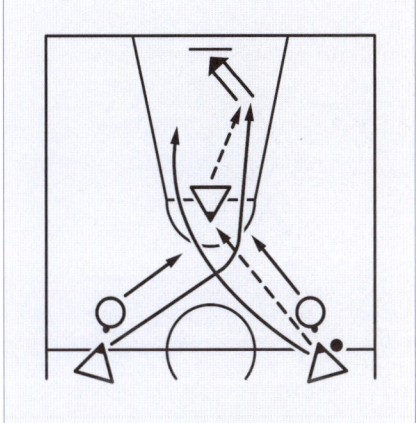

D180a

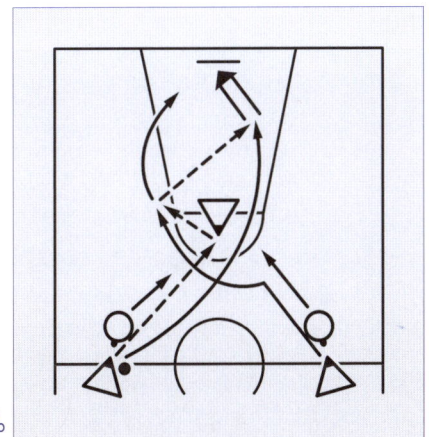

D180b

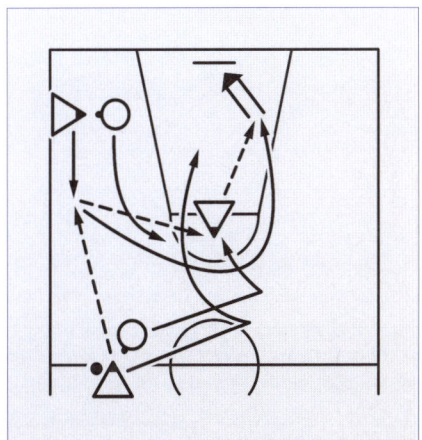

D180c

DRILLS

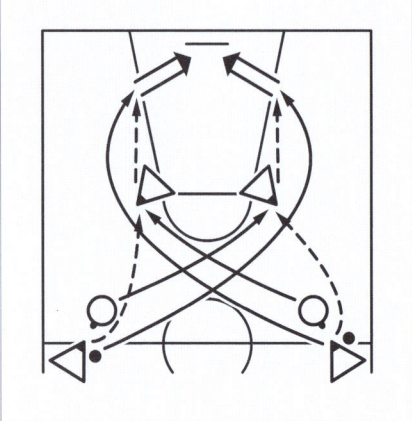
D180d

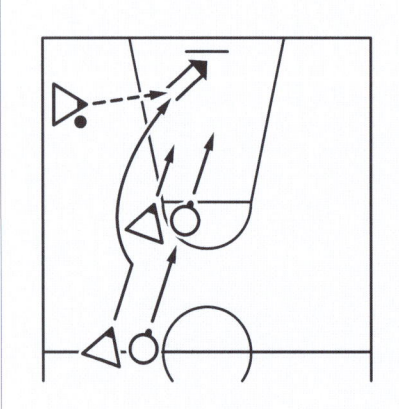
D181a

D181a,b,c Rubbing off by running or dribbling past a teammate One player runs past a slower teammate in such a way that his or her defender is rubbed off. These drills can be done without the ball (D181a,b) or with the ball (D181c).

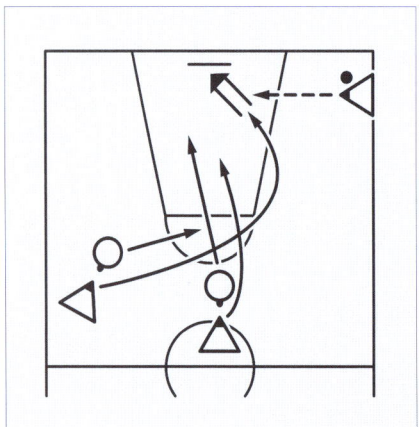
D181b

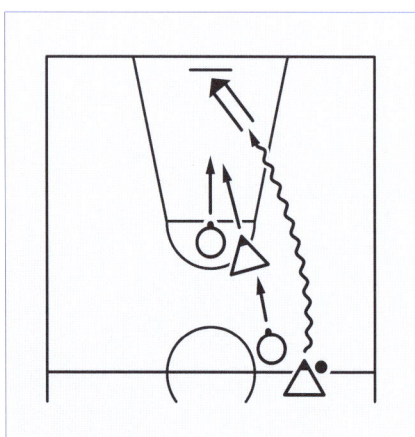
D181c

RUB SCREENS

DRILLS

Rebounding

Rebounding the ball after a missed shot is one of the most important elements in the game of basketball for both the offensive and defensive team. Successful rebounding depends on several factors, including predicting where the ball will bounce off the rim, getting into good rebounding position quickly, timing the jump at the right moment, and securing the ball with both hands whenever possible. Since rebounding is a skill utilized following a missed shot, it is often practiced during drills that also involve shooting.

Practicing rebounding during shooting drills helps players learn where the ball will bounce after missed shots from various positions on the floor. It is important to practice fighting for good inside position, blocking out (getting between the opponent and the basket), securing the ball with two hands, and either scoring or passing the ball out to a teammate. Offensive players have the important job of keeping the ball alive so they can gain another scoring opportunity. The more scoring opportunities a team gets the better chance they have to win the game. On the other hand, the defensive team must try to quickly rebound the ball after a missed shot, limiting scoring opportunities for the opponent and igniting an offensive counterattack. See **Chart 22** for a summary of rebounding skills.

Tips for defensive rebounding

- Always be aware of where offensive players and the ball are at all times.

- Rebounds following a missed shot can bounce in any direction, but generally close to the basket, giving taller players and good jumpers an initial advantage.

- Pay close attention to where the ball bounces off the rim for shots attempted from different spots on the floor. Rather than always reacting to the ball, try anticipating where the ball will bounce—gaining the inside position between your opponent and the basket is a great advantage.

- Try to gain and keep the inside position. If offensive players are able to gain the inside position, they will have an easy scoring opportunity if they are able to successfully rebound the ball.

- Coordinate your rebounding position with your teammates. If you have the inside position, always try setting up a defensive triangle with your teammates so no offensive player can get close to the basket.

- If the ball cannot be rebounded and secured with two hands, try tipping the ball to yourself or a teammate to control the rebound.

REBOUNDING

Chart 22

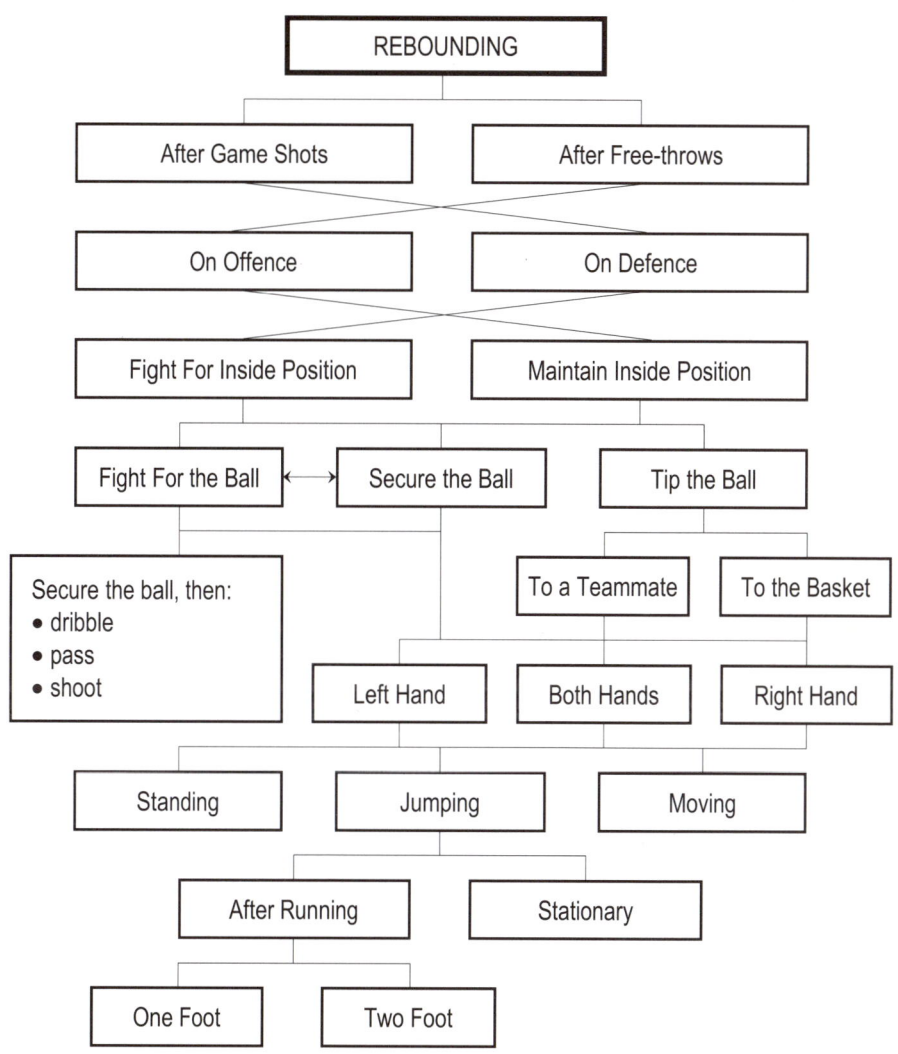

DRILLS

Tips for offensive rebounding

- Try to break through the defensive triangle and get inside position. Be aggressive and use your quickness.

- If you are not able to secure the rebound, try tipping the ball into the basket or keep the ball alive for another chance for you or a teammate to rebound the ball.

- Offensive rebounding can also be successful by screening the defensive players away from the basket.

Rebound two-on-one

D182a Two defensive players vs. one offensive player In this two-on-one situation under the basket, player 1 tries to prevent the offensive player from getting to the basket by boxing out and establishing inside position. The other defensive player (2) can focus on rebounding the ball when the shot comes from the outside.

REBOUNDING

D182b Two offensive players vs. one defensive player Again the shot comes from the outside, but this time the two-on-one situation under the basket favours the offense. One offensive player (1) tries to get inside position between the defensive player and the basket, increasing his or her chances of rebounding a missed shot and allowing his or her teammate (player 2) a clear shot at the rebound.

Rebound two-on-two

D183a Shoot and follow In this two-on-two rebounding drill, one player shoots and follows the shot, trying to gain inside position on the defender for a potential rebound. The other offensive player also tries to get inside position on his or her defender, who tries to box out for the rebound. The drill can be performed as a competition between offensive and defensive rebounders.

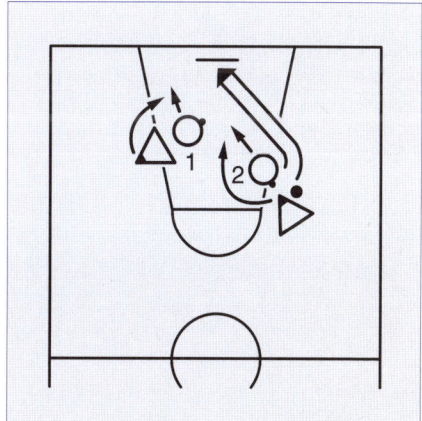

DRILLS

D183b Two-on-two box out and contest In this two-on-two rebounding drill, a shot comes from a fifth player on the perimeter, who does not try to rebound the ball. The two offensive players fight for inside position as the two defensive players try blocking them out for a potential rebound.

Rebound three-on-two

D184a,b,c Three-on-two rebounding Three-on-two rebounding drills can be performed either with defensive players outnumbering offensive players (D184a) or offensive players outnumbering defensive players (D184b,c). Drills may also be varied by having players follow their shots for a potential rebound (D184b), or by having a sixth player as a shooter from the perimeter who is not involved in rebounding the ball (D184a,c). Defensive players should concentrate on forming a defensive triangle (when outnumbering the opponent) and try to prevent the offensive players from getting inside position for the rebound. Offensive players must aggressively pursue the ball and try to use their quickness to get inside.

D184a

D184b

REBOUNDING

D184c

Rebound three-on-three

D185a Three-on-three under the basket
Three defensive players form a defensive rebounding triangle and the offensive players must try to get inside position for a rebound. The seventh player shooting the ball from the perimeter does not rebound.

DRILLS

D185b **Shooter rebounds** Three defensive players form a defensive rebounding triangle and the offensive players must try to get inside position for a rebound. The player shooting the ball becomes the third offensive player and also tries to rebound the ball.

Rebound after free-throw

D186 **Rebound the miss** Players are divided into teams of three and line up around the key at one basket. A player from one team starts with the ball and shoots a free-throw. As with regular free-throws during a game, all players are able to enter the lane for the rebound once the ball has been released from the shooter's hands. The same player can shoot several consecutive shots, or players may rotate after each shot.

REBOUNDING

D187 **Rotate right** Players are divided into three pairs (an offensive and defensive player in each pair) and line up around the key at one basket. Players in each pair alternately shoot two free-throws and then rotate around the key in a counterclockwise direction. If a shot is missed, players try to rebound the ball. If a player on the same team rebounds the ball, he or she can try to score. If a player on the other team rebounds the ball, the next free-throw is then taken. The next shot is taken only if a shot is made, the ball is rebounded by an opposing player, or the ball goes out of bounds. Pairs always rotate together.

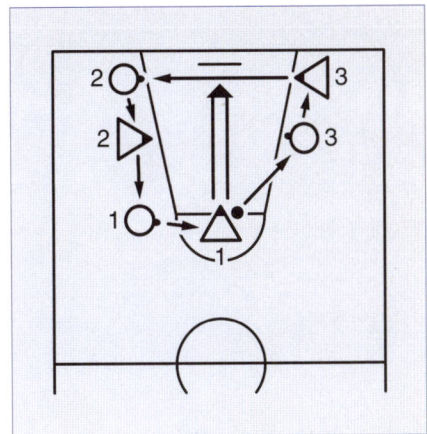

Variations:

- Players shoot free-throws until a shot is missed.

- Players of one pair alternate shooting free-throws until one player misses a shot. Only then do players rotate positions.

- The "team" that rebounds the ball after a missed free-throw shoots the next shot.

D188 **Free-throw and break** This drill is similar to D187, except the entire court is used and players are divided into five pairs. If a free-throw is missed and rebounded by a teammate, he or she can try to score. If a missed shot is rebounded by an opposing player, the ball is moved quickly downcourt on a fast break with his or her teammates, while the other team tries to stop the break. When all the players have arrived at the other end of the court and again set up around the key, the previous rebounder shoots the next free-throw, and so on. Players can wear pinnies to clearly identify the two teams.

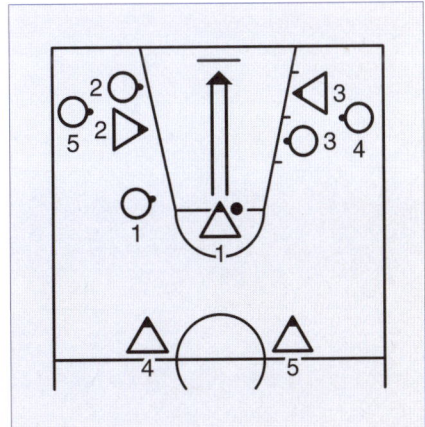

195

PART V

CIRCUIT 1 *198*

CIRCUIT 2 *199*

CIRCUIT 3 *200*

CIRCUIT 4 *201*

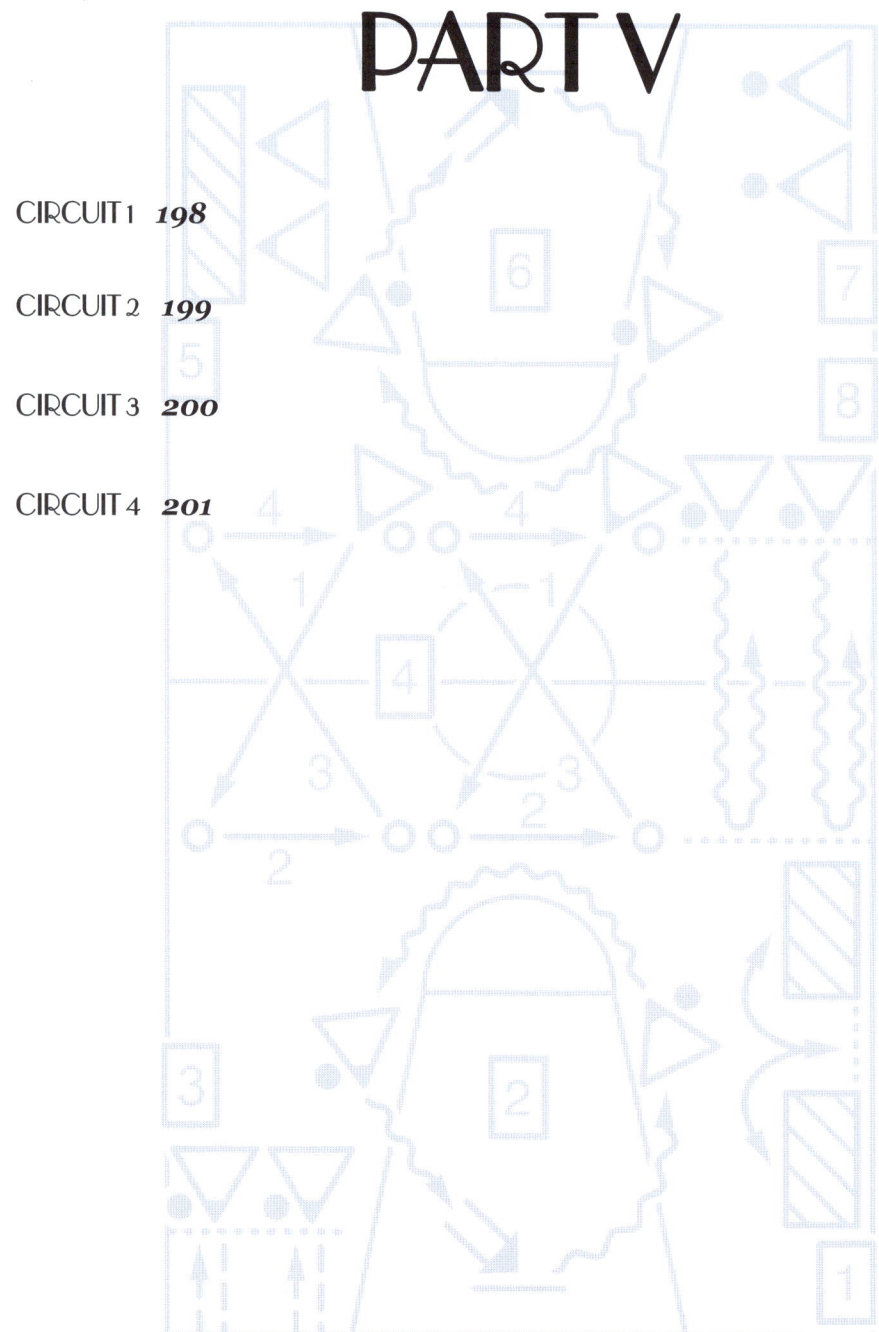

CIRCUIT TRAINING

Circuit training is designed to develop basketball-specific skills and fitness. It is a training program that incorporates a number of carefully selected exercises to practice several key basketball skills in one session.

Each exercise within the circuit is numbered and referred to as a station. The player progresses from one exercise station to another in sequence, completing a prescribed amount of work (repetitions) at each station.

The selection of exercises, number of repetitions, number of stations per circuit, etc. must be suited to the participants' age, training experience, and performance ability. Furthermore, depending upon the athletes' performance levels, training phase, and training objectives, each circuit can be repeated three to six times, with rest intervals between individual circuits ranging between zero and 240 seconds.

In circuit training, the loading of the main muscle groups (prime movers) changes as the player moves from one exercise to another. The loading at each station is normally below the player's maximum, which allows the athlete to move quickly from one station to another, requiring relatively little rest between exercises. The intensity of training remains relatively high throughout the circuit, which also generates a strong positive training effect on cardiovascular fitness.

Circuit training has many valuable organizational aspects. It can accommodate a relatively large number of participants at one time, requires relatively inexpensive equipment, and can be easily adapted to the individual needs and abilities of players. Coaches have found circuit training to be an excellent form of preparation during the preparatory phase of training; but due to its time efficiency, it can also be very effective for maintaining fitness during the pre-competitive and competitive phases of training.

Athletes should be introduced to a circuit training program in a highly organized manner. The coach must explain the objectives and the potential benefits of the program, as well as outline the structure and procedures. Individual performance cards must be prepared for each participant. They are used to record the achieved results, such as times per circuit and achieved number of repetitions/points per station, etc. Proper execution of each exercise, including the proper sequence of exercising and correct method of recording the results on the individual performance cards, must be emphasized.

Several forms of circuit training exist, depending on the goals to be achieved in training. Four different forms of circuit training are presented in this section. For more information on circuit training, refer to a Sport Books Publisher publication.

CIRCUIT TRAINING

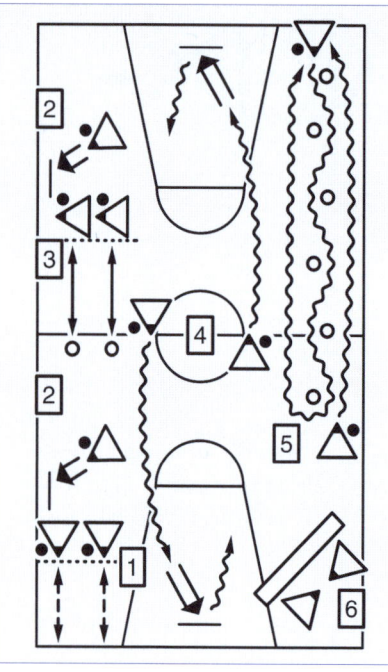

Circuit 1

Method: All athletes assume the starting position at their respective stations and begin at the same time at the given signal. Exercise duration at each station can be restricted to 30 to 40 seconds. Again, a given signal ends the exercise, which is followed by a rest interval of 30 to 60 seconds. During each break, participants enter the number of points achieved on their performance cards, then move to the next station and take up their new starting positions. At the given signal, they all start their respective exercises again at the same time.

Objectives: To develop several technical skills under physical and psychological stress.

Participants: 8 to 12.

Materials: One court, four baskets, eight basketballs, 10 medicine balls, a bench, a wall, a stopwatch.

Circuit stations:

Station 1:
   Chest pass with both hands against the wall from a four-metre distance. Each ball that rebounds back from the wall and is caught without touching the floor, counts for one point.

Station 2:
   Lay-ups at a "side" basket—shoot, rebound, shoot, and so on. Each successful shot is worth one point.

Station 3:
   Defensive shuffle between two lines three metres apart. A medicine ball is carried from one line to the other in a low defensive stance using shuffle steps. Touching each line with the ball counts for one point.

Station 4:
   Begin at the centre court line, dribble and shoot at one of the main baskets. Use a variety of shots. Each successful shot is worth one point.

Station 5:
   Zig-zag dribbling around six pylons (three-metre distance between pylons), dribble back in a straight line. Each full round (down and back) counts for one point.

Station 6:
   Jump back and forth over a bench with no intermediate jumps. Each successful jump counts for one point.

PROGRAMS

Circuit 2

Method: Participants perform a set number of repetitions at each station, completing the circuit as quickly as possible with no rest between exercises. Rest between circuits can range between zero and 240 seconds. Participants record the total time required to complete the entire circuit.

Objectives: To develop physical fitness and strengthen technical skills under physical stress.

Participants: 8 to 12.

Materials: One court, two baskets, six basketballs, three boxes, 12 medicine balls, one wall, two stopwatches.

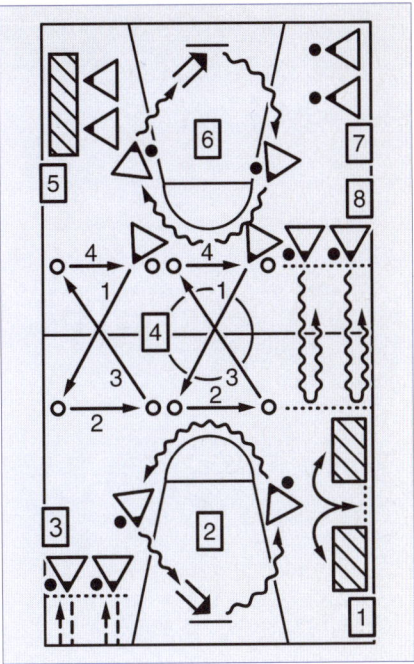

Circuit stations:
Station 1: Two-footed plyometric jumps between two boxes. *Task*: 10 jumps.
Station 2:
    Shoot a right-handed lay-up starting from the right side of the basket. Rebound the ball, dribble around the top of the key, and repeat the task. *Task*: 5 successful shots.
Station 3:
    Lying on their stomachs 1.5 metres away from a wall, participants hold up a medicine ball and throw it against the wall. *Task*: 10 wall shots.
Station 4:
    Participants run in the sequence shown, touching the medicine ball (or pylon) at each turn, alternating running forwards and backwards after each touch. *Task*: 20 ball touches.
Station 5:
    Participants start with the right foot on a box or bench and step up to a full upright position on the box. Return to original position. *Task*: 20 step-ups with each leg.
Station 6:
    Repeat the task from Station 2, shooting lay-ups from the left side of the basket with the left hand.
Station 7:
    Lying on their backs, participants hold a medicine ball up above the head, bring their extended legs to the medicine ball, and return to starting position (abdominal crunch). *Task*: 10 full crunches.
Station 8:
    Dribble with the right hand to a marked line (5 metres away from the starting line), and dribble back with the left hand. *Task*: 5 rounds back and forth.

CIRCUIT TRAINING

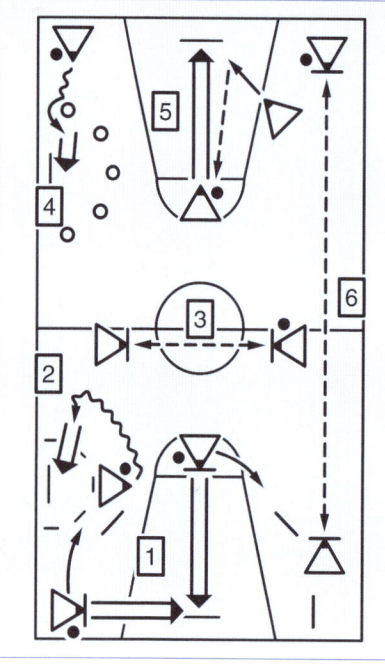

Circuit 3

Method: Participants perform a set number of repetitions at each station and switch stations on their own. Only successful shots or passes are counted. Exercises at stations 3, 5, and 6 are practiced in pairs. Shooting and passing distances should vary depending on the participants' age, abilities, and performance levels.

Objectives: To develop shooting and passing skills without a defender.

Participants: 8 to 12.

Materials: One court, four baskets, nine basketballs, five medicine balls or pylons.

Circuit stations:

Station 1:
  Each participant shoots 25 set or jump shots (five from each of five different positions on the floor). The ball is rebounded and taken back out after each shot. *Variation*: participants work in pairs—A shoots, B rebounds and passes the ball back out; participants switch roles after every five shots.

Station 2:
  Each participant shoots 25 overhead lay-ups off the dribble (five from each of five different positions on the floor) using both the left and the right hand. The ball is rebounded and taken back out after each shot. *Variation*: participants work in pairs—A shoots, B rebounds and passes the ball back out; participants switch roles after every five shots.

Station 3:
  Each participant completes 25 passes with each hand (a total of 50 passes each) while jumping.

Station 4:
  Each participant shoots 25 underhand lay-ups off the dribble (five from each of five different positions on the floor), side-stepping an obstacle before each shot. The ball is rebounded and taken back out after each shot. *Variation*: (a) participants alternate side-stepping the obstacles to the left and to the right; (b) participants work in pairs—A shoots, B returns the ball; participants switch roles after every five shots.

Station 5:
  Each participant shoots 25 free throws after a pass from a partner. Partners then switch roles. *Variation*: participants switch after every 5 shots or less.

Station 6:
  Each participant completes 50 long passes (25 with each hand) while standing.

PROGRAMS

Circuit 4

Methods: Each pair (Station 4 requires two pairs) practices 5 to 10 minutes per station. Only at station 4, one pair stays for an extra 5 to 10 minutes, while the other one moves on to station 5, so that each pair practices the two-on-two for a total of 10 to 20 minutes.

Objectives: To develop offensive and defensive technical and tactical skills.

Participants: 8 to 12.

Materials: One court, four baskets, five basketballs, four cones or pylons.

Circuit stations:

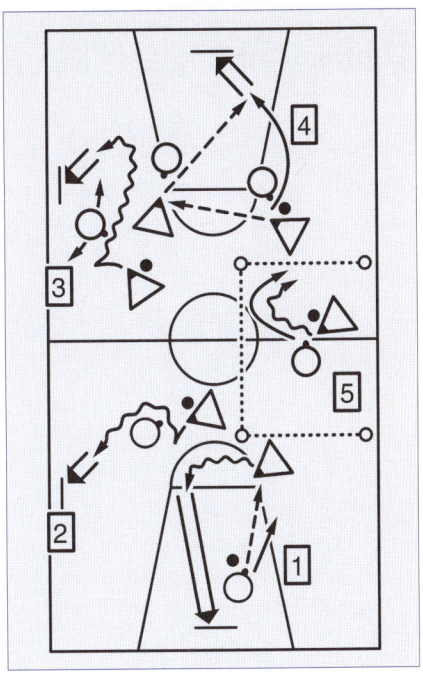

Station 1:
   Participants shoot set or jump shots against a defender—A shoots, B rebounds and passes back to A, and plays defense on A. They switch roles after 2.5 to 5 minutes.

Station 2:
   Participants play one-on-one at one basket. A tries to get as many baskets as possible, using various offensive fakes. B defends. They switch after 2.5 to 5 minutes.

Station 3:
   Participants practice hook shots (or other types of shots) against a defender (see Station 1). Participants switch roles after 2.5 to 5 minutes.

Station 4:
   Participants play two-on-two at one basket, trying to utilize group tactical offensive and defensive strategies. After 5 to 10 minutes, one team moves on to the next station, while the other stays.

Station 5:
   Participants dribble in a confined area against a defender. The defending player tries to get the ball without committing a foul. The participants switch roles after 2.5 to 5 minutes.

Notes

Notes

Notes